UTOPIAN LITERATURE

A Selection

MODERN LIBRARY COLLEGE EDITIONS

UTOPIAN

LITERATURE

A Selection

Edited, with Introductions, by

J. W. JOHNSON

Professor of English, University of Rochester

THE MODERN LIBRARY NEW YORK

Library of Congress Catalog Card Number: 68–16777

THE MODERN LIBRARY
is published by Random House, Inc.

Manufactured in the United States of America

FOR MIRANDA

So they sailed away, for a year and a day
To the land where the Bong-tree grows;
And there in the wood a piggy-wig stood . . .

Contents

IV The New Jerusalem

V The Middle Ages

VI The Renaissance

VII The Eighteenth Century

Preface

Although the word "utopia" was not coined until 1516, when Sir Thomas More published his political fantasy of that name, the idea which it embodies—the perfect state of human happiness—has existed from the era of prehistory. The term "utopia" is a combination of two Greek words: *ou*, meaning "no" or "not," and *topos*, "place." Thus "utopia" is "no place" or "nowhere" in the physical world; it cannot be located on a map. At the same time that he envisioned a society living in mutual harmony and individual happiness, More was wrily commenting that such a society did not, and possibly could not, exist. Perfect happiness was and is an elusive phenomenon. Nearly three hundred years after More's *Utopia*, the framers of the Declaration of Independence, bent on making America a possible utopia, realistically supposed only that men had a right to *pursue* happiness. But if no man has ever found his utopia, everyone conceives of complete happiness, and many writers have described the conditions they believe would effect it.

The very nature of the human mind is such as to foster utopian speculation. Human beings possess both hindsight and foresight: the ability to remember the past and to anticipate the future. As a result, none of us lives solely in the present, in his sensations and emotions of the moment. Our recollections, accurate or inaccurate, mingle with our thoughts of the present and our presentiments of what is to come; we naturally compare and evaluate the present in terms of yesterday and tomorrow. Almost always, today is somehow lacking whatever would make us completely free from worry.

Emotional tensions, sexual frustrations and anxieties, worry about money, disease, perhaps fear of death or death itself, intrude into our lives and destroy the happiness of the moment. At these times, it is humanly natural to think back to the tranquil days of last summer (so they seem now) or to look forward to the winter carnivals and the rites of spring. Habitual thinking of this kind produces nostalgia for "The Good Old Days" on the one hand and a "Tomorrow Will Be Better" hopefulness on the other.

Since desire is not a reasonable faculty, logicians cannot satisfactorily explain man's utopian dreams; nor can the modern scientist—the psychologist or physiologist—do much better, although a few of them have tried. Both Freud and Jung, the two great modern psychological theorists, have implied innate causes for utopian thinking in their hypotheses of human behavior. Freud's theory of the polymorphous sensuality of the infant, the many forms of the pleasure principle which the child experiences, explains why each of us has built into him a memory of a time when all wants were filled and there were no worries. Similarly, Jung's theory of a "collective unconscious," a racial memory present in everyone, would explain why the archetypal myths of a Garden of Eden and a Golden Age hold such appeal. These myths remind us of earlier stages in man's development, when cultures were more primitive and presumably less demanding than our own. Furthermore, Freud, Jung, and other psychologists predicate the betterment of men and society through psychoanalysis; and behavioral scientists have related visions. B. F. Skinner's interest in "human engineering" depends on such a vision, as do other modern proposals for improving the human race.

Whether the cause be genes, cultural tradition, or something else, recorded literature shows that for four thousand years, men have been dissatisfied with life as it *is*. They have conceived of life as it *ought* to be, as it *might* have been in the distant past or *may* be in the far future. Since their dissatisfaction is concentrated on present conditions, their conception of ideal conditions often is the opposite of actual circumstances. The ancient Hebrews, wandering in the sandy wastes of the Near East, repeated legends of a lush garden, watered by two great rivers, or they urged themselves onward with hopes for a fertile land flowing with milk and honey.

The roaming tribes of Doric Greeks, flying from the ravages of northern winters, searched for a paradise to the south or the west even as they told stories of a blessed tribe that lived back of the North Wind. The urban Romans celebrated festivals commemorating a vanished king and age or they idealized life in some rural glade far from the dusty streets of Rome. The Christian saw his perfect bliss in some heavenly city out of time. And so up to the present day, when migrants from Europe still look upon America as a Promised Land, when farm boys from Iowa yearn for New York, and sophisticated New Yorkers dream of happiness on an island lagoon in the Caribbean or South Pacific.

It would be wrong to think that man's utopian vision is mere escapism, the wish to be relieved of care and responsibility. On the contrary, the whole notion of progress in Western history is tied to the concept of utopia. In Judeo-Christian culture, some of the most sweeping historical, social, and religious movements have derived from men's dissatisfaction with the present and their determination to change things in the future, either by returning to the old ways or by developing entirely new ways of looking at themselves and doing things. The idea of utopia is a striking example of man's divine discontent: his refusal to admit that he has no say in his own destiny but must submit to the harsh, disagreeable facts of existence simply because they seem unconquerable.

The literature of utopia, from its earliest forms to those found in modern culture, is a record of some of the most profoundly cherished human ideals and some of the most pathetic and comic examples of human errors. From Homer to Dante to Shakespeare to Tolstoy, the master writers have incorporated utopian elements in their view of life and in their works. Philosophers have founded their systems in the conception of a utopia, and social reformers have determined their practices to fit plans for utopian living arrangements. Landscapes, climates, governments, education, human and animal nature have all been shown to be imperfect in utopian writings; proposals for altering them all have been advanced. The readings in the present anthology were se-

lected to show the linear development of the utopian concept from past to present, to indicate the chief variations
of the idea and relate these to other significant concepts,
and to open up some lines of reflection. To see the mutations
of the utopian dream through the centuries not only permits
us to understand the intellectual tradition that has formed
our own world; it reveals to us some of the deepest and most
desperate needs of the human race and, in doing this, dis-
closes the basic human drives that lie in our own hearts.

A Selective Bibliography

There is an enormous amount of material, both primary and critical, on the idea of utopia. Most of the important primary works are listed at the end of each chapter under the title "Suggested Additional Readings." These works are available in various editions and translations. Critical commentaries on utopianism are also numerous and increase yearly. Discussions of utopianism published in periodicals are listed in the *Reader's Guide to Periodical Literature* and the *International Index*. A recent issue of the literary journal *Daedalus*, 94 (Spring 1965), 271–517, provides a bibliography of utopian writing as well as critical articles on utopian thought. The books listed below serve as a broad guide to the range of utopian criticism; most contain further, detailed bibliographies.

Armytage, W. H. G. *Heavens Below: Utopian Experiments in England, 1560–1960.* Toronto, 1961.

Blum, R. H., and others. *Utopiates: The Use and Users of LSD-25.* New York, 1964.

Goodman, P. *Utopian Essays and Practical Proposals.* New York, 1963.

Hertzler, J. O. *The History of Utopian Thought.* New York, 1965.

Hinds, W. A. *American Utopias.* Gloucester, Mass., 1961.

Kateb, G. *Utopia and Its Enemies.* New York, 1963.

Manuel, F. E., ed. *Utopias and Utopian Thought.* New York, 1966.

Mumford, L. *The Story of Utopias.* Gloucester, Mass., 1963.

Negley, G. R., and J. M. Patrick. *The Quest for Utopia.* New York, 1962.

Tuveson, E. L. *Millennium and Utopia.* New York, 1964.

Walsh, C. *From Utopia to Nightmare.* New York, 1962.

UTOPIAN LITERATURE

A Selection

I

Prehistoric Myths

Introduction

Modern anthropologists have suggested that in the centuries immediately preceding the beginning of the historic era (about 4500 B.C.), many races were nomads, wandering from place to place according to the season, always in search of food. The great migrations of this period may have been caused by alterations in climate that changed grasslands into deserts or moderate valleys into glacial wastes. There is evidence that three groups of men—Semites, Caucasians, and Mongolians—roamed considerable distances from their sub-sistence-level homesites of the Stone Age. They must have been driven by despair and hope: despair for their lost way of life and hope of a new, better life someplace where food was plentiful and the ills and terrors of the nomadic life could be ended. In their search for the Happy Hunting Ground, some waves of Mongolians ventured across the Bering Straits and made their way down into two strange new continents. Some Caucasian peoples headed south toward the warm waters of the Mediterranean, where hopeful rumors claimed the trees bore fruit of shining gold and sheep had golden fleece.

South of the Mediterranean, small tribes of desert wanderers roamed from oasis to oasis, seeking enough water to keep their goats alive and fighting off other nomads and marauders in the process. One of these tribes, the Israelites or Jews, was enslaved during its wanderings by the Egyptians and the Babylonians; but it always managed to escape into the desert, succored by its belief in a protective God and its hope of finding someday the rich, fertile land promised by Yahweh (or Jehovah). The Jews sustained their hope with tales of a lost land of perfection, a Garden, where their ancestors had once lived in ease and plenty before that evil moment when man sinned against God and fell to his present state of misery and want.

The account of the Garden of Eden in the Old Testament book of Genesis (the first of the Hebrew Pentateuch, "five scrolls"), contains most of the utopian elements to be found in other versions of prehistoric myths and legends. Egyptian, Sumerian, and Babylonian legends included accounts of gardens, the symbol of fertility and plenty. Sir James Frazer's *The Golden Bough* contains material on the Gardens of Adonis, the worship of Ceres, and other pagan rituals that reflect the primitive emphasis on vegetation as the symbol of life and on the grove, oasis, or garden as a holy place. (It should be noted that the Greek word for garden is *paradisos*, or "paradise.") The Garden of Eden is a tale that displays most of the earliest notions of a lost utopia; and it has been used again and again as a source for utopian writers.

The Greek legend of Prometheus and Pandora has obvious resemblances to the story of Adam and Eve, although its stress on the garden-paradise is less great. Its myth of a Golden Age, however, is a vital one which has appealed to later generations and has affected man's view of history. The Roman story of Saturn also has had historical and religious significance. The modern celebration of Christmas, a microcosmic Golden Age of peace, plenty, and happiness, can be traced back to the Saturnalia. These ancient legends are still important in utopian thought for their archetypal meaning and their psychological insights.

✷

THE GARDEN OF EDEN

Thus the heavens and the earth were finished, and all the host of them. And on the seventh day God ended his work which he had made. And he rested on the seventh day from all his work which he had made. And God blessed the seventh day, and sanctified it: because that in it he had rested from all his work which God created and made.

These are the generations of the heavens and of the earth when they were created, in the day that the Lord God made the earth and the heavens, and every plant of the field before it was in the earth, and every herb of the field before it grew: for the Lord God had not caused it to rain upon the earth, and there was not a man to till the ground. But there went up a mist from the earth, and watered the whole face of the ground. And the Lord God formed man of the dust of the ground, and breathed into his nostrils the breath of life; and man became a living soul.

And the Lord God planted a garden eastward in Eden; and there he put the man whom he had formed. And out of the ground made the Lord God to grow every tree that is pleasant to the sight and good for food: the tree of life also in the midst of the garden, and the tree of knowledge of good and evil. And a river went out of Eden to water the garden, and from thence it was parted, and became into four heads. The name of the first is Pison: that is it which compasseth the whole land of Havilah, where there is gold. And the gold of that land is good: there is bdellium and the onyx stone. And the name of the second river is Gihon: the same is it that compasseth the whole land of Ethiopia. And the name of the third river is Hiddekel: that is it which goeth toward the east of Assyria: and the fourth river is Euphrates.

From *Genesis*, 1-3. King James translation.

And the Lord God took the man, and put him into the garden of Eden, to dress it and to keep it. And the Lord God commanded the man, saying, "Of every tree of the garden thou mayest freely eat. But of the tree of the knowledge of good and evil, thou shalt not eat of it: for in the day that thou eatest thereof thou shalt surely die."

And the Lord God said, "It is not good that the man should be alone: I will make him an help meet for him." And out of the ground the Lord God formed every beast of the field, and every fowl of the air, and brought them unto Adam, to see what he would call them: and whatsoever Adam called every living creature, that was the name thereof. And Adam gave names to all cattle, and to the fowl of the air, and to every beast of the field: but for Adam there was not found an help meet for him. And the Lord God caused a deep sleep to fall upon Adam, and he slept: and he took one of his ribs, and closed up the flesh instead thereof. And the rib which the Lord God had taken from man, made he a woman, and brought her unto the man. And Adam said, "This is now bone of my bones, and flesh of my flesh: she shall be called woman, because she was taken out of man." Therefore shall a man leave his father and his mother, and shall cleave unto his wife: and they shall be one flesh. And they were both naked, the man and his wife, and were not ashamed.

Now the serpent was more subtle than any beast of the field which the Lord God had made, and he said unto the woman, "Yea, hath God said, 'Ye shall not eat of every tree of the garden'?" And the woman said unto the serpent, "We may eat of the fruit of the trees of the garden: but of the fruit of the tree which is in the midst of the garden, God hath said, 'Ye shall not eat of it, neither shall ye touch it, lest ye die.' " And the serpent said unto the woman, "Ye shall not surely die. For God doth know that in the day ye eat thereof, then your eyes shall be opened: and ye shall be as gods, knowing good and evil." And when the woman saw that the tree was good for food, and that it was pleasant to the eyes, and a tree to be desired to make one wise, she took of the fruit thereof, and did eat, and gave also unto her husband with her, and he did eat. And the eyes of them both were opened, and they knew that they were naked, and they sewed fig leaves together, and made themselves aprons. And they heard the voice of the Lord God walking in the garden in the cool of the day: and Adam and his wife hid themselves from the presence of the Lord God, amongst the trees of the garden.

And the Lord God called unto Adam, and said unto him, "Where art thou?" And he said, "I heard thy voice in the garden: and I was afraid, because I was naked, and I hid myself." And he said, "Who told thee that thou wast naked? Hast thou eaten of the tree whereof I commanded thee that thou shouldst not eat?" And the man said, "The woman whom thou gavest to be with me, she gave me of the tree, and I did eat." And the Lord God said unto the woman, "What is this that thou hast done?" And the woman said, "The serpent beguiled me, and I did eat." And the Lord God said unto the serpent, "Because thou hast done this, thou art cursed above all cattle, and above every beast of the field: upon thy belly shalt thou go, and dust shalt thou eat, all the days of thy life. And I will put enmity between thee and the woman, and between thy seed and her seed: it shall bruise thy head, and thou shalt bruise his heel." Unto the woman he said, "I will greatly multiply thy sorrow and thy conception. In sorrow thou shalt bring forth children: and thy desire shall be to thy husband, and he shall rule over thee." And unto Adam he said, "Because thou hast hearkened unto the voice of thy wife, and hast eaten of the tree, of which I commanded thee, saying, 'Thou shalt not eat of it': cursed is the ground for thy sake: in sorrow shalt thou eat of it all the days of thy life. Thorns also and thistles shall it bring forth to thee: and thou shalt eat the herb of the field. In the sweat of thy face shalt thou eat bread, till thou return unto the ground: for out of it wast thou taken, for dust thou art, and unto dust shalt thou return." And Adam called his wife's name Eve, because she was the mother of all living. Unto Adam also, and to his wife, did the Lord God make coats of skins, and clothed them.

And the Lord God said, "Behold, the man is become as one of us, to know good and evil. And now, lest he put forth his hand, and take also of the tree of life, and eat and live for ever—": therefore the Lord God sent him forth from the garden of Eden, to till the ground from whence he was taken. So he drove out the man: and he placed at the east of the garden of Eden cherubim, and a flaming sword which turned every way, to keep the way of the tree of life.

Thomas Bulfinch

❉

THE GOLDEN AGE:
PROMETHEUS AND PANDORA

The creation of the world is a problem naturally fitted to excite the liveliest interest of man, its inhabitant. The ancient pagans, not having the information on the subject which we derive from the pages of Scripture, had their own way of telling the story, which is as follows:

Before earth and sea and heaven were created, all things wore one aspect, to which we give the name of Chaos—a confused and shapeless mass, nothing but dead weight, in which, however, slumbered the seeds of things. Earth, sea, and air were all mixed up together; so the earth was not solid, the sea was not fluid, and the air was not transparent. God and Nature at last interposed, and put an end to this discord, separating earth from sea, and heaven from both. The fiery part, being the lightest, sprang up, and formed the skies; the air was next in weight and place. The earth, being heavier, sank below; and the water took the lowest place, and buoyed up the earth.

Here some god—it is not known which—gave his good

From *Mythology*, by Thomas Bulfinch. First published in 1855.

offices in arranging and disposing the earth. He appointed
rivers and bays their places, raised mountains, scooped out
valleys, distributed woods, fountains, fertile fields, and stony
plains. The air being cleared, the stars began to appear, fishes
took possession of the sea, birds of the air, and four-footed
beasts of the land.

But a nobler animal was wanted, and Man was made.
It is not known whether the creator made him of divine
materials, or whether in the earth, so lately separated from
heaven, there lurked still some heavenly seeds. Prometheus
took some of this earth, and kneading it up with water,
made man in the image of the gods. He gave him an upright stature, so that while all other animals turn their faces
downward, and look to the earth, he raises his to heaven,
and gazes on the stars.

Prometheus was one of the Titans, a gigantic race, who
inhabited the earth before the creation of man. To him
and his brother Epimetheus was committed the office of
making man, and providing him and all other animals with
the faculties necessary for their preservation. Epimetheus
undertook to do this, and Prometheus was to overlook his
work, when it was done. Epimetheus accordingly proceeded
to bestow upon the different animals the various gifts of
courage, strength, swiftness, sagacity; wings to one, claws
to another, a shelly covering to a third, etc. But when man
came to be provided for, who was to be superior to all other
animals, Epimetheus had been so prodigal of his resources
that he had nothing left to bestow upon him. In his perplexity he resorted to his brother Prometheus, who, with
the aid of Minerva, went up to heaven, and lighted his
torch at the chariot of the sun, and brought down fire to
man. With this gift man was more than a match for all
other animals. It enabled him to make weapons wherewith
to subdue them; tools with which to cultivate the earth; to
warm his dwelling, so as to be comparatively independent
of climate; and finally to introduce the arts and to coin
money, the means of trade and commerce.

Woman was not yet made. The story (absurd enough!)
is that Jupiter made her, and sent her to Prometheus and

his brother, to punish them for their presumption in stealing fire from heaven; and man, for accepting the gift. The first woman was named Pandora. She was made in heaven, every god contributing something to perfect her. Venus gave her beauty, Mercury persuasion, Apollo music, etc. Thus equipped, she was conveyed to earth, and presented to Epimetheus, who gladly accepted her, though cautioned by his brother to beware of Jupiter and his gifts. Epimetheus had in his house a jar, in which were kept certain noxious articles, for which, in fitting man for his new abode, he had had no occasion. Pandora was seized with an eager curiosity to know what this jar contained; and one day she slipped off the cover and looked in. Forthwith there escaped a multitude of plagues for hapless man—such as gout, rheumatism, and colic for his body, and envy, spite, and revenge for his mind—and scattered themselves far and wide. Pandora hastened to replace the lid! but, alas! the whole contents of the jar had escaped, one thing only excepted, which lay at the bottom, and that was *hope*. So we see at this day, whatever evils are abroad, hope never entirely leaves us; and while we have *that*, no amount of other ills can make us completely wretched.

Another story is that Pandora was sent in good faith, by Jupiter, to bless man; that she was furnished with a box, containing her marriage presents, into which every god had put some blessing. She opened the box incautiously, and the blessings all escaped, *hope* only excepted. This story seems more probable than the former; for how could *hope*, so precious a jewel as it is, have been kept in a jar full of all manner of evils, as in the former statement?

The world being thus furnished with inhabitants, the first age was an age of innocence and happiness, called the *Golden Age*. Truth and right prevailed, though not enforced by law, nor was there any magistrate to threaten or punish. The forest had not yet been robbed of its trees to furnish timbers for vessels, nor had men built fortifications round their towns. There were no such things as swords, spears, or helmets. The earth brought forth all things necessary for man, without his labor in ploughing or sowing. Perpetual spring reigned, flowers sprang up without seed, the rivers flowed with milk and wine, and yellow honey distilled from the oaks.

Then succeeded the *Silver Age*, inferior to the golden, but better than that of brass. Jupiter shortened the spring, and divided the year into seasons. Then, first, men had to endure the extremes of heat and cold, and houses became necessary. Caves were the first dwellings, and leafy coverts of the woods, and huts woven of twigs. Crops would no longer grow without planting. The farmer was obliged to sow the seed, and the toiling ox to draw the plough.

Next came the *Brazen Age*, more savage of temper, and readier to the strife of arms, yet not altogether wicked. The hardest and worst was the *Iron Age*. Crime burst in like a flood; modesty, truth, and honor fled. In their places came fraud and cunning, violence, and the wicked love of gain. Then seamen spread sails to the wind, and the trees were torn from the mountains to serve for keels to ships, and vex the face of ocean. The earth, which till now had been cultivated in common, began to be divided off into possessions. Men were not satisfied with what the surface produced, but must dig into its bowels, and draw forth from thence the ores of metals. Mischievous *iron*, and more mischievous *gold*, were produced. War sprang up, using both as weapons; the guest was not safe in his friend's house; and sons-in-law and fathers-in-law, brothers and sisters, husbands and wives, could not trust one another. Sons wished their fathers dead, that they might come to the inheritance; family love lay prostrate. The earth was wet with slaughter, and the gods abandoned it, one by one, till Astraea[1] alone was left, and finally she also took her departure.

---

[1] The goddess of innocence and purity. After leaving earth, she was placed among the stars, where she became the constellation Virgo—the Virgin. Themis (Justice) was the mother of Astraea. She is represented as holding aloft a pair of scales, in which she weighs the claims of opposing parties.

It was a favorite idea of the old poets that these goddesses would

Sir James Frazer

SATURN AND THE SATURNALIA

We have seen that many peoples have been used to observe an annual period of license, when the customary restraints of law and morality are thrown aside, when the whole population give themselves up to extravagant mirth and jollity, and when the darker passions find a vent which would never be allowed them in the more staid and sober course of ordinary life. Such outbursts of the pent-up forces of human nature, too often degenerating into wild orgies of lust and crime, occur most commonly at the end of the year, and are frequently associated, as I have had occasion to point out, with one or other of the agricultural seasons, especially with the time of sowing or of harvest. Now, of all these periods of license the one which is best known and which in modern language has given its name to the rest, is the Saturnalia. This famous festival fell in December, the last month of the Roman year, and was popularly supposed to commemorate the merry reign of Saturn, the god of sowing and of husbandry, who lived on earth long ago

---

one day return, and bring back the Golden Age. Even in a Christian hymn, the "Messiah" of Pope, this idea occurs:

> All crimes shall cease, and ancient fraud shall fail,
> Returning Justice lift aloft her scale,
> Peace o'er the world her olive wand extend,
> And white-robed Innocence from heaven descend.

See, also, Milton's "Hymn on the Nativity," stanzas xiv and xv.

as a righteous and beneficent king of Italy, drew the rude
and scattered dwellers on the mountains together, taught
them to till the ground, gave them laws, and ruled in peace.
His reign was the fabled Golden Age: the earth brought
forth abundantly: no sound of war or discord troubled the
happy world: no baleful love of lucre worked like poison in
the blood of the industrious and contented peasantry. Slavery and private property were alike unknown: all men had
all things in common. At last the good god, the kindly king,
vanished suddenly; but his memory was cherished to distant ages, shrines were reared in his honor, and many hills
and high places in Italy bore his name. Yet the bright tradition of his reign was crossed by a dark shadow: his altars
are said to have been stained with the blood of human
victims, for whom a more merciful age afterwards substituted effigies. Of this gloomy side of the god's religion there
is little or no trace in the descriptions which ancient writers
have left us of the Saturnalia. Feasting and revelry and all
the mad pursuit of pleasure are the features that seem to
have especially marked this carnival of antiquity, as it went
on for seven days in the streets and public squares and
houses of ancient Rome from the seventeenth to the twenty-
third of December.

But no feature of the festival is more remarkable, nothing in it seems to have struck the ancients themselves more
than the license granted to slaves at this time. The distinction between the free and the servile classes was temporarily
abolished. The slave might rail at his master, intoxicate himself like his betters, sit down at table with them, and not
even a word of reproof would be administered to him for
conduct which at any other season might have been punished with stripes, imprisonment, or death. Nay, more, masters actually changed places with their slaves and waited on
them at table; and not till the serf had done eating and
drinking was the board cleared and dinner set for his master. So far was this inversion of ranks carried, that each
household became for a time a mimic republic in which
the high offices of state were discharged by the slaves, who
gave their orders and laid down the law as if they were in-

deed invested with all the dignity of the consulship, the praetorship, and the bench. Like the pale reflection of power thus accorded to bondsmen at the Saturnalia was the mock kingship for which freemen cast lots at the same season. The person on whom the lot fell enjoyed the title of king, and issued commands of a playful and ludicrous nature to his temporary subjects. One of them he might order to mix the wine, another to drink, another to sing, another to dance, another to speak in his own dispraise, another to carry a flute-girl on his back round the house.

Now, when we remember that the liberty allowed to slaves at this festive season was supposed to be an imitation of the state of society in Saturn's time, and that in general the Saturnalia passed for nothing more or less than a temporary revival or restoration of the reign of that merry monarch, we are tempted to surmise that the mock king who presided over the revels may have originally represented Saturn himself. The conjecture is strongly confirmed, if not established, by a very curious and interesting account of the way in which the Saturnalia was celebrated by the Roman soldiers stationed on the Danube in the reign of Maximian and Diocletian. The account is preserved in a narrative of the martyrdom of St. Dasius, which was unearthed from a Greek manuscript in the Paris library, and published by Professor Franz Cumont of Ghent. Two briefer descriptions of the event and of the custom are contained in manuscripts at Milan and Berlin; one of them had already seen the light in an obscure volume printed at Urbino in 1727, but its importance for the history of the Roman religion, both ancient and modern, appears to have been overlooked until Professor Cumont drew the attention of scholars to all three narratives by publishing them together some years ago. According to these narratives, which have all the appearance of being authentic, and of which the longest is probably based on official documents, the Roman soldiers at Durostorum in Lower Moesia celebrated the Saturnalia year by year in the following manner. Thirty days before the festival they chose by lot from amongst themselves a young and handsome man, who was then clothed in royal attire to resemble Saturn. Thus arrayed and attended by a multitude of soldiers he went about in public with full license to indulge his passions and to taste of every pleasure, however base and shameful. But if his reign was merry, it was short and ended tragically; for when the thirty days were up and the festival of Saturn had come, he cut his own throat on the altar of the god whom he personated. In the year A.D. 303 the lot fell upon the Christian soldier Dasius, but he refused to play the part of the heathen god and soil his last days by debauchery. The threats and arguments of his commanding officer Bassus failed to shake his constancy, and accordingly he was beheaded, as the Christian martyrologist records with minute accuracy, at Durostorum by the soldier John on Friday the twentieth day of November, being the twenty-fourth day of the moon, at the fourth hour.

Since this narrative was published by Professor Cumont, its historical character, which had been doubted or denied, has received strong confirmation from an interesting discovery. In the crypt of the cathedral which crowns the promontory of Ancona there is preserved, among other remarkable antiquities, a white marble sarcophagus bearing a Greek inscription, in characters of the age of Justinian, to the following effect: "Here lies the holy martyr Dasius, brought from Durostorum." The sarcophagus was transferred to the crypt of the cathedral in 1848 from the church of San Pellegrino, under the high altar of which, as we learn from a Latin inscription let into the masonry, the martyr's bones still repose with those of two other saints. How long the sarcophagus was deposited in the church of San Pellegrino, we do not know; but it is recorded to have been there in the year 1650. We may suppose that the saint's relics were transferred for safety to Ancona at some time in the troubled centuries which followed his martyrdom, when Moesia was occupied and ravaged by successive hordes of barbarian invaders. At all events it appears certain from the independent and mutually confirmatory evidence of the martyrology and the monuments that Dasius was no mythical saint, but a real man, who suffered death for his faith at Durostorum in one of the early centuries of the Christian era. Finding the narrative of the nameless martyrologist thus established as to the principal fact recorded, namely, the martyrdom of St. Dasius, we may reasonably accept his testimony as to the manner and cause of the martyrdom, all the more because his narrative is precise, circumstantial, and entirely free from the miraculous element. Accordingly I conclude that the account which he gives of the celebration of the Saturnalia among the Roman soldiers is trustworthy.

This account sets in a new and lurid light the office of the King of the Saturnalia, the ancient Lord of Misrule, who presided over the winter revels at Rome in the time of Horace and Tacitus. It seems to prove that his business had not always been that of a mere harlequin or merry-andrew whose only care was that the revelry should run high and the fun grow fast and furious, while the fire blazed and crackled on the hearth, while the streets swarmed with festive crowds, and through the clear frosty air, far away to the north, Soracte showed his coronal of snow. When we compare this comic monarch of the gay, the civilized metropolis with his grim counterpart of the rude camp on the Danube, and when we remember the long array of similar figures, ludicrous yet tragic, who in other ages and in other lands, wearing mock crowns and wrapped in sceptered palls, have played their little pranks for a few brief hours or days, then passed before their time to a violent death, we can hardly doubt that in the King of the Saturnalia at Rome, as he is depicted by classical writers, we see only a feeble emasculated copy of that original, whose strong features have been fortunately preserved for us by the obscure author of the *Martyrdom of St. Dasius*. In other words, the martyrologist's account of the Saturnalia agrees so closely with the accounts of similar rites elsewhere which could not possibly have been known to him, that the substantial accuracy of his description may be regarded as established; and further, since the custom of putting a mock king to death as a representative of a god cannot have grown out of a practice of appointing him to preside over a holiday revel, whereas the reverse may very well have happened, we are justified in assuming that in an earlier and more barbarous age it was the universal practice in ancient Italy, wherever the worship of Saturn prevailed, to choose a man who played the part and enjoyed all the traditionary privileges of Saturn for a season, and then died, whether by his own or another's hand, whether by the knife or the fire or on the gallows-tree, in the character of the good god who gave his life for the world. In Rome itself and other great towns the growth of civilization had probably mitigated this cruel custom long before the Augustan age, and transformed it into the innocent shape it wears in the writings of the few classical writers who bestow a passing notice on the holiday King of the Saturnalia. But in remoter districts the older and sterner practice may long have survived; and even if after the unification of Italy the barbarous usage was suppressed by the Roman government, the memory of it would be handed down by the peasants and would tend from time to time, as still happens with the lowest forms of superstition among ourselves, to lead to a recrudescence of the practice, especially among the rude soldiery on the outskirts of the empire over whom the once iron hand of Rome was beginning to relax its grasp.

The resemblance between the Saturnalia of ancient and the Carnival of modern Italy has often been remarked; but in the light of all the facts that have come before us, we may well ask whether the resemblance does not amount to identity. We have seen that in Italy, Spain, and France, that is, the countries where the influence of Rome has been deepest and most lasting, a conspicuous feature of the Carnival is a burlesque figure personifying the festive season, which after a short career of glory and dissipation is publicly shot, burnt, or otherwise destroyed, to the feigned grief or genuine delight of the populace. If the view here suggested of the Carnival is correct, this grotesque personage is no other than a direct successor of the old King of the Saturnalia, the master of the revels, the real man who personated Saturn and, when the revels were over, suffered a real death in his assumed character. The King of the Bean on Twelfth Night and the medieval Bishop of Fools, Abbot of Unreason, or Lord of Misrule are figures of the same sort and may perhaps have had a similar origin. Whether that was so or not, we may conclude with a fair degree of probability that if the King of the Wood at Aricia lived and died as an incarnation of a sylvan deity, he had of old a parallel at Rome in the men who, year by year, were slain in the character of King Saturn, the god of the sown and sprouting seed.

Suggested Additional Readings

The *Enuma Elish*
Sir James Frazer, *Folklore in the Old Testament*, Chaps. 1–2
     The Golden Bough, Chaps. 28–29, 33, 35, 40
The *Gilgamesh Epic*
Ovid, *Metamorphosis*
The *Prose Edda* (Snorri edition)

Hastings' *Encyclopedia of Religion and Ethics*, the *Larousse Encyclopedia of Mythology*, Robert Graves' *The Greek Myths*, Edith Hamilton's *Mythology*, Thomas Bulfinch's *Mythology*, the *Dictionary of Folklore*, and other reference works of similar kind contain articles about and indexes to other prehistoric utopian tales and legends as well as guides to secondary works about them.

Questions for Discussion and Writing

1. To what extent do the prehistoric ideas of utopia depend on conditions of climate? How do you account for this?

2. What is the place of physical labor in these utopias?

3. What conception of food and other physical needs is to be found in prehistoric utopias?

4. Considering their views of physical needs, may these

early utopian legends be considered entirely sensual in their ideal of perfection? Explain.

5. What is the place of disease and death in the Eden, Saturn, and Pandora stories? Is immortality a necessary condition of happiness in the accounts?

6. The qualities of permanence, safety, and freedom from care are stressed in the prehistoric utopian legends. What other qualities are presented as vital to utopia?

7. Consider the role played by women in these "perfect" societies. Are the visions of perfection essentially those of men or of women? How do you account for this?

8. Write (or present an oral report) on one of these subjects:
   a. The Garden legend
   b. The Happy Hunting Ground
   c. The Hyperboreans
   d. Saturnalia
   e. The Sacred Grove in Greek Literature
   f. The Legend of the Four Ages
   g. Arcady as Utopia
   h. Utopia and Pastoralism
   i. The Island Paradise in Homer's *Odyssey*

II

Greek and Roman Historiography

Introduction

Once the wandering tribes found their promised lands (of sorts) and ceased to be nomads, they became farmers, fishermen, and, in time, traders. With the rise of villages and towns, the arts of civilization developed, among them the writing down of old tales and legends as well as new accounts of the discoveries made by fishermen and traders on their journeys into distant lands.

Inevitably, the first historians drew upon the ancient accounts and upon the reports of travelers for the stuff of their histories, or "true narratives." The story of a land where people lived in peace and happiness continued to be popular, for man is perhaps the one animal whose wants are never entirely satisfied. Even when settled in the valleys of Canaan and Attica, people found something lacking in their lives. Food, shelter, and clothing proved not to be enough; the dreams of utopia in the histories of Herodotus, Strabo, and Diodorus Siculus emphasized the biological and moral elements in utopia rather than the geographical and climatic features of the prehistoric legends. Utopia still was not to be exactly located on maps, however, though it was called "Ethiopia," "Scythia," or "Hyperborea." These places, although geographically real, were known only through legends and fabulous accounts. Their reality was quite different from the account in Greek and Roman historiography.

Herodotus (c. 480–425 B.C.), the Greek "father of history," was something of a traveler himself, having journeyed to North Africa; but his experiences with real lands did not diminish his enthusiasm for fabulous countries that lay over the horizon. In Egypt, he heard tales of the Ethiopians, long thought to be beloved of the gods and the happiest race of mortals. Homer had spoken of the gods feasting with the Ethiopians; and Herodotus furnished some details of these utopian creatures who lived far beyond the mountains at the source of the Nile River. Herodotus also wrote of the Scythians, a nation beyond the Euxine Sea praised by Homer as well. And he mentioned the Hyperboreans who lived, as their name implies, at the back of the North Wind. Herodotus' account of the Ethiopians, however, had the most long-lasting effects.

Among the civilized Greeks in the period between 500 and 40 B.C., the Scythians were very popular symbols of the utopian life. Not only Herodotus but Hippocrates and Ephorus lauded them. It was the Greek historian and geographer Strabo (c. 64 B.C.–A.D. 19), who immortalized them for all time as examples of simplicity and virtue. Strabo's contrast of the hardy, virtuous Scythian and the luxury-loving, decadent Greek was a full-blown instance of "primitivism" (that is, idealizing an earlier stage of cultural development than one's own). Strabo's description of the Scythians, who supposedly lived as the ancestors of the modern Greeks had lived, is pervaded with the nostalgic backward look of many utopianists.

Diodorus Siculus (c. 40 B.C.), a native of Sicily, wrote a history of the world at the time Rome was undergoing changes at the hands of Julius Caesar. Like Herodotus,

Diodorus included many colorful versions of prehistoric myths and legends; but probably his most impressive use of the utopian concept can be found in his "historic" account of the early Egyptians and their government. Diodorus obviously intended ancient Egypt to be a model for modern Rome; he heightened the utopian character of Egypt in former centuries to contrast it with the decadent Egypt known to the Romans. Thus Diodorus' utopia was another instance of human perfection supposedly found long ago or far away.

To us, the Greek or Roman historian may appear close to the prehistoric teller of tales in his credulity and ignorance; but the changes in the concept of utopia introduced by Herodotus, Strabo, and Diodorus were significant ones. Their utopias may have been located back in time and past the horizon; but the historians asserted the truth of their existence and thus implicitly insisted that utopia was an actual, attainable state rather than a lost paradise or a future promise.

Herodotus

❈

THE ETHIOPIANS

When Cambyses, King of the Persians, determined to plan an expedition against the long-lived Ethiopians, who inhabited the Libyan coast of the southern sea, he first sent spies to investigate the truth of the story about a Table of the Sun in that country and to spy into other matters under the pretense of bringing gifts to the Ethiopian King. This is the story of the Table of the Sun:

Adapted from the *Histories,* III.17–26 *et passim.* Translation by J. W. Johnson.

Outside the city there is a meadow filled with the roasted flesh of every four-footed animal. The city authorities come here every night, setting out the meats with great care; and during the day, anyone who wishes may come there and feast. The Ethiopians say these meats are brought forth by the earth itself. Such is the story told about the Table of the Sun.

When Cambyses decided to send spies, he sent to fetch those of the tribe of Ichthyophagoi (Fish-Eaters) who could understand the Ethiopian tongue. When the Fish-Eaters arrived from the city of Elephantine in answer to his summons, Cambyses dispatched them to the Ethiopians, instructing them in what to say and providing them with gifts: a cloak of royal purple, a wrought gold necklace and armlets, an alabaster box of incense, and a cask of palm wine. The Ethiopians, to whom Cambyses sent these things, are reported to be the largest and most handsome of all men. In all their customs they differ from other men, including their manner of choosing a king. They consider most worthy to be king the citizen who is tallest and has strength appropriate to his stature.

Such were the men to whom the Fish-Eaters came, presenting gifts to the King and saying, "Cambyses, King of Persia, desiring to be your friend and guest, sends us as his spokesmen to give you gifts of the sort he takes delight in using himself." But the Ethiopian ruler, seeing that they came as spies, replied to them in this way: "The Persian King does not send you with gifts because he values my friendship, nor do you speak the truth (for you have come to spy on my kingdom), nor is your King a just man. If he were, he would not desire any country other than his own or would he try to make slaves of those who have done him no harm. Now, you take this bow back to him and say this: 'The King of the Ethiopians advises the King of the Persians to mount a massive attack on the long-lived Ethiopians only when he is able to draw a bow of this size as easily as I do. Until then, he should give thanks to the gods for not putting it into the minds of the Ethiopians to take more land than they already have.' "

So saying, he unstrung the bow and handed it to the messengers. Then he took the purple cloak and asked what it was and how it was made. When the Fish-Eaters told him the truth about the purple color and how the cloak was dyed, the King said both the men and their clothes were deceptive. Next he asked about the wrought gold necklace and armlets; and when the Fish-Eaters explained how they were made, the King, supposing them to be bonds, said smiling, "Our fetters are stronger than these." Thirdly, he asked about the incense and, when told how it was made and applied, said it was the same as the cloak—a deception. When he came to the wine, however, and asked how it was made, he was highly pleased with it and further inquired what food their King ate and what was the oldest age a Persian man might live to be. They answered, "Bread," and showed him how wheat grew from fertilized soil; and they said 80 years of life was the most a man could hope for in Persia. To this the Ethiopian remarked it was no wonder their years were few if they ate dung; they probably would not live that long if they did not have the power of the wine to strengthen them. Indicating the draught, he told the Fish-Eaters that the Persians surpassed the Ethiopians in making it.

In turn, the Fish-Eaters asked the King about the Ethiopians' life span and diet; he said that most of them lived 120 years and a few even longer, that they ate roasted meat and drank milk. The spies showed amazement at the account of their life span, whereupon the King led them to a spring where, it is said, by bathing one grows sleek as though it were ointment; the odor is that of violets. The spies later said the water of this spring was so light that nothing would float on it; wood and things lighter than wood all sank to the bottom. If this water was really the way the spies said, it is probably because of their regular use of it that the Ethiopians had such long lives. When they left the spring, the King led them to a prison, in which all the men were bound with golden chains. Nothing is so scarce and precious among the Ethiopians as bronze. After leaving the prison, they saw the so-called Table of the Sun.

Finally, they saw the Ethiopians' coffins, which are said to be made of porcelain in this fashion: they shrink the dead body in the same way the Egyptians do, or by some other process, then cover it with gypsum and paint it all as fully as possible in the likeness of the man when he was alive. They then place it in a hollow column made of porcelain, which they mine in large quantities from the earth and shape readily. The body may be seen through the porcelain there in the center of the column without any unpleasant odors or secretions coming from it; in its entirety it has the appearance of the dead man himself. His closest of kin keep the column in their household for a year, giving it the first fruits of the harvest and making sacrifices to it. Afterward, all the columns are brought out and placed around the city.

Having seen these things, the spies departed and reported everything to Cambyses. Furious, he set out against the Ethiopians without making any plans for providing food to his men or considering that he was leading them to the end of the earth. But before his army had gone even a part of the way toward Ethiopia, all their food was gone and then they ate their beasts of burden. At last, nothing was left; and if Cambyses had been a wise man, he would have led his army home again. But he was out of his mind and maddened, and he marched on, heeding nothing. So long as the soldiers could get anything from the soil, they stayed alive by eating grass; but then they came to a desert of sand, and some of them began a horrible practice, choosing one man out of ten by lot and eating him. When Cambyses learned of this, he became afraid his men would turn into cannibals and so he gave up and marched back to Thebes in Egypt. So ended the expedition against the Ethiopians.

Strabo

✠

THE SCYTHIANS

In the southern part of Germany, the section just next to
the Albis River is occupied by the Suevi tribes, and immediately next to it is the territory of the Getae, which reaches
from the Ister to the mountain border of the Hercynian
forests. I cannot tell the exact boundaries, however. Because
of a general ignorance of these regions, men have made up
the mythical Hyperboreans and the Rhipaean Mountains beyond which they supposedly live. These stories should not be
believed, nor should Sophocles when in his tragedy he describes the maiden Oreithyia being snatched up by Boreas
(the North Wind) and carried "over the entire ocean to
the end of the earth and the origin of night, to the begin-
nings of the heavens and the ancient garden of the Sun."

The Greeks used to think the Getae were Thracians or
Mysi, who lived beyond the Hellespont north of Troy.
Indeed, Homer connected them with the Hippemolgi (Mare-
Milkers) and Galactophagi (Cheese-Eaters) and Abioi, who
are truly the wagon-dwellers, the Scythians. Certainly now
all these tribes are mingled together. Poseidonius the geographer says that the Mysi tribe abstains from eating any
living thing, including their flocks; they use honey, milk,
and cheese for food, leading peaceful lives. Because of this,
they are called "god-fearing" and "smoke-eaters"; and certain of the Thracians who live apart from women are called
"Founders." Highly honored, they are dedicated to the gods
and live free of all fears. According to Poseidonius, Homer
thus speaks of all these Scythian peoples as "proud Mare-
Milkers, Cheese-Eaters, and Abioi, very just men," but he
calls them Abioi particularly because they live away from

Adapted from the *Geography*, VII.3 *et passim*. Translation by
J. W. Johnson.

women in a life that is half-complete. Homer also speaks of
the Mysi as hand to hand fighters because they battle most
nobly.

It is perhaps unnecessary to question this reading, which
has been approved for so long a time. It is much more
believable that the tribe originally called Mysi later had
their name changed to Getae. As for the name "Abioi," it
can just as well mean "those without hearths" or "those
living in wagons" as "those half-complete." Since injustices
usually result from contracts and too exaggerated an opinion
of property, it is reasonable to suppose that those like the
Abioi, who live frugally and with small resources, would be
called "very just."

The philosophers place moderation next to justice. As for
living without women, Homer does not suggest any such
thing, especially concerning the Thracians and Getae.
Compare Menander's statement about them: "All the
Thracians, and most of all we Getae (for I am proud to
belong to that tribe), are not very continent." And later he
sets down the proofs of their incontinence: "Each man
among us marries ten or eleven women, and some marry
twelve or more. If a man dies before he marries four or
five, he is mourned by the people as a miserable creature
without bride and marriage song." These facts are supported
by other writers as well.

Furthermore, it is not reasonable to suppose that a life
lived among many women and a life lived without them
can be equally pious and just. As for being both "god-
fearing" and "womanless," everyone knows that women are
the founders of religion and that they are responsible for
urging the men to be more respectful toward the gods and
holy days and prayers; it is a rare thing for a man living
alone to be devoted to such things. Thus, it is entirely
illogical to assume that womenless men among the Getae
are unusually pious, for Poseidonius and other authorities
tell us that this tribe as a whole is extremely religious and
therefore refuses to eat living creatures.

Apollodorus says that although Homer was familiar with
nearby places, he was ignorant of those farther away from

Greece, which is shown by his not mentioning the Scythians by name but inventing tribal names such as "Mare-
Milkers" and so on. Homer learned from travelers who had
gone on foot to parts of Scythia but he knew nothing of the
distant coasts on the Euxine Sea. Indeed, according to Apollodorus, travel by water to these regions was impossible in
Homer's time because the seas were not navigable. That is
why the sea was called "Euxine," because of its wintry storms
and the ferocity of the tribes living beside it, especially the
Scythians, who sacrificed strangers, then ate their flesh and
used their skulls for drinking cups. But this ignorance in
Homer's case is not surprising since many who lived later
than he were equally ignorant and invented fabulous tales.
So says Apollodorus.

In truth, it is Apollodorus who is ignorant. Even today in
the areas described by Homer there are people who live in
wagons and are nomads, who live off their herds on milk
and cheese, particularly the cheese made from the milk of
mares. These people know nothing about storing up food or
peddling merchandise apart from exchanging goods for other
goods. It is the ancestors of these people, the Scythians, that
Homer called "Mare-Milkers," "Cheese-Eaters," and "Very
Just." The Greeks of Homer's time were accustomed to
calling them that. It is no wonder that with the prevalent
cheating in business among the Greeks, Homer called
"proud" and "most just" men who do not spend their lives
in moneymaking but who actually own everything in common—except their drinking cups and swords. The Scythians
even own wives and children in common, in the way Plato
praises.[1]

Aeschylus the playwright supports Homer when he calls
the Scythians "law-abiding eaters of cheese from the milk of
mares." And even now the belief is common among the
Greeks that the Scythians are the most straightforward of
men and the least inclined to evildoing, as well as more independent and frugal than we are. Unfortunately, our Greek
way of life has spread among other people, changing them

[1] In *The Republic*. See p. 46 below.

for the worse, leading them to sensual and luxurious pleasures; to satisfy their new vices, they take up deceitfulness and cunning and so commit countless acts of greed. Wickedness of this kind has spread even to the modern Scythians.

But those who lived before our time, nearer to Homer's time, were just such people as Homer described and the Greeks believed them to be. See what Herodotus says about the King of the Scythians, when Darius, the Persian King, made an expedition against Scythia and the Scythians retreated in their wagons. Darius sent a message to King Idanthyrsus, reproaching him for fleeing, to which the Scythian replied that he was not retreating but simply moving around as his tribe was accustomed to do during times of peace. If Darius wanted a fight, he might try to locate the ancestral tombs of the Scythians and defile them; then he would learn whether or not the Scythians could fight. As for Darius' assertion that he was the master of the Scythians, Idanthyrsus answered, "Howl on!"

Ephorus, in his book of history entitled *Europe*—and he had traveled as far as Scythia—says that the way of living differed among the various Scythian tribes, some being so fierce as to be cannibals and others abstaining from eating any living thing at all. Ephorus thought that other writers told only about the savage tribes because the terrible and shocking are more exciting; but he himself would give the opposite side of the picture and make the Scythians models of conduct, so he told of those who were "very just," and lived as nomads, feeding on mare's milk and excelling all other people in justice. Ephorus explains that since the Scythians were thrifty in their way of living and were not moneymakers, they were therefore orderly in their arrangements with one another and held wives and children in common, together with all their relatives and possessions. They were invincible and never conquered by outsiders because they had nothing to be enslaved for. Anarcharsis, the Scythian sage, was called "wise" by Ephorus and was considered one of the ancient Seven Wise Men because of his complete self-control and good sense.

The Scythian peoples have always been fierce in battle.

Although they have lately been conquered several times by the Romans, one tribe, the Dacians, who live north of the Danube River, is able to send forth an army of 40,000 men. Another tribe, living north of the Caspian Sea, sent 50,000 men against the forces of Mithradates. Their soldiers use helmets and chestguards made of raw ox-hide, carry wicker shields, and have the spear, bow, and sword for weapons. The nomadic tents are made of felt and fastened on the wagons in which the Scythians spend their lives. Around the tents graze the herds that supply the milk, cheese, and meat the people live on. The wagons follow the trails of the grazing herds as they move on from time to time to other grassy areas, living in the marshes near Lake Maeotis in the winter but on the plains as well during the summer.

The entire country has very severe winters. The coldness of these regions is evident, even though the people inhabit the plains, for the Scythians do not breed asses, animals that are most sensitive to cold. As for their cattle, some are born without horns, while the horns of others are filed off since this part of the beast is sensitive to cold. Their horses are small, but their sheep are large. It is so cold that the bronze water jars of the Scythians burst and their contents freeze solid. The cold is so severe that the rivers freeze and become both ice and roadways. Fish caught in the ice are gotten by digging with an instrument like a trident; sturgeon as large as dolphins may be caught this way. It is said that the general of Mithradates won two victories over the barbarians in the same strait, a naval victory in the summer and a cavalry battle in the winter. It is also said that the people bury their vines during the winter in the region of the Bosporus, piling much earth upon it. It is said, too, that the heat in these regions is extreme as well, perhaps because the people are not used to heat and thus feel it more, or else because the air, being very dense, becomes overheated in warm weather.

Diodorus Siculus

✠

THE EGYPTIANS

The Egyptians say that in the beginning, when the earth came into existence, the first men came into being in Egypt because of the favorable climate there and the nature of the Nile. This river, producing many forms of life and providing a spontaneous supply of food, can readily maintain the life procreated there, for the root of the reed and the lotus, as well as the Egyptian bean and the tubers of the water lily, provide ready-made nourishment for the human race. As proof that animal life first appeared in their land, they argue that even now the soil in the Thebaid generates mice, so numerous and large as to amaze those witnessing the process; some of these creatures are fully formed in their breasts and front feet and are able to move, while the lower part of their bodies remains unformed, still keeping the character of a lump of earth. From this it is obvious that since the formation of the world, this country was the best suited to produce human beings because of the even-tempered character of its soil, for even now while the soil of no other country generates anything like them, in Egypt alone certain forms of life are still being generated in an amazing manner.

When the men of Egypt came into being long ago, they contemplated the heavens and, being struck with wonder and awe, they believed in two gods, the first and everlasting sun and moon, which they called Osiris and Isis. These names were based on the inner meanings of the words, Osiris being translated into "many-eyed" since in diffusing his rays, he looks with many eyes upon all the land and sea. Isis, in turn, meant "ancient" since she was born from the everlasting and ancient heavens. These two gods rule the

Adapted from *The Library of History*, I.10, 16–20, 70–71. Translation by J. W. Johnson.

universe, giving growth and sustenance to everything through a regulated cycle of three seasons, which rotate unobserved through spring to summer to winter and so complete in total symphony the yearly cycle.

It was Osiris who first made the race of men stop being cannibals. When Isis discovered the produce of the wheat and barley plants that grew wild throughout the land along with other plants and when Osiris devised the system of cultivating fruits, mankind was happy to change their food, both because the nature of the new foods pleased them and because they saw it was to their own benefit to stop slaughtering each other. When Osiris had finished setting up affairs in Egypt, he set off on a campaign and so went into Ethiopia. In Ethiopia, according to the story, he had brought before him the Satyrs, who reputedly have hairy loins, for Osiris loved laughter and music and dancing, and the Satyrs were accomplished in dancing and singing and every sort of amusement. Osiris was not a warrior and did not have to plan battles or engagements; the people received him as a god because of his generous deeds. He taught the Ethiopians agriculture, established some famous cities, then left behind him men to administer the country and collect the taxes.

[*Diodorus then describes the reigns of the kings following Osiris*]

At this point, we shall give an account of the customs of Egypt, both the peculiar and those useful to our readers. Many of the ancient customs of the Egyptians not only have been handed down to their present-day descendants but have been accepted as admirable among the Greeks. For that reason, men who have gained the highest reputation for their intellectual accomplishments are very eager to visit Egypt and study its customs and institutions as worthy of notice. The Egyptians themselves say that writing was first invented by them and they began the study of the stars as well as discovering the basic principles of geometry and most of the arts and establishing the best laws. The proof of all this, they say, is the fact that Egypt was ruled for over 4,700 years by kings, most of them native Egyptians, and the land was the most prosperous one in the inhabited world; this could not have happened unless the people followed the most excellent customs and practices and the institutions had promoted culture of every sort. As for the far-fetched stories of Herodotus and others about the Egyptians, they are inventions rather than truth. But this account is taken from the written records of the Egyptian priests, which we have carefully examined.

In the first place, the Egyptian kings did not lead their lives in the same way as other men who exercise monarchic power, doing everything according to their own pleasure without any control. The actions of the king in Egypt were entirely proscribed by law, not only his administrative acts but his daily behavior and diet. Among his servants there were no slaves at all who had been purchased or born in the palace; instead, all those who served the king were sons of the most honored priests, more than twenty in age, the best educated of their group, so that the king, being constantly attended by the best men available, would never follow any base practices. No ruler goes very far into evil unless he is served by those who indulge his passions. The hours of both day and night were carefully planned for the Egyptian monarch, and he was absolutely required to do at the specified time what the law stated and not what he wanted. In the morning when he first awoke, he had to receive all letters that had come from everywhere, the reason being that he might be fully informed of the business of his kingdom and thus take care of his administrative duties promptly and properly. Then he bathed; and after he was dressed in the proper elaborate garments and the trappings of his office, he had to offer a sacrifice to the gods.

Once the sacrificial animals had been brought to the altar, it was the custom for the head priest, standing next to the king, with the crowd of commoners near at hand, to pray in a loud voice that health and every other blessing be granted the king so long as he ruled his subjects justly. The king's virtues were also mentioned by the priest, who declared him respectful toward the gods, generous to men, self-restrained, just, magnanimous, truthful, open-handed with kindnesses, and above all base emotions. The king also was lenient with evil-doers, punishing them less than they deserved, and he repaid those who bestowed gifts on him with greater gifts. Proclaiming these and many more sentiments of the same sort, the priest ended by cursing all done in error, eliminating the king from any blame, and asking the gods to punish those responsible for serving the king wrongly and teaching him wicked ways. All this the priest did, partly to induce the king to fear and honor the gods and partly to condition him to proper conduct, not by hard criticism but by pleasant praise that would lead him to virtue.

After the sacrifices, a scribe read aloud to the assembly from some of the holy books about the inspiring words and deeds of their famous men so that the king, their supreme leader, might contemplate high principles and then the specific actions related to his prescribed role.

There was an established time for every action of his life; and his diet was prescribed with such an emphasis on continence and moderation that it seemed less the work of the lawmaker than a physician of the greatest skill whose only concern was the king's health. Odd as it seems that the king did not control his own diet, even more remarkable was the fact that he could not hand down any legal decision, carry on any incidental business or punish anybody out of malice, anger, or anything but the legal principles established to treat the offense. Nor were the kings of Egypt indignant or secretly offended by this; on the contrary, they considered themselves to lead a very happy life. Whereas other men committed many evil acts, misled by their passions even to the point of doing things they knew very well to be foolish and wrong, the kings cultivated a way of life established by the most wise and prudent men and thus avoided making mistakes. Consequently, the people loved their kings for their uprightness more than they did their own wives and children; the concern of the population was the safety of the ruler. As a result, the Egyptians throughout their long recorded history preserved an orderly government and had a happy life so long as the system of laws was followed. In addition, they conquered more nations and gained greater wealth than other races, and they decorated their country with monuments and adornments that are unsurpassed and their cities with expensive works of dedication of all kinds.

As a whole, the territory of Egypt is divided into three parts. The first is controlled by the priests, who are the most respected not only because they serve the gods and direct their worship but also because they are superior in education and thus intelligence to others. The priests are the first to consider important matters and are always beside the king, to assist him or to suggest actions or instruct him. They can also predict the future, because of their knowledge of astrology and divination; and they aid the king by reading from their sacred records. It is not the same with the Egyptians as with the Greeks, who confine the priesthood only to single men and women; many Egyptians participate in sacred rituals and transmit to their children this way of life. They pay no taxes whatsoever and rank only after the king in honor and authority.

The second part of the country is controlled by the king. He uses this income to pay the cost of wars, support the court, and give rewards to those who have distinguished themselves. In this way, the king avoids overburdening his subjects with taxes, since his land revenues provide him with a large income.

The last part is controlled by the warriors, as they are called, who are available for military service. The idea is that those who risk their lives to serve their country will be especially loyal to the realm where they own land and will engage in war with added fervor, for it would be foolish to trust the safety of the country to men who had no part in it and owned no property valuable enough to make them arduous to defend it. Most importantly, the warriors will sire many children, if they are well enough off, and so increase the military to a size where mercenaries will not be needed. Since the military caste is hereditary, like the priestly, the warriors are incited to heroism by the achievements of their fathers and are unconquerable because of their skill and daring, having been raised up to warfare from childhood.

There are three other classes of free citizens: herdsmen, farmers, and craftsmen. All of these are brought up from infancy to know the trade of their caste; and the legendary experience of their ancestors, together with their own innovations, have made them the best workers and the most knowledgeable on earth. The craftsmen, living in the cities, are forbidden to engage in actions of the public and political kind, as artisans in democratic states are permitted to do. As a result, the Egyptian craftsmen spend their time perfecting their arts, while in other lands the artisans waste time attending public assemblies and meetings and not only lose their skill but stir up all sorts of confusion and political unrest. Such, therefore, are the orders of the citizens, maintained by the first inhabitants of Egypt, and such is their dedication to the class each inherits from his forefathers.

Suggested Additional Readings

Herodotus, *Histories*, I.201–216; II.2–35.
Hippocrates, *Airs, Waters, Places*, XVII–XXII
Justin, *History of the World*, I–XV
Diodorus Siculus in *The Library of History*, I.6–9; II. 35–37, 47–55, 55–60; III.2–17

Questions for Discussion and Writing

1. Prehistoric legends of utopian tribes emphasized the relationship of the state of blessedness to man's dependence on God or the gods. To what extent do the Ethiopians, Scythians, and Egyptians derive their perfect happiness from their relationship with divinities?

2. In what significant way does Herodotus' account of the Ethiopians stress qualities or conditions for perfection that

differ from those set forth in earlier legends? What does this shift in emphasis suggest to you about the idea of utopia as it was changing?

3. In what obvious ways do the Egyptians (as Diodorus describes them) resemble the Ethiopians of Herodotus? In what important ways do they differ?

4. The Scythians (in the accounts by Herodotus, Strabo, Hippocrates, and others) are unlike most utopian peoples. Compare and contrast them with the Egyptians and Ethiopians and list their unique characteristics.

5. A number of modern scholarly works have dealt with the ideas of primitivism in the ancient world, notably *Primitivism and Related Ideas in Antiquity* by Arthur O. Lovejoy and George Boas. Consult this or other works for a working definition of primitivism, and suggest how the primitivistic concept became involved with utopian thinking.

6. The Scythians are "noble savages" to Strabo—that is, in their state of cultural simplicity, even crudity, they are believed to have moral qualities superior to more civilized peoples. What moral qualities do the Scythians supposedly possess? Are these qualities derived from the Scythians' relationship to God or from other sources?

7. To what extent does the idea of physical invulnerability —because of geographical location, military prowess, or divine protection—appear in Greco-Roman historiography? How do you explain this?

8. In the main, do the early historians show the Ethiopians *et al.* as practical working models of behavior for Greeks and Romans who wish to attain an organized (political) utopia? Why? Do they supply a working model for individual men to attain perfect happiness? Discuss.

9. Choose some aspect of the utopian vision in Greco-Roman history—the sensual or physical, the political, the moral, the religious—and trace its development from the earlier utopias in prehistoric legend.

10. Write (or report orally) on one of these subjects:
    a. The Fountain of Youth
    b. The Tree of Life
    c. The Autochthonous Theory of Man's Origin
    d. "Mother" Nature
    e. The Scythians in Hebrew History
    f. The Ichthyophagoi (Fish-Eaters)
    g. Ethiopia in Roman History
    h. The Scythians and the American Indian
    i. Scythia, Egypt, and the Age of the World
    j. Utopia and Death

III

Classical
Political Theorists

Introduction

The attainability of a perfect society assumed by Greek and
Roman historians was accepted eagerly by political theorists
of the classical period. Some of these theorists—for instance,
Polybius (c. 202–120 B.C.), a Greek military man who composed an inclusive history of Rome—were also historians.
Polybius' theory of a balanced, three-part government was
advanced as a proposal for an improved Roman government;
it was taken up by later historians (Diodorus, Livy); and in
time it influenced the making of the Constitution of the
United States. Similarly, utopian political theory was written by classical philosophers and biographers.

The most famous of these was the Greek philosopher
Plato (c. 427–348 B.C.). A pupil of the equally famous
Socrates, whom Plato made spokesman in his work, this
Greek thinker was concerned with every branch of philoso-
phy but especially with modes of conduct, private and pub-
lic. In one of his dialogues, the *Timaeus*, Plato used the

fable of a utopian country, Atlantis, located somewhere past the bounds of known geography, the Pillars of Hercules or Gibraltar. Atlantis was probably Plato's adaptation of an earlier legend of Elysium, or the Happy Islands, supposedly far west of the Pillars, out in the Atlantic Ocean.

In his full-scale treatment, *The Republic*, Plato systematically developed his blueprint of ways to bring into existence the ideal state. This state could be realized by living men, provided they developed proper—that is, rational or "reasonable"—ways of thinking about the universe, the gods, human society, each other, and themselves. A rational, orderly, virtuous society must be well-regulated; Plato worked out a hierarchy of classes, three in number, defining the duties and responsibilities of each class. The state must transcend its citizens. The state would raise most children, regulate all economic and social activities, and protect some rights by denying others. In some ways, Plato seems to have been trying to make human societies into the passionless, functioning societies of bees or ants, which he often used as analogies. When he was invited by the rulers of Syracuse, the Greek colony on Sicily, to put his plans into practice, he found that human beings were not yet ready for the utopia he had planned.

Plutarch (c. 46–120), a Greek biographer who subscribed to Plato's philosophy, was also much concerned with moral and ethical matters. In the *Lives*, a group of comparative biographies, and the *Moralia*, he set up a number of models of behavior, suggesting ways for his readers to better themselves as men and citizens. In his life of Lycurgus, he not only showed a model ruler of a model state in the historical past; he also suggested that utopia was a practicable way of life, since it had once been attained. Both Plato and Plutarch asserted that men had only to think clearly in order to see ways of perfecting themselves and society and then to set about achieving their utopian goal. One thought the means to utopia lay in contemplating the past; but both postulated a progression toward an obtainable perfection. Striving for utopia meant willing, working, and attaining in stages: "progress." Since Plato, the link between the idea of progress and achieving perfection in the future has become vital in much utopian thought.

Plato

✳

THE REPUBLIC

Here Adeimantus interposed a question: How would you answer, Socrates, said he, if a person were to say that you are making[1] these people miserable, and that they are the cause of their own unhappiness; the city in fact belongs to them, but they are none the better for it; whereas other men acquire lands, and build large and handsome houses, and have everything handsome about them, offering sacrifices to the gods on their own account, and practicing hospitality; moreover, as you were saying just now, they have gold and silver, and all that is usual among the favorites of fortune; but our poor citizens are no better than mercenaries who are quartered in the city and are always mounting guard?

Yes, I said; and you may add that they are only fed, and not paid in addition to their food, like other men; and therefore they cannot, if they would, take a journey of pleasure; they have no money to spend on a mistress or any other luxurious fancy, which, as the world goes, is thought to be happiness; and many other accusations of the same nature might be added.

But, said he, let us suppose all this to be included in the charge.

You mean to ask, I said, what will be our answer?

Yes.

From Book IV of *The Republic*. Translation by Benjamin Jowett.
[1] Or, 'that for their own good you are making these people miserable.'

If we proceed along the old path, my belief, I said, is that we shall find the answer. And our answer will be that, even as they are, our guardians may very likely be the happiest of men; but that our aim in founding the State was not the disproportionate happiness of any one class, but the greatest happiness of the whole; we thought that in a State which is ordered with a view to the good of the whole we should be most likely to find justice, and in the ill-ordered State injustice: and, having found them, we might then decide which of the two is the happier. At present, I take it, we are fashioning the happy State, not piecemeal, or with a view of making a few happy citizens, but as a whole; and by-and-by we will proceed to view the opposite kind of State. Suppose that we were painting a statue, and some one came up to us and said, Why do you not put the most beautiful colors on the most beautiful parts of the body— the eyes ought to be purple, but you have made them black —to him we might fairly answer, Sir, you would not surely have us beautify the eyes to such a degree that they are no longer eyes; consider rather whether, by giving this and the other features their due proportion, we make the whole beautiful. And so I say to you, do not compel us to assign to the guardians a sort of happiness which will make them anything but guardians; for we too can clothe our husbandmen in royal apparel, and set crowns of gold on their heads, and bid them till the ground as much as they like, and no more. Our potters also might be allowed to repose on couches, and feast by the fireside, passing round the winecup, while their wheel is conveniently at hand, and working at pottery only as much as they like; in this way we might make every class happy—and then, as you imagine, the whole State would be happy. But do not put this idea into our heads; for, if we listen to you, the husbandman will be no longer a husbandman, the potter will cease to be a potter, and no one will have the character of any distinct class in the State. Now this is not of much consequence where the corruption of society, and pretension to be what you are not, is confined to cobblers; but when the guardians of the laws and of the government are only seemingly and not real guardians, then see how they turn the State upside down; and on the other hand they alone have the power of giving order and happiness to the State. We mean our guardians to be true saviors and not the destroyers of the State, whereas our opponent is thinking of peasants at a festival, who are enjoying a life of revelry, not of citizens who are doing their duty to the State. But, if so, we mean different things, and he is speaking of something which is not a State. And therefore we must consider whether in appointing our guardians we would look to their greatest happiness individually, or whether this principle of happiness does not rather reside in the State as a whole. But if the latter be the truth, then the guardians and auxiliaries, and all others equally with them, must be compelled or induced to do their own work in the best way. And thus the whole State will grow up in a noble order, and the several classes will receive the proportion of happiness which nature assigns to them.

I think that you are quite right.

I wonder whether you will agree with another remark which occurs to me.

What may that be?

There seem to be two causes of the deterioration of the arts.

What are they?

Wealth, I said, and poverty.

How do they act?

The process is as follows: When a potter becomes rich, will he, think you, any longer take the same pains with his art?

Certainly not.

He will grow more and more indolent and careless?

Very true.

And the result will be that he becomes a worse potter?

Yes; he greatly deteriorates.

But, on the other hand, if he has no money, and cannot provide himself with tools or instruments, he will not work equally well himself, nor will he teach his sons or apprentices to work equally well.

Certainly not.

Then, under the influence either of poverty or of wealth, workmen and their work are equally liable to degenerate?

That is evident.

Here, then, is a discovery of new evils, I said, against which the guardians will have to watch, or they will creep into the city unobserved.

What evils?

Wealth, I said, and poverty; the one is the parent of luxury and indolence, and the other of meanness and viciousness, and both of discontent.

That is very true, he replied; but still I should like to know, Socrates, how our city will be able to go to war, especially against an enemy who is rich and powerful, if deprived of the sinews of war.

There would certainly be a difficulty, I replied, in going to war with one such enemy; but there is no difficulty where there are two of them.

How so? he asked.

In the first place, I said, if we have to fight, our side will be trained warriors fighting against an army of rich men.

That is true, he said.

And do you not suppose, Adeimantus, that a single boxer who was perfect in his art would easily be a match for two stout and well-to-do gentlemen who were not boxers?

Hardly, if they came upon him at once.

What, not, I said, if he were able to run away and then turn and strike at the one who first came up? And supposing he were to do this several times under the heat of a scorching sun, might he not, being an expert, overturn more than one stout personage?

Certainly, he said, there would be nothing wonderful in that.

And yet rich men probably have a greater superiority in the science and practice of boxing than they have in military qualities.

Likely enough.

Then we may assume that our athletes will be able to fight with two or three times their own number?

I agree with you, for I think you right.

And suppose that, before engaging, our citizens send an embassy to one of the two cities, telling them what is the truth: Silver and gold we neither have nor are permitted to have, but you may; do you therefore come and help us in war, and take the spoils of the other city: Who, on hearing these words, would choose to fight against lean wiry dogs, rather than, with the dogs on their side, against fat and tender sheep?

That is not likely; and yet there might be a danger to the poor State if the wealth of many States were to be gathered into one.

But how simple of you to use the term State at all of any but our own!

Why so?

You ought to speak of other States in the plural number; not one of them is a city, but many cities, as they say in the game. For indeed any city, however small, is in fact divided into two, one the city of the poor, the other of the rich; these are at war with one another; and in either there are many smaller divisions, and you would be altogether beside the mark if you treated them all as a single State. But if you deal with them as many, and give the wealth or power or persons of the one to the others, you will always have a great many friends and not many enemies. And your State, while the wise order which has now been prescribed continues to prevail in her, will be the greatest of States, I do not mean to say in reputation or appearance, but in deed and truth, though she number not more than a thousand defenders. A single State which is her equal you will hardly find, either among Hellenes or barbarians, though many that appear to be as great and many times greater.

That is most true, he said.

And what, I said, will be the best limit for our rulers to fix when they are considering the size of the State and the amount of territory which they are to include, and beyond which they will not go?

What limit would you propose?

I would allow the State to increase so far as is consistent with unity; that, I think, is the proper limit.

Very good, he said.

Here then, I said, is another order which will have to be conveyed to our guardians: Let our city be accounted neither large nor small, but one and self-sufficing.

And surely, said he, this is not a very severe order which we impose upon them.

And the other, said I, of which we were speaking before is lighter still—I mean the duty of degrading the offspring of the guardians when inferior, and of elevating into the rank of guardians the offspring of the lower classes, when naturally superior. The intention was, that, in the case of the citizens generally, each individual should be put to the use for which nature intended him, one to one work, and then every man would do his own business, and be one and not many; and so the whole city would be one and not many.

Yes, he said; that is not so difficult.

The regulations which we are prescribing, my good Adeimantus, are not, as might be supposed, a number of great principles, but trifles all, if care be taken, as the saying is, of the one great thing—a thing, however, which I would rather call, not great, but sufficient for our purpose.

What may that be? he asked.

Education, I said, and nurture: If our citizens are well educated, and grow into sensible men, they will easily see their way through all these, as well as other matters which I omit; such, for example, as marriage, the possession of women and the procreation of children, which will all follow the general principle that friends have all things in common, as the proverb says.

That will be the best way of settling them.

Also, I said, the State, if once started well, moves with accumulating force like a wheel. For good nurture and education implant good constitutions, and these good constitutions taking root in a good education improve more and more, and this improvement affects the breed in man as in other animals.

Very possibly, he said.

Then to sum up: This is the point to which, above all, the attention of our rulers should be directed—that music and gymnastic be preserved in their original form, and no innovation made. They must do their utmost to maintain them intact. And when any one says that mankind most regard

The newest song which the singers have,[2]

they will be afraid that he may be praising, not new songs, but a new kind of song; and this ought not to be praised, or conceived to be the meaning of the poet; for any musical innovation is full of danger to the whole State, and ought to be prohibited. So Damon tells me, and I can quite believe him;—he says that when modes of music change, the fundamental laws of the State always change with them.

Yes, said Adeimantus; and you may add my suffrage to Damon's and your own.

Then, I said, our guardians must lay the foundations of their fortress in music?

Yes, he said; the lawlessness of which you speak too easily steals in.

Yes, I replied, in the form of amusement; and at first sight it appears harmless.

Why, yes, he said, and there is no harm; were it not that little by little this spirit of license, finding a home, imperceptibly penetrates into manners and customs; whence, issuing with greater force, it invades contracts between man and man, and from contracts goes on to laws and constitutions, in utter recklessness, ending at last, Socrates, by an overthrow of all rights, private as well as public.

Is that true? I said.

That is my belief, he replied.

Then, as I was saying, our youth should be trained from

[2] Odyssey, i, 352.

the first in a stricter system, for if amusements become lawless, and the youths themselves become lawless, they can never grow up into well-conducted and virtuous citizens.

Very true, he said.

And when they have made a good beginning in play, and by the help of music have gained the habit of good order, then this habit of order, in a manner how unlike the lawless play of the others! will accompany them in all their actions and be a principle of growth to them, and if there be any fallen places in the State will raise them up again.

Very true, he said.

Thus educated, they will invent for themselves any lesser rules which their predecessors have altogether neglected.

What do you mean?

I mean such things as these:—when the young are to be silent before their elders; how they are to show respect to them by standing and making them sit; what honor is due to parents; what garments or shoes are to be worn; the mode of dressing the hair; deportment and manners in general. You would agree with me?

Yes.

But there is, I think, small wisdom in legislating about such matters—I doubt if it is ever done; nor are any precise written enactments about them likely to be lasting.

Impossible.

It would seem, Adeimantus, that the direction in which education starts a man, will determine his future life. Does not like always attract like?

To be sure.

Until some one rare and grand result is reached which may be good, and may be the reverse of good?

That is not to be denied.

And for this reason, I said, I shall not attempt to legislate further about them.

Naturally enough, he replied.

Well, and about the business of the agora, and the ordinary dealings between man and man, or again about agreements with artisans; about insult and injury, or the commencement of actions, and the appointment of juries, what would you say? there may also arise questions about any impositions and extractions of market and harbor dues which may be required, and in general about the regulations of markets, police, harbors, and the like. But, oh heavens! shall we condescend to legislate on any of these particulars?

I think, he said, that there is no need to impose laws about them on good men; what regulations are necessary they will find out soon enough for themselves.

Yes, I said, my friend, if God will only preserve to them the laws which we have given them.

And without divine help, said Adeimantus, they will go on for ever making and mending their laws and their lives in the hope of attaining perfection.

You would compare them, I said, to those invalids who, having no self-restraint, will not leave off their habits of intemperance?

Exactly.

Yes, I said; and what a delightful life they lead! they are always doctoring and increasing and complicating their disorders, and always fancying that they will be cured by any nostrum which anybody advises them to try.

Such cases are very common, he said, with invalids of this sort.

Yes, I replied; and the charming thing is that they deem him their worst enemy who tells them the truth, which is simply that, unless they give up eating and drinking and wenching and idling, neither drug nor cautery nor spell nor amulet nor any other remedy will avail.

Charming! he replied. I see nothing charming in going into a passion with a man who tells you what is right.

These gentlemen, I said, do not seem to be in your good graces.

Assuredly not.

Nor would you praise the behavior of States which act like the men whom I was just now describing. For are there not ill-ordered States in which the citizens are forbidden under pain of death to alter the constitution; and yet he who most sweetly courts those who live under this régime and indulges them and fawns upon them and is skillful in anticipating and gratifying their humors is held to be a great and good statesman—do not these States resemble the persons whom I was describing?

Yes, he said; the States are as bad as the men; and I am very far from praising them.

But do you not admire, I said, the coolness and dexterity of these ready ministers of political corruption?

Yes, he said, I do; but not of all of them, for there are some whom the applause of the multitude has deluded into the belief that they are really statesmen, and these are not much to be admired.

What do you mean? I said; you should have more feeling for them. When a man cannot measure, and a great many others who cannot measure declare that he is four cubits high, can he help believing what they say?

Nay, he said, certainly not in that case.

Well, then, do not be angry with them; for are they not as good as a play, trying their hand at paltry reforms such as I was describing; they are always fancying that by legislation they will make an end of frauds in contracts, and the other rascalities which I was mentioning, not knowing that they are in reality cutting off the heads of a hydra?

Yes, he said; that is just what they are doing.

I conceive, I said, that the true legislator will not trouble himself with this class of enactments whether concerning laws or the constitution either in an ill-ordered or in a well-ordered State; for in the former they are quite useless, and in the latter there will be no difficulty in devising them; and many of them will naturally flow out of our previous regulations.

What, then, he said, is still remaining to us of the work of legislation?

Nothing to us, I replied; but to Apollo, the God of Delphi, there remains the ordering of the greatest and noblest and chiefest things of all.

Which are they? he said.

The institution of temples and sacrifices, and the entire service of gods, demigods, and heroes; also the ordering of the repositories of the dead, and the rites which have to be observed by him who would propitiate the inhabitants of the world below. These are matters of which we are ignorant ourselves, and as founders of a city we should be unwise in trusting them to any interpreter but our ancestral deity. He is the god who sits in the center, on the navel of the earth, and he is the interpreter of religion to all mankind.

You are right, and we will do as you propose.

But where, amid all this, is justice? son of Ariston, tell me where. Now that our city has been made habitable, light a candle and search, and get your brother and Polemarchus and the rest of our friends to help, and let us see where in it we can discover justice and where injustice, and in what they differ from one another, and which of them the man who would be happy should have for his portion, whether seen or unseen by gods and men.

Nonsense, said Glaucon: did you not promise to search yourself, saying that for you not to help justice in her need would be an impiety?

I do not deny that I said so, and as you remind me, I will be as good as my word; but you must join.

We will, he replied.

Well, then, I hope to make the discovery in this way: I mean to begin with the assumption that our State, if rightly ordered, is perfect.

That is most certain.

And being perfect, is therefore wise and valiant and temperate and just.

That is likewise clear.

And whichever of these qualities we find in the State, the one which is not found will be the residue?

Very good.

If there were four things, and we were searching for one of them, wherever it might be, the one sought for might be known to us from the first, and there would be no further trouble; or we might know the other three first, and then the fourth would clearly be the one left.

Very true, he said.

And is not a similar method to be pursued about the virtues, which are also four in number?

Clearly.

First among the virtues found in the State, wisdom comes into view, and in this I detect a certain peculiarity.

What is that?

The State which we have been describing is said to be wise as being good in counsel?

Very true.

And good counsel is clearly a kind of knowledge, for not by ignorance, but by knowledge, do men counsel well?

Clearly.

And the kinds of knowledge in a State are many and diverse?

Of course.

There is the knowledge of the carpenter; but is that the sort of knowledge which gives a city the title of wise and good in counsel?

Certainly not; that would only give a city the reputation of skill in carpentering.

Then a city is not to be called wise because possessing a knowledge which counsels for the best about wooden implements?

Certainly not.

Nor by reason of a knowledge which advises about brazen pots, I said, nor as possessing any other similar knowledge?

Not by reason of any of them, he said.

Nor yet by reason of a knowledge which cultivates the earth; that would give the city the name of agricultural?

Yes.

Well, I said, and is there any knowledge in our recently founded State among any of the citizens which advises, not about any particular thing in the State, but about the whole, and considers how a State can best deal with itself and with other States?

There certainly is.

And what is this knowledge, and among whom is it found? I asked.

It is the knowledge of the guardians, he replied, and is

found among those whom we were just now describing as perfect guardians.

And what is the name which the city derives from the possession of this sort of knowledge?

The name of good in counsel and truly wise.

And will there be in our city more of these true guardians or more smiths?

The smiths, he replied, will be far more numerous.

Will not the guardians be the smallest of all the classes who receive a name from the profession of some kind of knowledge?

Much the smallest.

And so by reason of the smallest part or class, and of the knowledge which resides in this presiding and ruling part of itself, the whole State, being thus constituted according to nature, will be wise; and this, which has the only knowledge worthy to be called wisdom, has been ordained by nature to be of all classes the least.

Most true.

Thus, then, I said, the nature and place in the State of one of the four virtues has somehow or other been discovered.

And, in my humble opinion, very satisfactorily discovered, he replied.

Again, I said, there is no difficulty in seeing the nature of courage, and in what part that quality resides which gives the name of courageous to the State.

How do you mean?

Why, I said, every one who calls any State courageous or cowardly, will be thinking of the part which fights and goes out to war on the State's behalf.

No one, he replied, would ever think of any other.

Certainly not.

The rest of the citizens may be courageous or may be cowardly but their courage or cowardice will not, as I conceive, have the effect of making the city either the one or the other.

The city will be courageous in virtue of a portion of herself which preserves under all circumstances that opinion about the nature of things to be feared and not to be feared in which our legislator educated them; and this is what you term courage.

I should like to hear what you are saying once more, for I do not think that I perfectly understand you.

I mean that courage is a kind of salvation.

Salvation of what?

Of the opinion respecting things to be feared, what they are and of what nature, which the law implants through education; and I mean by the words 'under all circumstances' to intimate that in pleasure or in pain, or under the influence of desire or fear, a man preserves, and does not lose this opinion. Shall I give you an illustration?

If you please.

You know, I said, that dyers, when they want to dye wool for making the true sea-purple, begin by selecting their white color first; this they prepare and dress with much care and pains, in order that the white ground may take the purple hue in full perfection. The dyeing then proceeds; and whatever is dyed in this manner becomes a fast color, and no washing either with lyes or without them can take away the bloom. But, when the ground has not been duly prepared, you will have noticed how poor is the look either of purple or of any other color.

Yes, he said; I know that they have a washed-out and ridiculous appearance.

Then now, I said, you will understand what our object was in selecting our soldiers, and educating them in music and gymnastic; we were contriving influences which would prepare them to take the dye of the laws in perfection, and the color of their opinion about dangers and of every other opinion was to be indelibly fixed by their nurture and training, not to be washed away by such potent lyes as pleasure —mightier agent far in washing the soul than any soda or lye; or by sorrow, fear, and desire, the mightiest of all other solvents. And this sort of universal saving power of true opinion in conformity with law about real and false dangers I call and maintain to be courage, unless you disagree.

But I agree, he replied; for I suppose that you mean to

exclude mere uninstructed courage, such as that of a wild beast or of a slave—this, in your opinion, is not the courage which the law ordains, and ought to have another name.

Most certainly.

Then I may infer courage to be such as you describe?

Why, yes, said I, you may, and if you add the words 'of a citizen,' you will not be far wrong;—hereafter, if you like, we will carry the examination further, but at present we are seeking not for courage but justice; and for the purpose of our enquiry we have said enough.

You are right, he replied.

Two virtues remain to be discovered in the State—first temperance, and then justice which is the end of our search.

Very true.

Now, can we find justice without troubling ourselves about temperance?

I do not know how that can be accomplished, he said, nor do I desire that justice should be brought to light and temperance lost sight of; and therefore I wish that you would do me the favor of considering temperance first.

Certainly, I replied, I should not be justified in refusing your request.

Then consider, he said.

Yes, I replied; I will; and as far as I can at present see, the virtue of temperance has more of the nature of harmony and symphony than the preceding.

How so? he asked.

Temperance, I replied, is the ordering or controlling of certain pleasures and desires; this is curiously enough implied in the saying of 'a man being his own master'; and other traces of the same notion may be found in language.

No doubt, he said.

There is something ridiculous in the expression 'master of himself'; for the master is also the servant and the servant the master; and in all these modes of speaking the same person is denoted.

Certainly.

The meaning is, I believe, that in the human soul there is a better and also a worse principle; and when the better has the worse under control, then a man is said to be master of himself; and this is a term of praise: but when, owing to evil education or association, the better principle, which is also the smaller, is overwhelmed by the greater mass of the worse—in this case he is blamed and is called the slave of self and unprincipled.

Yes, there is reason in that.

And now, I said, look at our newly created State, and there you will find one of these two conditions realized; for the State, as you will acknowledge, may be justly called master of itself, if the words 'temperance' and 'self-mastery' truly express the rule of the better part over the worse.

Yes, he said, I see that what you say is true.

Let me further note that the manifold and complex pleasures and desires and pains are generally found in children and women and servants, and in the freemen so called who are of the lowest and more numerous class.

Certainly, he said.

Whereas the simple and moderate desires which follow reason, and are under the guidance of mind and true opinion, are to be found only in a few, and those the best born and best educated.

Very true.

These two, as you may perceive, have a place in our State; and the meaner desires of the many are held down by the virtuous desires and wisdom of the few.

That I perceive, he said.

Then if there be any city which may be described as master of its own pleasures and desires, and master of itself, ours may claim such a designation?

Certainly, he replied.

It may also be called temperate, and for the same reasons?

Yes.

And if there be any State in which rulers and subjects will be agreed as to the question who are to rule, that again will be our State?

Undoubtedly.

And the citizens being thus agreed among themselves, in

which class will temperance be found—in the rulers or in the subjects?

In both, as I should imagine, he replied.

Do you observe that we were not far wrong in our guess that temperance was a sort of harmony?

Why so?

Why, because temperance is unlike courage and wisdom, each of which resides in a part only, the one making the State wise and the other valiant; not so temperance, which extends to the whole, and runs through all the notes of the scale, and produces a harmony of the weaker and the stronger and the middle class, whether you suppose them to be stronger or weaker in wisdom or power or numbers or wealth, or anything else. Most truly then may we deem temperance to be the agreement of the naturally superior and inferior, as to the right to rule of either, both in states and individuals.

I entirely agree with you.

And so, I said, we may consider three out of the four virtues to have been discovered in our State. The last of those qualities which make a state virtuous must be justice, if we only knew what that was.

The inference is obvious.

The time then has arrived, Glaucon, when, like huntsmen, we should surround the cover, and look sharp that justice does not steal away, and pass out of sight and escape us; for beyond a doubt she is somewhere in this country: watch therefore and strive to catch a sight of her, and if you see her first, let me know.

Would that I could! but you should regard me rather as a follower who has just eyes enough to see what you show him—that is about as much as I am good for.

Offer up a prayer with me and follow.

I will, but you must show me the way.

Here is no path, I said, and the wood is dark and perplexing; still we must push on.

Let us push on.

Here I saw something: Halloo! I said, I begin to perceive a track, and I believe that the quarry will not escape.

Good news, he said.

Truly, I said, we are stupid fellows.

Why so?

Why, my good sir, at the beginning of our enquiry, ages ago, there was justice tumbling out at our feet, and we never saw her; nothing could be more ridiculous. Like people who go about looking for what they have in their hands—that was the way with us—we looked not at what we were seeking, but at what was far off in the distance; and therefore, I suppose, we missed her.

What do you mean?

I mean to say that in reality for a long time past we have been talking of justice, and have failed to recognize her.

I grow impatient at the length of your exordium.

Well then, tell me, I said, whether I am right or not: You remember the original principle which we were always laying down at the foundation of the State, that one man should practice one thing only, the thing to which his nature was best adapted;—now justice is this principle or a part of it.

Yes, we often said that one man should do one thing only.

Further, we affirmed that justice was doing one's own business, and not being a busybody; we said so again and again, and many others have said the same to us.

Yes, we said so.

Then to do one's own business in a certain way may be assumed to be justice. Can you tell me whence I derive this inference?

I cannot, but I should like to be told.

Because I think that this is the only virtue which remains in the State when the other virtues of temperance and courage and wisdom are abstracted; and, that this is the ultimate cause and condition of the existence of all of them, and while remaining in them is also their preservative; and we were saying that if the three were discovered by us, justice would be the fourth or remaining one.

That follows of necessity.

If we are asked to determine which of these four qualities by its presence contributes most to the excellence of the

State, whether the agreement of rulers and subjects, or the preservation in the soldiers of the opinion which the law ordains about the true nature of dangers, or wisdom and watchfulness in the rulers, or whether this other which I am mentioning, and which is found in children and women, slave and freeman, artisan, ruler, subject—the quality, I mean, of every one doing his own work, and not being a busybody, would claim the palm—the question is not so easily answered.

Certainly, he replied, there would be a difficulty in saying which.

Then the power of each individual in the State to do his own work appears to compete with the other political virtues, wisdom, temperance, courage.

Yes, he said.

And the virtue which enters into this competition is justice?

Exactly.

Let us look at the question from another point of view: Are not the rulers in a State those to whom you would entrust the office of determining suits at law?

Certainly.

And are suits decided on any other ground but that a man may neither take what is another's, nor be deprived of what is his own?

Yes; that is their principle.

Which is a just principle?

Yes.

Then on this view also justice will be admitted to be the having and doing what is a man's own, and belongs to him?

Very true.

Think, now, and say whether you agree with me or not. Suppose a carpenter to be doing the business of a cobbler, or a cobbler of a carpenter; and suppose them to exchange their implements or their duties, or the same person to be doing the work of both, or whatever be the change; do you think that any great harm would result to the State?

Not much.

But when the cobbler or any other man whom nature

designed to be a trader, having his heart lifted up by wealth or strength or the number of his followers, or any like advantage, attempts to force his way into the class of warriors, or a warrior into that of legislators and guardians, for which he is unfitted, and either to take the implements or the duties of the other; or when one man is trader, legislator, and warrior all in one, then I think you will agree with me in saying that this interchange and this meddling of one with another is the ruin of the State.

Most true.

Seeing then, I said, that there are three distinct classes, any meddling of one with another, or the change of one into another, is the greatest harm to the State, and may be most justly termed evil-doing?

Precisely.

And the greatest degree of evil-doing to one's own city would be termed by you injustice?

Certainly.

This then is injustice; and on the other hand when the trader, the auxiliary, and the guardian each do their own business, that is justice, and will make the city just.

I agree with you.

We will not, I said, be over-positive as yet; but if, on trial, this conception of justice be verified in the individual as well as in the State, there will be no longer any room for doubt; if it be not verified, we must have a fresh enquiry. First let us complete the old investigation, which we began, as you remember, under the impression that, if we could previously examine justice on the larger scale, there would be less difficulty in discerning her in the individual. That larger example appeared to be the State, and accordingly we constructed as good a one as we could, knowing well that in the good State justice would be found. Let the discovery which we made be now applied to the individual —if they agree, we shall be satisfied; or, if there be a difference in the individual, we will come back to the State and have another trial of the theory. The friction of the two when rubbed together may possibly strike a light in which justice will shine forth, and the vision which is then revealed we will fix in our souls.

That will be in regular course; let us do as you say.

I proceeded to ask: When two things, a greater and less, are called by the same name, are they like or unlike in so far as they are called the same?

Like, he replied.

The just man then, if we regard the idea of justice only, will be like the just State?

He will.

And a State was thought by us to be just when the three classes in the State severally did their own business; and also thought to be temperate and valiant and wise by reason of certain other affections and qualities of these same classes?

True, he said.

And so of the individual; we may assume that he has the same three principles in his own soul which are found in the State; and he may be rightly described in the same terms, because he is affected in the same manner?

Certainly, he said. . . .

And so, after much tossing, we have reached land, and are fairly agreed that the same principles which exist in the State exist also in the individual, and that they are three in number.

Exactly.

Must we not then infer that the individual is wise in the same way, and in virtue of the same quality which makes the State wise?

Certainly.

Also that the same quality which constitutes courage in the State constitutes courage in the individual, and that both the State and the individual bear the same relation to all the other virtues?

Assuredly.

And the individual will be acknowledged by us to be just in the same way in which the State is just?

That follows, of course.

We cannot but remember that the justice of the State

consisted in each of the three classes doing the work of its own class?

We are not very likely to have forgotten, he said.

We must recollect that the individual in whom the several qualities of his nature do their own work will be just, and will do his own work?

Yes, he said, we must remember that too.

And ought not the rational principle, which is wise, and has the care of the whole soul, to rule, and the passionate or spirited principle to be the subject and ally?

Certainly.

And, as we were saying, the united influence of music and gymnastic will bring them into accord, nerving and sustaining the reason with noble words and lessons, and moderating and soothing and civilizing the wildness of passion by harmony and rhythm.

Quite true, he said.

And these two, thus nurtured and educated, and having learned truly to know their own functions, will rule over the concupiscent, which in each of us is the largest part of the soul and by nature most insatiable of gain; over this they will keep guard, lest, waxing great and strong with the fullness of bodily pleasures, as they are termed, the concupiscent soul, no longer confined to her own sphere, should attempt to enslave and rule those who are not her natural-born subjects, and overturn the whole life of man?

Very true, he said.

Both together will they not be the best defenders of the whole soul and the whole body against attacks from without; the one counseling, and the other fighting under his leader, and courageously executing his commands and counsels?

True.

And he is to be deemed courageous whose spirit retains in pleasure and in pain the commands of reason about what he ought or ought not to fear?

Right, he replied.

And him we call wise who has in him that little part which rules, and which proclaims these commands; that part too being supposed to have a knowledge of what is for the interest of each of the three parts and of the whole?

Assuredly.

And would you not say that he is temperate who has these same elements in friendly harmony, in whom the one ruling principle of reason, and the two subject ones of spirit and desire are equally agreed that reason ought to rule, and do not rebel?

Certainly, he said, that is the true account of temperance whether in the State or individual.

And surely, I said, we have explained again and again how and by virtue of what quality a man will be just.

That is very certain.

And is justice dimmer in the individual, and is her form different, or is she the same which we found her to be in the State?

There is no difference in my opinion, he said.

Because, if any doubt is still lingering in our minds, a few commonplace instances will satisfy us of the truth of what I am saying.

What sort of instances do you mean?

If the case is put to us, must we not admit that the just State, or the man who is trained in the principles of such a State, will be less likely than the unjust to make away with a deposit of gold or silver? Would any one deny this?

No one, he replied.

Will the just man or citizen ever be guilty of sacrilege or theft, or treachery either to his friends or to his country?

Never.

Neither will he ever break faith where there have been oaths or agreements?

Impossible.

No one will be less likely to commit adultery, or to dishonor his father and mother, or to fail in his religious duties?

No one.

And the reason is that each part of him is doing its own business, whether in ruling or being ruled?

Exactly so.

Are you satisfied then that the quality which makes such men and such states is justice, or do you hope to discover some other?

Not I, indeed.

Then our dream has been realized; and the suspicion which we entertained at the beginning of our work of construction, that some divine power must have conducted us to a primary form of justice, has now been verified?

Yes, certainly.

And the division of labor which required the carpenter and the shoemaker and the rest of the citizens to be doing each his own business, and not another's, was a shadow of justice, and for that reason it was of use?

Clearly.

But in reality justice was such as we were describing, being concerned however, not with the outward man, but with the inward, which is the true self and concernment of man: for the just man does not permit the several elements within him to interfere with one another, or any of them to do the work of others—he sets in order his own inner life, and is his own master and his own law, and at peace with himself; and when he has bound together the three principles within him, which may be compared to the higher, lower, and middle notes of the scale, and the intermediate intervals—when he has bound all these together, and is no longer many, but has become one entirely temperate and perfectly adjusted nature, then he proceeds to act, if he has to act, whether in a matter of property, or in the treatment of the body, or in some affair of politics or private business; always thinking and calling that which preserves and cooperates with this harmonious condition, just and good action, and the knowledge which presides over it, wisdom, and that which at any time impairs this condition, he will call unjust action, and the opinion which presides over it ignorance.

You have said the exact truth, Socrates.

Very good; and if we were to affirm that we had discovered the just man and the just State, and the nature of justice in each of them, we should not be telling a falsehood?

Most certainly not.
May we say so, then?
Let us say so.

Plutarch

✖

LYCURGUS AND
THE SPARTANS

Of Lycurgus the lawgiver we have nothing to relate that is certain and uncontroverted. For there are different accounts of his birth, his travels, his death, and especially of the laws and form of government which he established. But least of all are the times agreed upon in which this great man lived. As the history of those times is very involved, in relating the circumstances of Lycurgus' life we shall endeavor to select such as are least controverted, and follow authors of the greatest reputation.

The most distinguished of his ancestors was Soüs, under whom the Lacedaemonians [*the Spartans*] made the Helots their slaves and gained an extensive tract of land from the Arcadians. Of Soüs it is related that, being besieged by the Clitorians in a difficult post where there was no water, he agreed to give up all his conquests, provided that himself and all his army should drink of the neighboring spring. When these conditions were sworn to, he assembled his forces and offered his kingdom to the man that would forebear drinking. Not one of them, however, could deny himself—they all drank. Then Soüs went down to the spring himself, and having only sprinkled his face in the sight of the enemy, he

From Plutarch's *Lives*. Translation by John and William Langhorne.

marched off and still held the country, because *all* had not drunk. Though Soüs was highly honored for this, the family did not take their name from him, but were called Eurypon-tids. This was because his son, Eurypon, seems to be the first who relaxed the strictness of kingly government, inclining to the interests of the people and ingratiating himself to them. Upon this relaxation their encroachments increased and the succeeding kings—either by treating them with greater rigor, or else giving way through weakness, or in hopes of favor—brought anarchy and confusion to Sparta; by which one of its kings, Eunomus, the father of Lycurgus, lost his life. For, while he was endeavoring to part some persons who were involved in a fray, he received a fatal wound by a kitchen knife, leaving the kingdom to his eldest son, Polydectes.

But Polydectes dying soon after, the general voice called for Lycurgus to ascend the throne; and he actually did so until it appeared that his brother's widow was pregnant. As soon as Lycurgus perceived this he declared that the kingdom belonged to her issue, provided it were male, and he kept the administration in his hands only as a guardian. This he did with the title of Prodicus, which the Lacedaemonians gave to the guardians of infant kings.

The Queen later revealed to him privately that she would destroy her child upon condition that he would marry her when King of Sparta. Though he detested her wickedness, he said nothing against the proposal, pretending to approve it. He charged her not to take any drugs to procure an abortion lest she should endanger her own health or life, saying he would take care that the newborn child would be destroyed. Thus he artfully drew on the woman to her full time. When he heard she was in labor he sent persons to attend and watch her delivery, with orders, if it were a girl, to give it to the women, but if a boy, to bring it to him. It happened that he was at supper with the magistrates when she was delivered of a boy, and his servants, who were present, carried the child to him. When he received it, he is reported to have said to the company: "Spartans, see here your newborn King." Lycurgus then laid him down upon the chair of state and named him Charilaus—Joy of the People

—for the admiration of his magnanimity and justice was testified to by all present.

Thus the reign of Lycurgus lasted only eight months. But the citizens had a great veneration for him on other accounts, and there were more that paid him their attentions and were ready to execute his commands, out of regard for his virtues, than those that obeyed him as a guardian of the King and director of the administration. There were also those who envied him and opposed his advancement as being too high for so young a man, and particularly the relations and friends of the queen-mother, who seemed to have been treated with contempt. Her brother Leonidas one day boldly attacked him with virulent language, going so far as to tell him that he was well assured he would soon be King—thus paving the way for suspicions and accusations against Lycurgus in case any accident should befall the infant King. Insinuations of the same kind were spread by the queen-mother. Moved by this ill treatment, and fearing some dark design, Lycurgus determined to get clear of all suspicion by traveling into other countries until his nephew should grow up and have a son to succeed him in the kingdom.

He set sail and landed in Crete. There, having observed the forms of government and conversed with the most illustrious personages, he was struck with admiration for some of their laws and resolved at his return to make use of them in Sparta. Some others he rejected. Among the friends he gained in Crete was Thales, with whom he had interest enough to persuade him to go and settle at Sparta. Thales was famed for his wisdom and political abilities; he was withal a lyric poet who, under color of exercising his art, performed as great things as the most excellent lawgivers. For his odes were exhortations to obedience and unanimity. By their sheer melody they had great grace and power, they softened insensibly the manners of the audience, drew them off from the animosities which then prevailed, and united them in zeal for excellence and virtue. So, in some measure, Thales prepared the way for Lycurgus toward the instruction of the Spartans.

From Crete Lycurgus passed to Asia, desirous, as is said,

to compare Ionian luxury with the Cretan frugality and hard diet, so as to judge what effect each had on their manners and governments—just as physicians compare bodies that are weak and sickly with the healthy and robust. There also probably, he met with Homer's poems, which were preserved by the posterity of Creophylus. Observing that many moral sentences and much political knowledge were intermixed with his stories, which had an irresistible charm, he collected them into one work in order to take them home with him. Homer's glorious poetry was not yet fully known in Greece, for only some scattered pieces were in a few hands. Lycurgus was the first to make them generally known.

The Egyptians likewise suppose Lycurgus visited them, and that of all their institutions he was pleased most with their distinguishing the military men from the rest of the people. He adopted the same method in Sparta and, by separating from these the mechanics and artificers, he rendered the constitution more noble and more of a piece. This assertion of the Egyptians is confirmed by some of the Greek writers. But we know of no one, except Aristocrates, son of Hipparchus and a Spartan, who has affirmed that Lycurgus went to Libya and Spain and in his Indian excursions conversed with the Gymnosophists.

The Lacedaemonians missed Lycurgus and sent many emissaries to entreat him to return. They perceived that their kings had barely the title and outward appendages of royalty but in nothing else differed from the multitude; whereas Lycurgus had natural abilities to guide the measures of government, and powers of persuasion that drew the hearts of men to him. The kings, consulted about his return, were agreeable, for they hoped that his presence would serve as a bulwark against the insolence of the people.

Returning then to a city thus disposed, he immediately applied himself to alter the whole frame of the constitution. He was aware that a partial change and the introduction of some new laws would be of no advantage, but, as in the case of a body diseased and full of bad humors, whose temperament is to be corrected and newly formed by medicines, it was necessary to begin a new regimen. With these sentiments he went to Delphi, and when he had offered sacrifice and consulted the god he returned with that celebrated oracle in which the priestess called him: "Beloved of the gods, and rather a god than a man." As to his wish that he might enact good laws, she told him Apollo had heard his request and promised that the constitution he should establish would be the most excellent in the world. Thus encouraged, he applied to the nobility and desired them to put their hands to the work. He addressed himself privately at first to his friends, and afterwards, by degrees, trying the disposition of others and preparing them to concur in the business.

When matters were ripe he ordered thirty of the principal citizens to appear armed in the market-place by break of day to strike terror into such as might desire to oppose him. Hermippus has given us the names of twenty of the most eminent of them, but he who had the greatest share in the whole enterprise and gave Lycurgus the best assistance in establishing his laws was called Arthmiadas.

Upon the first alarm, King Charilaus, apprehending it to be a design against his person, took refuge in the Temple of Minerva. But he was soon satisfied and accepted their oath. Far from being obstinate, he joined in the undertaking. Indeed, he was so remarkable for the gentleness of his disposition that Archelaus, his partner on the throne, is reported to have said to some who were praising the young King: "Yes, Charilaus is a good man, to be sure, who cannot find in his heart to punish the bad."

Among the many new institutions of Lycurgus, the first and most important was that of a senate, which—sharing, as Plato says, in the power of the kings, too imperious and unrestrained before, and having equal authority with them—was the means of keeping them within the bounds of moderation and highly contributed to the preservation of the state. Before, it had been veering and unsettled, sometimes inclining to arbitrary power, and sometimes toward a pure democracy, but this establishment of a senate, an intermediate body, like ballast, kept it in a just equilibrium; the twenty-eight senators adhering to the kings whenever they

saw the people too encroaching and, on the other hand, supporting the people when the kings attempted to make themselves absolute. This, according to Aristotle, was the number
of senators fixed upon because two of the thirty associates
of Lycurgus deserted the business through fear. But Sphaerus
tells us there were only twenty-eight at first entrusted with
the design. Something, perhaps, there is in its being a
perfect number formed of seven multiplied by four, and
being the first number after six that is equal to all its parts.
But I rather think that many senators were created so that,
together with the two kings, the whole body might consist
of thirty members.

A second and bolder political enterprise of Lycurgus was
a new division of lands, for he found a prodigious inequality,
the city overcharged with many indigent persons who had no
land and the wealth centered in the hands of a few. Determined, therefore, to root out the evils of insolence, envy,
avarice and luxury, and those distempers of a state still
more inveterate and fatal, I mean poverty and riches, he
persuaded them to cancel all former divisions of land and
to make new ones in such a manner that they be perfectly
equal in their possessions and way of living. Hence, if they
were ambitious of distinction, they might seek it in virtue,
as no other difference was left between them but that which
arises from the dishonor of base actions and the praise of
good ones. His proposal was put into practice. He made
nine thousand lots for the territory of Sparta which he distributed among so many citizens, and thirty thousand for
the inhabitants of the rest of Laconia. Each lot was capable
of producing, one year with another, seventy bushels of grain
for each man and twelve for each woman, besides a quantity
of wine and oil in proportion. Such a provision they thought
sufficient for health and a good habit of body, and they
wanted nothing more. A story goes of our legislator returning
from a journey through the fields just reaped and seeing the
shocks standing parallel and equal. He smiled and said:
"How like is Laconia to an estate newly divided among
many brothers!"

After this, Lycurgus attempted also to divide the movables in order to take away all appearance of inequality, but he soon perceived that they could not bear to have their goods taken directly from them and therefore he adopted another method, counter-working their avarice by a stratagem. First, he stopped the currency of the gold and silver coin and ordered that they should make use of iron money only. Then to a great quantity and weight of this he assigned but a very small value so that to lay up ten minas a whole room was required, and to remove it, nothing less than a yoke of oxen. When this became current many kinds of injustice ceased in Lacedaemon. Who would steal or take a bribe, who would defraud or rob, when he could not conceal the booty, when he could neither be dignified by the possession of it, nor, if cut in pieces, be served by its use? For we are told that when hot, they quenched it in vinegar to make it brittle and unmalleable and consequently unfit for any other service.

In the next place, Lycurgus excluded unprofitable and superfluous arts. Indeed, if he had not done this, most of them would have fallen of themselves when the new money took place, as the manufactures could not be disposed of. Their iron coin would not pass in the rest of Greece, but was ridiculed and despised, so that the Spartans had no means of purchasing any foreign or curious wares. Nor did any merchant ship unload in their harbors. There were not even to be found in all their country either sophists, wandering fortune-tellers, keepers of infamous houses, or dealers in gold and silver trinkets, because there was no money. Thus luxury, losing by degrees the means that cherished and supported it, died away of itself. Even those who had great possessions had no advantage of them since they could not be displayed in public but must lie useless in unregarded repositories. Hence it was that excellent workmanship was shown in their useful and necessary furniture, as beds, chairs and tables. The Lacedaemonian cup called *cothon*, as Critias informs us, was highly valued, particularly in campaigns, for the water which must then of necessity be drunk, though it would often otherwise offend the sight, had its muddiness concealed by the color of the cup, and, the sediment stopping at the shelving brim, it came clearer to the lips. For these improvements the lawgiver was responsible, and the workmen, having no more employment in matters of mere curiosity, showed the excellence of their art in necessary things.

Desirous to complete the conquest of luxury and exterminate the love of riches, he introduced a third institution which was wisely enough and ingeniously contrived. This was the use of public tables where all were to eat in common of the same meat and such kinds of it as were appointed by law. At the same time the citizens were forbidden to eat at home upon expensive couches and tables, to call in the assistance of butchers and cooks or to fatten like voracious animals in private. For then not only their manners would be corrupted but their bodies disordered, and, abandoned to all manner of sensuality and dissoluteness, they would require long sleep, warm baths, and the same indulgence as in perpetual sickness.

The public repasts were called by the Lacedaemonians *Phiditia*, or friendship and benevolence. There were fifteen persons to a table, or a few more or less. Each of them was obliged to bring in monthly a bushel of meal, eight gallons of wine, five pounds of cheese, two pounds and a half of figs, and a little money to buy flesh and fish. If any of them happened to offer a sacrifice of fresh fruits or to kill venison, he sent a part of it to the public table. Only after a sacrifice or hunting was he at liberty to sup at home, but the rest were to appear at the usual place. For a long time this eating in common was observed with great exactness.

Children also attended these public tables, as if sent to schools of sobriety, and there they heard discourses concerning government. They were allowed to jest without scurrility and were not to take it ill when the raillery was returned. For it was reckoned worthy of a Lacedaemonian to bear a jest, but if anyone's patience failed, he had only to desire them to be quiet and they left off immediately. When they first entered, the oldest man present pointed to the door and said: "Not a word spoken in this company goes out there."

The admittance of any man to a particular table was under the following regulation: each member of that small society took a little ball of soft bread in his hand, and this he was to drop, without saying a word, into the vessel called *caddos* which the waiter carried upon his head. In case he approved of the candidate he did it without altering the figure; if not, he first pressed it flat in his hand. A flattened ball was considered as a negative, and if but one such was found the person was not admitted, as they thought it proper that the whole company should be satisfied with each other. He who was thus rejected was said to have no luck in the *caddos*.

Lycurgus left none of his laws in writing. It was ordered in one of the *rhetrae* that none should be written: for what he thought most conducive to the virtue and happiness of a city was principles interwoven with the manners and breeding of the people. These would remain immovable, as founded in inclination, and be the strongest and most lasting tie, and the habits which education produced in the youth would answer in each the purpose of a lawgiver. As for smaller matters, contracts about property, and whatever occasionally varied, it was better not to reduce these to a written form and unalterable method but to allow them to change with the times, and to admit of additions or retrenchments at the pleasure of persons so well educated. For he resolved the whole business of legislation into the bringing up of youth. And this, as we have observed, was the reason why one of his ordinances forbade them to have any written laws.

Another ordinance of Lycurgus was that the Spartans should not often make war against the same enemy, lest by being frequently put upon to defend themselves, they too should become able warriors in their turn. And this they most blamed King Agesilaus for afterwards, that by frequent and continued incursions into Boeotia he taught the Thebans to stand firm against the Lacedaemonians. This made Antalcidas say, when he saw Agesilaus wounded: "The Thebans pay you well for making them good soldiers, who neither were willing nor able to fight you before." These ordinances Lycurgus called *rhetrae*, as if they had been oracles and decrees of the Deity himself.

As for the education of youth, which he looked upon as the greatest and most glorious work of a lawgiver, he began at the very source, taking into consideration their conception and birth by regulating the marriages. For he did not, as Aristotle says, desist from his attempt to bring the women under sober rules. They had, indeed, assumed great liberty and power on account of the frequent expeditions of their husbands, during which they were left sole mistresses at home and so gained an undue deference and improper titles, but, notwithstanding this, he took all possible care of them. He ordered the virgins to exercise themselves in running, wrestling, and throwing quoits and darts so that, their bodies being strong and vigorous, the children afterwards produced from them might be the same; and that, thus fortified by exercise, they might the better support the pangs of child-birth and be delivered with safety.

In order to take away the excessive tenderness and delicacy of the sex, the consequence of a recluse life, he accustomed the virgins occasionally to be seen naked, as well as the young men, and to dance and sing in their presence on certain festivals. There they sometimes indulged in a little raillery upon those that had misbehaved themselves and sometimes they sang encomiums on such as deserved them, thus exciting in the young men a useful emulation and love of glory. For he who was praised for his bravery and celebrated among the virgins went away perfectly happy, while their satirical glances, thrown out in sport, were no less cutting than serious admonitions—especially as the kings and senate went with the other citizens to see all that passed.

As for the virgins appearing naked, there was nothing disgraceful in it because everything was conducted with modesty and without one indecent word or action. Nay, it caused a simplicity of manners and an emulation for the best habit of body. Their ideas too were naturally enlarged while they were not excluded from their share of bravery and honor. Hence they were furnished with sentiments and language such as Gorgo, the wife of Leonidas, is said to have used. When a woman of another country said to her: "You of Lacedaemon are the only women in the world who rule the men," she answered: "We are the only women who bring forth men."

These public dances and other exercises of the young maidens naked in sight of the young men were, moreover, incentives to marriage and, to use Plato's expression, drew them almost as necessarily by the attractions of love as a geometrical conclusion follows from the premises. To encourage it still more, some marks of infamy were set upon those that continued bachelors. They were not permitted to see these exercises of the naked virgins, and the magistrates commanded them to march naked round the market-place in the winter and to sing a song composed against themselves which expressed how justly they were punished for their disobedience to the laws. They were also deprived of that honor and respect which the younger people paid to the old, so that nobody found fault with what was said to Dercyllidas, though he was an eminent commander. It seems when he came one day into company a young man, instead of rising and giving him place, told him: "You have no child to give place to me, when I am old."

When Lycurgus had thus established a proper regard for modesty and decorum with respect to marriage, he was equally studious to drive from that state the vain and womanish passion of jealousy by making it quite as reputable to have children in common with persons of merit, as to avoid all offensive freedom in their own behavior to their wives. He laughed at those who revenge with wars and bloodshed the communication of a married woman's favors, and allowed that if a man in years should have a young wife, he might introduce to her some handsome and honest young man whom he most approved of, and when she had a child of this generous race, bring it up as his own. On the other hand, he allowed that if a man of character should entertain a passion for a married woman, on account of her modesty and the beauty of her children, he might treat with her husband for admission to her company, that so planting in a beauty-bearing soil he might produce excellent children, the congenial offspring of excellent parents.

For, in the first place, Lycurgus considered children not so much the property of their parents as of the state, and therefore he would not have them begot by ordinary persons but by the best men in it. In the next place, he observed the vanity and absurdity of other nations where people study to have their horses and dogs of the finest breed they can procure, either by interest or money, and yet keep their wives shut up that they may have children by none but themselves, though they may happen to be doting, decrepit or infirm.

These regulations tending to secure a healthy offspring, and consequently beneficial to the state, were so far from encouraging the licentiousness of the women, which prevailed afterwards, that adultery was not known amongst them. A saying upon this subject of Geradas, an ancient Spartan, is thus related: A stranger had asked him what punishment their law appointed for adulterers. He answered: "My friend, there are no adulterers in our country." The other replied: "But what if there should be one?" "Why, then," said Geradas, "he must forfeit a bull so large that he might drink of the Eurotas from the top of Mount Taygetus." When the stranger expressed his surprise at this, and said: "How can such a bull be found?", Geradas answered with a smile: "How can an adulterer be found in Sparta?" This is the account we have of their marriages.

It was not left to the father to rear what children he pleased, but he was obliged to carry the child to a place called Lesche, to be examined by the most ancient men of the tribe who were assembled there. If it was strong and well proportioned, they gave orders for its education and assigned it one of the nine thousand shares of land; but if the child was weak and deformed, they ordered it to be thrown into the place called Apothetae, a deep cavern near the mountain Taygetus, concluding that its life could be no advantage either to itself or to the public since nature had not given it at first any strength or resilient constitution. For the same reason, the women did not wash their newborn infants with water but with wine, imagining that sickly and epileptic children sink and die under the experiment while the healthy become more vigorous and hardy. Great care and art was also exerted by the nurses, for, as they never swathed the infants, their limbs had a freer turn, and their countenances a more liberal air. Besides, they accustomed them to any sort of meat, to have no terrors in the dark, nor to be afraid of being alone, and to desist from all ill humor and unmanly crying. Hence people of other countries purchased Lace-daemonian nurses for their children.

The Spartan children were not in any manner under tutors purchased or hired with money, nor were the parents at liberty to educate them as they pleased. As soon as they were seven years old Lycurgus ordered them to be enrolled in companies where they were all kept under the same order and discipline and had their exercises and recreations in common. He who showed the most conduct and courage amongst them was made captain of the company. The rest kept their eyes upon him, obeyed his orders, and bore with patience the punishments he inflicted; so that their whole education was an exercise of obedience. The old men were present at their diversions and often suggested some occasion for dispute or quarrel, so that they might observe with exactness the spirit of each and their firmness in battle.

As for learning, they had just what was absolutely necessary. All the rest of their education was calculated to make them subject to command, to endure labor, to fight and conquer. They added, therefore, to the children's discipline as they advanced in age, cutting their hair very close, making them go barefoot and play for the most part quite naked. At twelve years of age their undergarment was taken away and but one upper garment a year allowed them. Hence they were necessarily dirty in their persons and did not indulge the great favor of baths and oil, except on some particular days of the year. They slept in companies in beds made of the tops of reeds which they gathered with their own hands, without knives, and brought from the banks of the Eurotas. In winter, they were permitted to add a little thistledown as that seemed to have some warmth in it.

At this age the most distinguished amongst them became favorite companions of the elder. The old men attended more constantly their places of exercise, observing their trials of strength, not slightly or in a cursory manner, but as their fathers, guardians and governors, so that there was neither time nor place where persons were wanting to instruct and chastise them. One of the best and ablest men in the city was, moreover, appointed inspector of the youth, and he gave the command of each company to the discreetest and most spirited of those called Irens. An Iren was one who had been two years out of the class of boys, a Melliren was one of the oldest lads. This Iren, when a youth twenty years old, gave orders to those under his command in their little battles and had them to serve him at his house. He sent the oldest of them to fetch wood and the younger to gather potherbs, which they stole where they could find them either slyly getting into gardens or else craftily and warily creeping to the common tables—but if anyone was caught, he was severely flogged for negligence or want of dexterity.

They stole also whatever victuals they possibly could, ingeniously contriving to do it when persons were asleep or kept but indifferent watch. If they were discovered, they were punished, not only with whipping, but with hunger. Indeed, their supper was but slender at all times, so that, to fence against want, they were forced to exercise their courage and adroitness. This was the first intention of their spare diet; a subordinate one was to make them grow tall, for when the animal spirits are not too much oppressed by a great quantity of food, which stretches itself out in breadth and thickness, they mount upwards by their natural lightness and the body easily and freely shoots up in height. This also contributed to make them handsome, for thin and slender habits yield more freely to nature, which then gives a fine proportion to the limbs, while the heavy and gross resist her by their weight. Just as women who take physic during their pregnancy have slighter children, but of a finer and more delicate turn because the suppleness of the matter more readily obeys the plastic power. However, these are speculations which we shall leave to others.

The boys stole with so much caution that one of them, having hidden a young fox under his garment, suffered the creature to tear out his bowels with its teeth and claws, choosing rather to die than to be detected. Nor does this appear incredible if we consider what their young men can endure to this day, for we have seen many of them expire under the lash at the altar of Diana Orthia.

When the King advanced against the enemy he had always with him someone that had been crowned in the public games of Greece. And they tell us that a Lacedaemonian, when large sums were offered him on condition that he would not enter the Olympic lists, refused them. Having with much difficulty thrown his antagonist, a question was put to him: "Spartan, what will you get by this victory?" He answered with a smile: "I shall have the honor to fight foremost in the ranks before my prince." When they had routed the enemy they continued the pursuit until they were assured of the victory. After that they immediately desisted, deeming it neither generous nor worthy of a Grecian to destroy those who made no further resistance. This was not only a proof of magnanimity but of great service to their cause. For when their adversaries found that they killed such as stood it out but spared the fugitives, they concluded it was better to fly than to meet their fate upon the spot.

The discipline of the Lacedaemonians continued after they had arrived at years of maturity. For no man was at liberty to live as he pleased, the city being like one great camp where all had their stated allowance and knew their public charge, each man concluding that he was born, not for himself, but for his country. Hence, if they had no particular orders, they employed themselves in inspecting the boys and teaching them something useful, or in learning from those that were older than themselves. One of the greatest privileges that Lycurgus procured for his countrymen was the enjoyment of leisure, the consequence of his forbidding them to exercise any mechanical trade. It was not worth their while to take great pains to raise a fortune since riches there were of no account, and the Helots who tilled the ground were answerable for the produce. We have a story of a Lacedaemonian who, happening to be at Athens while the court sat, was informed of a man who was fined for idleness; and when the poor fellow was returning home in great dejection, attended by his consoling friends, this Spartan desired the company to show him the person who was condemned for keeping up his dignity. So much beneath them they reckoned all attention to mechanical arts and all desire of riches!

Lawsuits were banished from Lacedaemon along with money. The Spartans knew neither riches nor poverty but possessed complete equality and had a cheap and easy way of supplying their few wants. Hence, when they were not engaged in war their time was taken up with dancing, feasting, hunting, or meeting to exercise or converse. Those under thirty years of age did not go to market, all their necessary concerns being managed by their relations or adopters. Nor was it reckoned a credit to the old to be seen sauntering in the market-place, for it was deemed more suitable for them to pass a great part of the day in the schools of exercise or in places of conversation. Their discourse seldom turned upon money or business or trade, but upon the praise of the excellent or the contempt of the worthless, and the last was expressed with that pleasantry and humor which conveyed instruction and correction, without seeming to intend it. Nor was Lycurgus himself immoderately severe in his manner; but, as Sosibius tells us, he dedicated a little statue to the god of laughter in each hall. He considered facetiousness as a seasoning of their hard exercise and diet and therefore ordered it to take place on all proper occasions, in their common entertainments and parties of pleasure.

Upon the whole, he taught his citizens to think nothing more disagreeable than to live by, or for, themselves. Like bees, they acted with one impulse for the public good and always assembled about their prince. They were possessed with a thirst for honor, an enthusiasm bordering on insanity, and had no other wish but for their country.

For the same reason he would not permit all who desired it to go abroad and see other countries, lest they should contract foreign manners, acquaint themselves with a life of little discipline, and with a different form of government. He also forbade strangers to go to Sparta who could not assign a good reason for their coming; not, as Thucydides says, out of fear they should imitate the constitution of that city and make improvements in virtue, but lest they should teach his own people some evil. For along with foreigners come new subjects of discourse, new discourse produces new opinions, and from these there necessarily spring new passions and desires which, like discords in music, would disturb the established government. He, therefore, thought it even more expedient for the city to keep from it corrupt customs and manners than to prevent the introduction of a plague.

When his principal institutions had taken root in the manners of the people and the government had reached such maturity as to be able to support and preserve itself, then—as Plato says of the Deity who rejoiced after he had created the world and given it its first motion—Lycurgus likewise was charmed with the beauty and greatness of his political establishment when he saw it accomplished in fact and continuing in good order. He was next desirous to make it immortal, so far as human wisdom could effect it, and to deliver it down unchanged to the latest times. For this purpose he assembled all the people and told them the provisions he had already made for the state were indeed sufficient for virtue and happiness, but the greatest and most important matter was still behind which he could not disclose to them until he had consulted the oracle—that they must therefore inviolably observe his laws without altering anything in them until he returned from Delphi, and then he would acquaint them with the pleasure of Apollo. When they had all promised to do so and desired him to set forward he took an oath of the kings and senators, and afterwards of all the citizens, that they would abide by the present establishment until Lycurgus came back. He then took his journey to Delphi.

When he arrived there, he offered sacrifice to the gods and consulted the oracle as to whether his laws were sufficient to promote virtue and secure the happiness of the state. Apollo answered that the laws were excellent and that the city which kept to the constitution he had established would be the most glorious in the world. This oracle Lycurgus took down in writing and sent it to Sparta. He then offered another sacrifice and embraced his friends and his son, determined never to release his citizens from their oath, but voluntarily to end his life there, when he was yet of an age when life was not a burden, when death was not desirable, and while he was not unhappy in any one circumstance. He, therefore, destroyed himself by abstaining from food, persuaded that the very death of lawgivers should have its use, and their exit, so far from being insignificant, have its share of virtue to be considered as a great action.

To him, indeed, whose performances were so illustrious, the conclusion of life was the crown of happiness, and his death was left guardian of those invaluable blessings he had secured for his countrymen through life, as they had taken an oath to maintain his laws until his return. Nor was he deceived in his expectations. Sparta continued superior to the rest of Greece, both in its government at home and reputation abroad, so long as it retained the institutions of Lycurgus, and this it did during the space of five hundred years through the reign of fourteen successive kings, down to Agis the son of Archidamus. As for the appointment of the Ephori, far from weakening the constitution, it gave it additional vigor, and though it seemed to be established in favor of the people, it strengthened the aristocracy.

But in the reign of Agis money found its way into Sparta, and with money came its inseparable attendant, avarice. This was caused by Lysander, who, though himself incapable of being corrupted by money, filled his country with the love of it, and with luxury too. He brought both gold and silver from the wars and thereby broke through the laws of Lycurgus. While these were in force Sparta was not so much under the political regulations of a commonwealth as under the strict rules of a philosophic life. Just as the poets imagine of Hercules that only with a club and lion's skin he traveled over the world clearing it of lawless ruffians and cruel tyrants, so the Lacedaemonians with a piece of parchment kept Greece in voluntary obedience, destroyed usurpation and tyranny in the states, put an end to wars and laid seditions asleep, very often without either shield or lance, and only by sending one ambassador, to whose direction all parties concerned immediately submitted. Thus bees, when their queen appears, compose their quarrels and unite in one swarm.

It was not, however, the principal design of Lycurgus that his city should govern many others. He considered its happiness, like that of a private man, as flowing from virtue and self-consistency. His aim was that, by the freedom and sobriety of its inhabitants and their having a sufficiency within themselves, its continuance might be the more secure. Plato, Diogenes, Zeno and other writers upon government have taken Lycurgus for their model; and they have attained great praise, though they have left only an idea of something excellent. Yet Lycurgus, who not in idea and in words, but in fact, produced a most inimitable form of government and showed a whole city of philosophers, confounded those who imagine that the so much talked-of strictness of a philosophic life is impracticable. Lycurgus, I say, stands in rank of glory high above the founders of all the other Grecian states. And so Aristotle is of the opinion that the honors paid him in Lacedaemon were very great, for he has a temple there, and they offer him a yearly sacrifice, as a god. It is also said that when his remains were brought home his tomb was struck with lightning—a seal of divinity which no other man, however eminent, has had except Euripides, who died and was buried at Arethusa in Macedonia.

We are told he left an only son named Antiorus, and, as he died without issue, the family became extinct. His friends and relations observed his anniversary, which subsisted for many ages, and the days on which they met for that purpose they called Lycurgidae. Aristocrates, the son of Hipparchus, relates that the friends of Lycurgus, with whom he lived and died in Crete, burned his body and, at his request, threw his ashes into the sea. Thus he guarded against the possibility of his remains being brought back to Sparta by the Lacedae-monians, lest they should then think themselves released from their oath on the pretense that he had returned, and make innovations in the government. This is what we had to say of Lycurgus.

Suggested Additional Readings

Aristophanes, *The Birds*
Aristotle, *Politics*
Plato, *Critias, Timaeus, The Laws*
Plutarch, *Life of Solon*
Polybius, *Histories*, VI

Questions for Discussion and Writing

1. Political theory, which is concerned with a regulated, collective group of human beings, must sink its roots into a basic theory of human nature. What is Plato's theory of human nature? Is it optimistic or pessimistic?

2. Compare Plato's and Plutarch's concept of essential human nature with the views in Genesis. Are they like or unlike? Explain.

3. Are the views of human nature in *The Republic* and the *Life of Lycurgus* the same as in Herodotus' account of the Ethiopians? What does this mean in terms of theorizing about a perfect human society?

4. Which is closer to the legendary civilization of the Scythians: Plato's ideal republic or Plutarch's Sparta? Discuss.

5. Compare and contrast in some detail the virtues of the Spartans with those of the Scythians. Do the same for the Platonic Republicans and the Diodoran Egyptians.

6. Does Plutarch's Lycurgus fit Plato's requirements for a philosopher-king? Explain why or why not.

7. Is Plato's idea of utopian perfection one that emphasizes the "happiness" of the individual or something else? What does Plato seem to think "happiness" is?

8. How important is religion (or divine institutions) in Plutarch's Sparta? In Plato's Republic? How do you interpret this fact?

9. Does Plato think that utopia can be found by the individual or must it be attained by men working together? What necessity does Plato see for formal political institutions in the eventual perfect state?

10. Both Plato and Plutarch include in their utopian states many elements thought of today as "communistic." Enumerate these and discuss their variations in the two writers.

11. Plato's view of man has been termed "dualistic"; that is, he sees men as composed of two parts, spirit and body or reason and passion, always contending with each other so long as men live on earth. Can a society of men hope to attain collective stability when it is made up of individuals incapable of attaining personal stability?

12. Spartan society is shown as static and unchanging by Plutarch, at least up to a point. What, then, causes it to fall apart: internal or external factors? How does this affect the idea of utopia as a stable or permanent condition?

13. Plato has been accused of growing increasingly authoritarian, even totalitarian, in his political views as he became older. Is his philosopher-king really a political dictator? Is Lycurgus a dictator in the Roman or twentieth-century sense?

14. Write or report on one of these topics:
    a. Was there an Atlantis?
    b. The Bee Hive as a Political Model
    c. The Ant Hill as a Political Model
    d. Atlantis and the Republic as Ideals

IV

The New Jerusalem

Introduction

As the Greeks were developing their utopian theories with an emphasis on man's *nous* (intellect or reason) and its use to solve human problems, the Jews continued to stress the need for faith in Jehovah, the supernatural being who planned and supervised human destiny. In general, Hellenic utopias were constructed on man's ability to find his own perfection; the Hebrew writer, however, envisioned God's benevolence as the way to happiness.

The Old Testament book of Exodus (Chapters 3, 23), envisioned the Promised Land and its abundance, and described how the wandering Jew could hope to attain it only by trusting and obeying Jehovah. But once the children of Israel came into the Promised Land and began to prosper, the evils of life, though changed, did not completely vanish. United under King David, strengthened under King Solomon, and with all the wealth and glory of Israel, the Jews still found life imperfect and happiness eluding them. They fought among themselves as outside powers armed against them. Replete with luxuries and leisure, they adopted the practices of the infidels; and a series of prophets arose to warn that Israel was doomed to fall before the Babylonians, Assyrians, and other nations.

Along with their castigations of the conduct of the Jews and their predictions of disaster, the Hebrew prophets began to develop a distinctive concept of a utopia less material and economic than moral and spiritual. Amos, Hosea, and Jeremiah combined attacks on Jewish decadence and immorality with visions of a "new" Jerusalem that would rise from the ruins of the old. But this utopia of the future would not simply be a land of milk and honey. It could come into existence only by a drastic alteration in men, who must seek it by turning again to Jehovah. The result of such a reliance on faith would be a perfect society, pastoral and simple, where man and God could live in harmony as they had in Eden.

The most beautiful of the utopian prophecies may be found in the sayings of the three prophets gathered in the book of Isaiah. The Deutero (Second)-Isaiah foresaw a king, a messiah, who would rule over the perfect kingdom to come (compare the pagan legend of Saturn); the nature of men and animals would be changed; and the New Jerusalem would conquer the world with peace and love instead of swords. Later prophets stressed that this peaceful kingdom would come *after* the destruction of present empires: Daniel, among other diviners or prophets of revelation, held an apocalyptic vision of successive kingdoms that reflected pagan notions.

With the proclamation of himself as the long-awaited Messiah, Jesus of Nazareth preached of a kingdom not of this earth but of heaven. The spiritual utopia anticipated by the ancient prophets would come only to men of faith after their deaths. Jesus' promise of eternal life in the blessed kingdom of God was the culmination and combination of many utopian visions of both Greek and Jew: the pastoral land of milk and honey; Plato's vision of an Ideal realm of the Soul; the apocalyptic visions of Isaiah. Jesus' teachings were codified, after his crucifixion, by the apostle Paul, himself a reader of Plato, and supplemented by the mystic Revelations of John the Divine.

In the first centuries of the Christian era, the followers of Jesus believed that their messiah would soon return to earth and establish the Heavenly City for his followers, perhaps in an altered world or else in the heavens. As the years passed and the Second Coming did not take place, the founders of the Christian church began to work out various historical-eschatological systems of belief based on the utopian concepts handed down to them. One group traced the origins of time and historical sequence back to the Garden of Eden. Thus Clement of Alexandria, Eusebius, and Jerome subscribed to the retrospective view of utopia. Other Church Fathers, anticipating the eventual establishment of Christ's kingdom on earth, took the prospective view; these included Minucius Felix, Orosius, and most importantly, Augustine.

Saint Augustine (A.D. 354–430), a North African educated as a pagan, is the most important thinker marking the end of the classical period of utopian thought. A follower of Plato as well as of Jesus, Augustine tried to combine in his masterpiece, *The City of God*, Christian ideals with elements of pagan ethics, history, and philosophy that he considered useful. When he saw the mighty Roman Empire collapsing before the invading Goths and Huns, he recalled the prophecies of Daniel and John the Divine about the course of worldly empires. From the Hebrew prophets he drew the predictions of a mighty catastrophe presaging the coming of the spiritual kingdom of God. From the Gospels of the New Testament he derived a faith in Jesus as the ruler of the New Jerusalem, the "Second Adam," come to reestablish God's early pact with man. And from Plato, Augustine took the concept of an Ideal Realm beyond time for which men could prepare themselves by proper thought and conduct. He saw the fall of Rome as the end of man's vain hopes for a worldly utopia based on political and economic principles. *The City of God* pictures a utopia that surpasses the pastoral idylls, the political theories of the pagans. It predicates an infinitely blessed, eternally lasting happiness that comes when man is united with God. With Augustine's utopian vision, the classical world gives way to the medieval.

Isaiah

✠

PROPHECIES

And there shall come forth a rod out of the stem of Jesse, and a branch shall grow out of his roots; and the spirit of the Lord shall rest upon him, the spirit of wisdom and understanding, the spirit of counsel and might, the spirit of knowledge and of the fear of the Lord; and shall make him of quick understanding in the fear of the Lord; and he shall not judge after the sight of his eyes, neither reprove after the hearing of his ears. But with righteousness shall he judge the poor, and reprove with equity for the meek of the earth: and he shall smite the earth with the rod of his mouth, and with the breath of his lips shall he slay the wicked. And righteousness shall be the girdle of his loins, and faithfulness the girdle of his reins. The wolf also shall dwell with the lamb, and the leopard shall lie down with the kid; and the calf and the young lion and the fatling together; and a little child shall lead them. And the cow and the bear shall feed; their young ones shall lie down together: and the lion shall eat straw like the ox. And the suckling child shall put his hand on the cockatrice's den.

And it shall come to pass in that day, that the Lord shall set his hand again the second time to recover the remnant of his people, which shall be left, from Assyria, and from Egypt, and from Pathros, and from Cush, and from Elam, and from Shinar, and from Hamath, and from the islands of

Adapted from Isaiah, 11–12, 34–35. King James translation.

the sea. And he shall set up an ensign for the nations, and shall assemble the outcasts of Israel, and gather together the dispersed of Judah from the four corners of the earth.

And in that day thou shalt say, O Lord, I will praise thee: though thou wast angry with me, thine anger is turned away, and thou comfortest me. Behold, God is my salvation: I will trust and not be afraid; for the Lord Jehovah is my strength and my song; he also is become my salvation. Therefore with joy shall ye draw water out of the wells of salvation, and in that day shall ye say, Praise the Lord, call upon his name, declare his doings among the people, make mention that his name is exalted. Sing unto the Lord, for he hath done excellent things: this is known in all the earth. Cry out and shout, thou inhabitant of Zion; for great is the Holy One of Israel in the midst of thee.

THE DAY OF THE LORD: ARMAGEDDON

Come near, ye nations, to hear; and hearken, ye people. Let the earth hear, and all that is therein; the world and all things that come forth of it. For the indignation of the Lord is upon all nations, and his fury upon all their armies; he hath utterly destroyed them, he hath delivered them to the slaughter. Their slain also shall be cast out, and their stink shall come up out of their carcasses, and the mountains shall be melted with their blood. And all the host of heaven shall be dissolved, and the heavens shall be rolled together as a scroll; and all their host shall fall down, as the leaf falleth off from the vine, and as a falling fig from the fig tree. For it is the day of the Lord's vengeance, and the year of recompenses for the controversy of Zion.

And the streams thereof shall be turned into pitch, and the dust thereof into brimstone, and the land thereof shall become burning pitch. It shall not be quenched night nor day; the smoke thereof shall go up forever: from generation to generation it shall lie waste; none shall pass through it for ever and ever. But the cormorant and the bittern shall possess it; the owl also and the raven shall dwell in it; and he shall stretch out upon it the line of confusion, and the stones of emptiness. They shall call the nobles thereof to the kingdom, but none shall be there, and all her princes shall be nothing. And thorns shall come up in her palaces, nettles and brambles in the fortresses thereof: and it shall be a habitation of dragons, and a court of owls. The wild beasts of the desert shall also meet with the wild beasts of the island, and the satyr shall cry to his fellow; the screech owl also shall rest there, and find for herself a place of rest; there shall the vultures also be gathered, every one with her mate.

Say to them that are of a fearful heart, Be strong and fear not: behold, your God will come with vengeance, even God with a recompense; he will come and save you. Then the eyes of the blind shall be opened, and the ears of the deaf shall be unstopped. Then shall the lame man leap as a hart, and the tongue of the dumb sing: for in the wilderness shall waters break out, and streams in the desert. And the parched ground shall become a pool, and the thirsty land springs of water: in the habitation of dragons, where each lay, shall be grass with reeds and rushes. And a highway shall be there, and a way, and it shall be called The Way of Holiness; the unclean shall not pass over it, but it shall be for those: the wayfaring men, though fools, shall not err therein. No lion shall be there, nor any ravenous beast shall go up thereon, it shall not be found there. But the redeemed shall walk there, and the ransomed of the Lord shall return, and come to Zion with songs and everlasting joy upon their heads. They shall obtain joy and gladness, and sorrow and sighing shall flee away.

Jesus of Nazareth

✖

MY FATHER'S KINGDOM

Now when Jesus had heard that John [*the Baptist*] was cast into prison, he departed into Galilee; from that time Jesus began to preach, and to say, Repent: for the kingdom of heaven is at hand.

And seeing the multitudes, he went up into a mountain: and when he was set, his disciples came unto him, and he opened his mouth and taught them, saying:

Blessed are the poor in spirit: for theirs is the kingdom of heaven. Blessed are they that mourn: for they shall be comforted. Blessed are the meek: for they shall inherit the earth. Blessed are they which do hunger and thirst after righteousness: for they shall be filled. Blessed are the merciful: for they shall obtain mercy. Blessed are the pure in heart: for they shall see God. Blessed are the peacemakers: for they shall be called the children of God. Blessed are they which are persecuted for righteousness' sake: for their's is the kingdom of heaven. Blessed are ye, when men shall revile you, and persecute you, and shall say all manner of evil against you falsely, for my sake. Rejoice and be exceeding glad: for great is your reward in heaven: for so persecuted were the prophets which were before you.

Lay not up for yourselves treasures upon earth, where moth and rust doth corrupt, and where thieves break through and steal: but lay up for yourselves treasures in heaven, where neither moth nor rust doth corrupt, and where thieves do not break through nor steal: for where your treasure is, there will your heart be also. Therefore I say unto you, Take no thought for your life, what ye shall eat, or what ye shall drink; nor yet for your body, what ye shall put on.

Adapted and abridged from the Gospel of St. Matthew, 4, 5, 6, 7, 13. King James translation.

Is not life more than meat, and the body more than raiment? Therefore take no thought, saying What shall we eat? or What shall we drink? or, Wherewithal shall we be clothed? (For after all these things do the Gentiles seek:) for your heavenly Father knoweth that ye have need of all these things. But seek ye first the kingdom of God, and his righteousness; and all these things shall be added unto you. Take therefore no thought for the morrow: for the morrow shall take thought for the things of itself. Ask and it shall be given you: seek, and ye shall find; knock, and it shall be opened to you. For every one that asketh receiveth; and he that seeketh findeth; and to him that knocketh it shall be opened. If ye, then, being evil, know how to give good gifts unto your children, how much more shall your Father, which is in heaven, give good things to them that ask him?

And Jesus spake many things unknown to them in parables, saying:

Behold, a sower went forth to sow; and when he sowed, some seeds fell by the wayside, and the fowls came and devoured them up. Some fell upon stony places, where they had not much earth; and forthwith they sprung up, because they had no deepness of earth. And when the sun was up, they were scorched; and because they had no root, they withered away. And some fell among thorns; and the thorns sprung up and choked them. But others fell into good ground, and brought forth fruit, some a hundredfold, some sixtyfold, some thirtyfold.

When any one heareth the word of the kingdom, and understandeth it not, then cometh the wicked one, and catcheth away that which was sown in his heart. This is he which received seed by the wayside. But he that received seed into stony places, the same is he that heareth the word, and anon with joy receiveth it; yet hath he not root in himself, but dureth for a while: for when tribulation or persecution ariseth because of the word, by and by he is offended. He also that received seed among the thorns is he that heareth the word; and the care of this world, and the deceitfulness of riches, choke the word, and he becometh unfruitful. But he that received seed into the good ground is he that heareth the word, and understandeth it; which also beareth fruit, and bringeth forth, some a hundredfold, some sixty, and some thirty.

Another parable put he forth unto them, saying:

The kingdom of heaven is likened unto a man which sowed good seed in his field; but while men slept, his enemy came and sowed tares among the wheat, and went his way. But when the blade was sprung up, and brought forth fruit, then appeared the tares also. So the servants of the householder came and said unto him, Sir, didst thou not sow good seed in thy field? from whence came the tares? He said unto them, An enemy hath done this. The servants said unto him, Wilt thou then that we go and gather them up? But he said, Nay; lest while ye gather up the tares, ye root up also the wheat with them. Let both grow together until the harvest: and in the time of harvest I will say to the reapers, Gather ye together first the tares and bind them into bundles to burn them: but gather the wheat into my barn.

Another parable put he forth unto them, saying:

The kingdom of heaven is like to a grain of mustard seed, which a man took, and sowed in his field: which indeed is the least of all seeds; but when it is grown, it is the greatest among herbs, and becometh a tree, so that the birds of the air come and lodge in the branches thereof.

Another parable spake he unto them:

The kingdom of heaven is like unto leaven, which a woman took, and hid in three measures of meal, till the whole was leavened.

All these things spake Jesus unto the multitude in parables; and his disciples came unto him saying, Declare unto us the parable of the tares of the field. He answered and said unto them, He that soweth the good seed is the Son of man;[1] the field is the world; the good seed are the children of the kingdom; but the tares are the children of the wicked one.[2] The enemy that sowed them is the devil; the harvest is the end of the world; and the reapers are the angels. As

---

[1] Jesus customarily referred to himself in this way.
[2] Satan or the Devil.

therefore the tares are gathered and burned in the fire, so shall it be in the end of this world. The Son of man shall send forth his angels, and they shall gather out of his kingdom all things that offend, and them which do iniquity, and shall cast them into a furnace of fire: there shall be wailing and gnashing of teeth. Then shall the righteous shine forth as the sun in the kingdom of their Father. Who hath ears to hear, let him hear.

Again, the kingdom of heaven is like unto a treasure hid in a field, the which when a man hath found, he hideth, and for joy thereof goeth and selleth all that he hath and buyeth that field.

Again, the kingdom of heaven is like unto a merchant man, seeking goodly pearls, who, when he had found one pearl of great price, went and sold all that he had and bought it.

Again, the kingdom of heaven is like unto a net, that was cast into the sea and gathered of every kind, which, when it was full, they drew to shore, and sat down, and gathered the good unto vessels but cast the bad away. So shall it be at the end of the world: the angels shall come forth and sever the wicked from among the just, and shall cast them into the furnace of fire: there shall be wailing and gnashing of teeth.

Jesus saith unto them, Have ye understood all these things? They say unto him, Yea, Lord.

St. John the Divine

✠

THE NEW JERUSALEM

And I saw heaven opened, and behold a white horse; and he that sat upon him was called Faithful and True, and

Adapted from the Book of Revelation, 19, 20, 21, 22. Translated by S. P. Tregelles.

in righteousness he doth judge, and make war. His eyes were as a flame of fire, and on his head were many diadems: and he had a name written, that no man knoweth but He himself. And he was clothed with a vesture dipped in blood: and his name hath been called THE WORD OF GOD. And the armies in heaven followed him upon white horses, clothed in fine linen, white and pure. And out of his mouth proceedeth a sharp sword, that with it he might smite the nations; and He shall rule them with a rod of iron: and He treadeth the winepress of the fierceness of the wrath of God the Almighty. And he hath on his garment and on his thigh a name written: KING OF KINGS, AND LORD OF LORDS.

And I saw an angel standing in the sun; and he cried with a loud voice, saying to all the fowls that fly in the mid-heaven, "Come, be gathered together unto the great supper of God; that ye may eat the flesh of kings; and the flesh of chief-captains, and the flesh of mighty men, and the flesh of horses, and of those that sit on them, and the flesh of all men, both free and bond, both small and great."

And I saw the beast, and the kings of the earth, and their armies, gathered together to make war with him that sat on the horse, and with his army. And the best was taken, and he who was with him, the false prophet that wrought the miracles in his presence, with which he deceived those that had received the mark of the beast, and those that worship his image. These both were cast alive into the lake of fire which burneth with brimstone. And the rest were killed with the sword of him that sat upon the horse, which sword proceeded out of his mouth; and all the fowls were filled with their flesh.

And I saw an angel coming down from heaven, having the key to the abyss and a great chain in his hand. And he laid hold on the dragon—the old serpent, which is the Devil and Satan—and bound him a thousand years, and cast him into the abyss, and shut him up, and set a seal upon him that he should deceive the nations no more till the thousand years should be completed; afterwards he must be loosed a season.

And I saw thrones, and they sat upon them, and judgment was given unto them: and I saw the souls of those that were beheaded because of the testimony of Jesus and because of the word of God; and those who had not worshipped the beast, neither his image, and had not received the mark on their forehead and on their hand, they lived and reigned with Christ a thousand years. And the rest of the dead lived not until the thousand years were completed. This is the first resurrection. Blessed and holy is he that hath part in the first resurrection: over these the second death hath no power, but they shall be priests of God and of Christ and shall reign with him the thousand years.

And when the thousand years are completed, Satan shall be loosed out of his prison and shall go out to deceive the nations which are in the four corners of the earth, Gog and Magog, to gather them together to battle: the number of whom is as the sand of the sea. And they went up on the breadth of the earth and compassed the citadel of the saints about, and the beloved city; and the fire came down out of heaven from God and devoured them. And the devil that deceived them was cast into the lake of fire and brimstone, where both the beast and the false prophet are, and they shall be tormented day and night for ever and ever.

And I saw a great white throne, and him that sat on it, from whose face the earth and heaven fled away; and no place was found for them. And I saw the dead, the great and the small, standing before the throne; and books were opened, which is the Book of Life: and the dead were judged out of the things which had been written in the books, according to their works. And the sea gave up the dead that were in it; and death and Hades gave up the dead that were in them: and they were judged every one according to their works. And death and Hades were cast into the lake of fire. And whosoever was not found written in the Book of Life was cast into the lake of fire.

And I saw a new heaven and a new earth; for the first heaven and the first earth passed away, and the sea no longer is. And I saw the holy city, New Jerusalem, coming down out of heaven from God, prepared as a bride adorned for her husband. And I heard a great voice out of heaven saying, "Behold, the tabernacle of God is with men, and he will dwell with them, and they shall be his peoples, and God himself shall be with them. And God shall wipe away every tear from their eyes; and death shall be no more, neither sorrow, nor crying, neither shall there be any more pain, because the former things passed away."

And there came one of the seven angels who had the seven bowls full of the seven last plagues, and talked with me, saying, "Come hither, I will show thee the bride, the Lamb's wife." And he carried me away in the spirit to a great and high mountain, and showed me the City, the holy Jerusalem, descending out of heaven from God, having the glory of God: her light was like unto a stone most precious, even like a jasper stone, clear as crystal. And it had a wall, great and high, and twelve gates, and at the gates, twelve angels, and names written thereon, which are the names of the twelve tribes of the children of Israel: on the east three gates, and on the north three gates, and on the south three gates, and on the west three gates. And the wall of the city had twelve foundations, and on them twelve names of the twelve apostles of the Lamb.

And he that talked with me had a measuring reed of gold to measure the city and the gates thereof. And the city lieth four-square, and its length is as large as the breadth; and he measured the city with the reed, twelve thousand furlongs. The length and the breadth and the height of it are equal. And he measured the wall thereof, a hundred and forty and four cubits, according to the measure of a man, that is, of the angel.

And the structure of the wall of it was of jasper; and the city was pure gold, like unto clear glass. The foundations of the wall were adorned with every precious stone. The first foundation was a jasper; the second, a sapphire; the third, a chalcedony; the fourth, an emerald; the fifth, a sardonyx; the sixth, a sardine; the seventh, a chrysolite; the eighth, a beryl; the ninth, a topaz; the tenth, a chrysoprasus; the eleventh, a jacinth; the twelfth, an amethyst. And the twelve gates were twelve pearls; each one of the gates severally was of one pearl: and the street of the city was pure gold, as if it were transparent glass.

And I saw no temple therein: for the Lord God the Almighty and the Lamb are the temple of it. And the city hath no need of the sun, neither of the moon, that they might illumine it: for the glory of God did lighten it, and the Lamb is the light thereof. And the nations shall walk by means of the light thereof; and the kings of the earth shall do their glory unto it. And the gates of it shall not be shut at all by day: for there shall be no night there. And they shall bring the glory and honor of the nations unto it. And there shall in no wise enter into it anything common, neither whosoever worketh abomination and a lie, but those who have been written in the Lamb's Book of Life.

And he showed me a river of water of life, bright as crystal, proceeding out of the throne of God and the Lamb. In the midst of the street of it, and of the river, on this side and on that side, was there the tree of life, which bare twelve manner of fruits and yielded its fruit every month; and the leaves of the tree were for the healing of the nations. And no curse shall any longer be: and the throne of God and the Lamb shall be in it; and his servants shall serve him: and they shall see his face; and his name shall be on their foreheads. And there shall be no more night, and they have no need of the light of the candle; because the Lord God will lighten them, and they shall reign for ever and ever.

St. Augustine

✠

THE CITY OF GOD

This is that House of God more glorious than the former for all the precious material: for Haggai's prophecy was not

The City of God, from XIX–XX. Translation by J. Hervey.

fulfilled in the repairing of the Temple, which never had that glory after the restoring that it had in Solomon's time: but rather lost it all, the prophets ceasing, and destruction ensuing, which was performed by the Romans as I formerly related. But the House of the New Testament is of another luster, the workmanship being more glorious, and the stones being more precious. But it was figured in the reparation of the old Temple, because the whole New Testament was figured in the Old one. God's prophecy, therefore, that saith, "In that place will I give peace," is to be meant of the place signified, not of the place significant: that is, as the restoring that house prefigured the Church which Christ was to build, so God said, "in this place" (that is, in the place that this prefigures), "will I give peace," for all things signifying, seem to support the persons of the things signified, as St. Peter said: "the Rock was Christ:" for it signified Christ. So then, far is the glory of the House of the New Testament above the glory of the Old, as shall appear in the final dedication. Then shall the Desire of all nations appear (as it is in the Hebrew): for His first coming was not desired of all the nations, for some knew not whom to desire, nor in whom to believe. And then also shall they that are God's elect out of all nations come (as the LXX read it),[1] for none shall come truly at that day but the elect, of whom the apostle says, "As He hath elected us in Him, before the beginning of the world:" for the Architect Himself, that said, "Many are called, but few are chosen," He spake not of those that were called to the feast and then cast out: but meant to shew that He had built a house of His elect, which time's worst spite could never ruin. But being altogether in the Church as yet, to be hereafter sifted, the corn from the chaff, the glory of this House cannot be so great now, as it shall be then, where every man shall be always there where he once comes.

Therefore in these mischievous days, wherein the Church works for His future glory in present humility, in fears, in

---

[1] The LXX are the seventy Jewish scholars who prepared the Septuagint version of the Old Testament.

sorrows, in labors, and in temptations, joying only in hope when she joys as she should, many reprobate live amongst the elect: both come into the Gospel's net, and both swim at random in the sea of mortality, until the fishers draw them to shore, and then the bad are thrown from the good, in whom as in His temple, God is all in all. We acknowledge therefore His words in the Psalm, "I would declare and speak of them, but they are more than I am able to express, to be truly fulfilled." This multiplication began at that instant when first John His messenger, and then Himself in person began to say, "Repent ye, for the kingdom of God is at hand." He chose Him disciples, and named the apostles: poor, ignoble, unlearned men, that what great work soever was done He might be seen to do it in them. He had one, who abused His goodness,[2] yet used He this wicked man to a good end, to the fulfilling of His passion, and presenting His Church an example of patience in tribulation. And having sown sufficiently the seed of salvation, He suffered, was buried, and rose again; shewing by His suffering what we ought to endure for the truth, and by His resurrection what we ought to hope for from eternity, besides the ineffable sacrament of His blood, shed for the remission of sins. He was forty days on earth with His disciples afterwards, and in their sight ascended to heaven, ten days later sending down His promised Spirit upon them: which in the coming, gave that manifest and necessary sign of the knowledge in languages of all nations, to signify that it was but one catholic Church, that in all those nations should use all those tongues.

Now the devil seeing his temples empty and all running unto this Redeemer, set heretics on foot to subvert Christ, in a Christian mask, as if there were that allowance for them in the heavenly Jerusalem which there was for contrariety of philosophers in the devil's Babylon. Such therefore as in the Church of God do distaste anything, and being checked and advised to beware, do obstinately oppose themselves against good instructions, and rather defend their abominations than discard them, those become heretics, and going forth out of

[2] Judas Iscariot.

God's house, are to be held as our most eager enemies: yet they do the members of the catholic Church this good, that their fall makes them take better hold upon God, who uses evil to a good end, and works all for the good of those that love Him. So then the Church's enemies whatsoever, if they have the power to impose corporal affliction, they exercise her patience: if they bait her with opposition only verbal, they practice her in her wisdom: and she in loving these enemies exercises His benevolence and bounty, whether she go about them with gentle persuasion or severe correction: and therefore though the devil her chief opponent, move all his vassals against her virtues, still he cannot injure her an inch. Comfort she has in prosperity, to be confirmed, and constant in adversity: and exercised is she in this, to be kept from corruption in that: God's providence managing the whole: and so tempering the one with the other that the Psalmist said fitly: "In the multitude of the cares of mine heart Thy comforts have rejoiced my soul." And the apostle also: "Rejoicing in hope and patient in tribulation." For the same apostle's words, saying, "All that will live godly in Christ shall suffer persecution," must be held to be in continual action: for though *ab externo* abroad, all seem quiet, no gust of trouble appearing, and that is a great comfort, to the weak especially: yet at home, *ab intus*, there do we never want those that offend and molest the godly pilgrim by their devilish demeanor, blaspheming Christ and the catholic name, which how much dearer the godly esteem, so much more grief they feel to hear, if less respected by their pernicious brethren than they desire it should be: and the heretics themselves, being held to have Christ, and the sacraments amongst them, grieve the hearts of the righteous extremely, because many that have a good desire to Christianity, stumble at their dissensions, and again many that oppose it, take occasion hereby to burden it with greater calamities: the heretics bearing the name of Christians also. These persecutions befall God's true servants by the vanity of others' errors, although they be quiet in their bodily estate: this persecution touches the heart, and not the body: as the Psalm says, "In the multitude of the cares of mine heart," not of my body. But then again, when we revolve the immutability of God's promises, who, as the apostle says, "knoweth them that are His, whom He has predestinate to be made like the image of His Son," there shall not one of these be lost: therefore the Psalm adds, "Thy comforts have rejoiced my soul." Now the sorrow that the godly feel for the perverseness of evil, or false Christians, is good for their own souls, if it proceed from charity, not desiring their destruction nor the hindrance of their salvation: and the reformation of such, yields great comfort to the devout soul, redoubling the joy now, for the grief that it felt before for their errors. So then in these malignant days, not only from Christ and His apostles' time, but even from holy Abel whom his wicked brother slew, so along unto the world's end, does the Church travel on her pilgrimage, now suffering worldly persecutions, and now receiving divine consolations.

But yet notwithstanding in this heavy yoke that lies upon Adam's children from their birth to their burial, we have this one means left us, to live soberly, and to weigh that our first parents' sin has made this life but a pain to us, and that all the promises of the New Testament belong only to the heritage laid up for us in the world to come: pledges we have here, but the performance due thereto we shall not have till then. Let us now therefore walk in hope, and profiting day by day let us mortify the deeds of the flesh, by the Spirit, for God knows all that are His, and as many as are led by the Spirit of God, are the sons of God, but by grace, not by nature, for God's only Son by nature, was made the Son of man for us, that we being the sons of men by nature might become the sons of God in Him by grace, for He remaining changeless, took our nature upon Him, and keeping still His own divinity, that we being changed might leave our frailty and aptness to sin, through the participation of His righteousness and immortality and keep that which He had made good in us, by the perfection of that good which is in Him: for as we all fell into this misery by one man's sin, so shall we ascend unto that glory by one (deified) Man's righteousness. Nor may any imagine that he has had this pass, until he be there where there is no temptation, but all full of that peace which we seek by these conflicts of the spirit against the flesh, and the flesh against the spirit. This war had never been, had man kept his will in that right way wherein it was first placed. But refusing that, now he fights in himself, and yet this inconvenience is not so bad as the former, for happier far is he that strives against sin, than he that allows it sovereignty over him. Better is war with hope of eternal peace, than thraldom without any thought of freedom. We wish the want of this war though, and God inspires us to aim at that orderly peace wherein the inferior obeys the superior in all things: but if there were hope of it in this life (as God forbid we should imagine) by yielding to sin, yet ought we rather to stand out against it, in all our miseries, than to give over our freedoms to sin, by yielding to it.

Every part therefore of the bodies, perishing either in death, or after it, in the grave, or wheresoever, shall be restored, renewed, and of a natural and corruptible body, it shall become immortal, spiritual, and incorruptible. Be it all made into powder and dust, by chance, or cruelty, or dissolved into air or water, so that no part remain undispersed, yet shall it not, yet can it not, be kept hidden from the omnipotency of the Creator, who will not have one hair of the head to perish. Thus shall the spiritual flesh become subject to the spirit, yet shall it be flesh still, as the carnal spirit before was subject to the flesh, and yet a spirit still.

A proof of which we have in the deformity of our penal estate. For they were carnal in respect of the spirit indeed (not merely of the flesh) to whom Saint Paul said, "I could not speak unto you as unto spiritual men, but as unto carnal." So man in this life is called "spiritual," though he be "carnal" still, and have a law in his members, rebelling against the law of his mind. But he shall be spiritual in body, when he rises again, "So that it is sown a natural body, but raised a spiritual body," as the said Apostle says.

But of the measure of this spiritual grace, what and how great it shall be in the body, I fear to determine: for it were rashness to go about it.

But seeing we may not conceal the joy of our hope for the glorifying of God, and seeing that it was said from the very bowels of divine rapture, "Lord, I have loved the habitation of Thine house!" we may by God's help make a conjecture from the goods imparted to us in this transitory life, how great the glories shall be that we shall receive in the other, which as yet we neither have tried, nor can any way truly describe. I omit man's estate before his fall; our first parents' happiness in the fertile Paradise, which was so short, that their offspring had no taste of it. Who is he that can express the boundless mercies of God shewn unto mankind, even in this life that we all try, and wherein we suffer temptations, or rather a continual temptation (be we never so vigilant) all the time that we enjoy it?

Concerning man's first origin, our present life (if such a miserable estate can be called a life) does sufficiently prove that all his children were condemned in him. What else does that horrid gulf of ignorance confirm, whence all error has birth, and wherein all the sons of Adam are so deeply drenched, that none can be freed without toil, fear and sorrow? what else does our love of vanities affirm, whence there arises such a tempest of cares, sorrows, repinings, fears, mad exultations, discords, altercations, wars, treasons, furies, hates, deceits, flatteries, thefts, rapines, perjuries, pride, ambition, envy, murder, parricide, cruelty, villainy, luxury, impudence, unchastity, fornications, adulteries, incests, several sorts of sins against nature (filthy even to be named), sacrilege, heresy, blasphemy, oppression, calumnies, circumventions, cozenages, false witnesses, false judgments, violence, robberies, and such like, out of my remembrance to reckon, but not excluded from the life of man? All these evils are belonging to man, and arise out of the root of that error and perverse affection which every son of Adam brings into the world with him. For who does not know in what a mist of ignorance (as we see in infants) and with what a crew of vain desires (as we see in boys) all mankind enters this world? so that might he be left unto his own election, he would fall into most of the foresaid mischiefs.

But the hand of God bearing a rein upon our condemned souls, and pouring out His mercies upon us (not shutting them up in displeasure), law, and instruction were revealed unto the capacity of man, to awake us out of those lethargies of ignorance, and to withstand those former incursions, which notwithstanding is not done without great toil and trouble. For what imply those fears whereby we keep little children in order? what do teachers, rods, the strap, thongs, and such like, but confirm this? And that discipline of the Scriptures that says that our sons must be beaten on the sides while they are children, lest they wax stubborn, and either past, or very near past reformation? What is the end of all these, but to abolish ignorance, and to bridle corruption both which we come wrapped into the world withal? what is our labor to remember things, our labor to learn, and our ignorance without this labor; our agility got by toil, and our dullness if we neglect it? does it not all declare the promptness of our nature (in itself) unto all viciousness, and the care that must be had in reclaiming it? Sloth, dullness, and negligence, are all vices that avoid labor, and yet labor itself is but a profitable pain.

But to omit the pains that enforce children to learn the (scarcely useful) books that please their parents, how huge a band of pains attend the firmer state of man, and be not peculiarly inflicted on the wicked, but generally impendent over us all, through our common estate in misery? who can recount them, who can conceive them? What fears, what calamities does the loss of children, of goods or of credit, the false dealing of others, false suspicion, open violence, and all other mischiefs inflicted by others, heap upon the heart of man? being generally accompanied with poverty, imprisonment, bands, banishments, tortures, loss of limbs or senses, prostitution to beastly lust, and other such horrid events? So are we afflicted on the other side with chances *ab externo*, with cold, heat, storms, showers, deluges, lightning, thunder, earthquakes, falls of houses, fury of beasts, poisons of airs, waters, plants, and beasts of a thousand sorts, stinging of serpents, biting of mad dogs, a strange accident, wherein a beast most sociable and familiar with man, shall sometimes become more to be feared than a lion or a dragon, infecting him whom he bites, with such a furious madness, that he is to be feared by his family worse than any wild beast? what misery do navigators now and then endure? or travelers by land? what man can walk anywhere free from sudden accidents? One coming home from the court (being sound enough on his feet) fell down, broke his leg, and died of it; who would have thought this that had seen him sitting in the court? Eli the priest fell from his chair where he sat, and broke his neck. What fears are husbandmen, yea all men subject unto, that the fruits should be hurt by the heavens, or earth, or caterpillars, or locusts or such other pernicious things! yet when they have gathered them and laid them up, they are secured: notwithstanding I have known granaries full of corn borne quite away with an inundation.

Who can be secured by his own innocency against the innumerable incursions of the devils, when we see that they do sometimes afflict little baptized infants (who are as innocent as can be) and (by the permission of God) even upon their harmless bodies, do shew the miseries of this life, and excite us all to labor for the bliss of the other? Besides, man's body we see how subject it is to diseases, more than physic can either cure or comprehend. And in most of these, we see how offensive the very medicines are that cure them, nay even our very meat we eat, during the time of the malady's domination. Has not extremity of heat made man to drink his own urine, and others' too? Has not hunger enforced man to eat man, and to kill one another to make meat of; yea even the mother to massacre and devour her own child? Nay is not our very sleep (which we term rest) sometimes so fraught with disquiet, that it disturbs the soul, and all her powers at once, by the appearance of such horrid terrors to the phantasy, and with such an expression, that she cannot discern them from true terrors? This is ordinary in some diseases: besides the deceitful fiends sometimes will so delude the eye of a sound man with such apparitions, that although they make no farther impression into him, yet they persuade the sense that they are truly so as they seem, and the devil's desire is ever to deceive. From all these miserable engagements (representing a kind of direct hell) we are freed only by the grace of Jesus Christ. For this is His name; Jesus is a Savior, and He it is that will save us from a worse life, or rather a perpetual death, after this life: for although we have many and great comforts by the saints in this life, yet the benefits hereof are not given at every one's request, lest we should apply our faith unto those transitory respects, whereas it rather concerns the purchase of a life which shall be absolutely free from all inconvenience. And the more faithful that one is in this life, the greater confirmation has he from grace, to endure those miseries without fainting, whereunto the Paynim authors refer their true philosophy; which their gods, as Tully says, revealed unto some few of them. "There was never," says he, "nor could there be a greater gift given unto man, than this." Thus our adversaries are fain to confess that true philosophy is a divine gift: which being (as they confess) the only help against our human miseries, and coming from above, hence then it appears that all mankind was condemned to suffer miseries. But as they confess that this help was the greatest gift that God ever gave, so do we avow and believe, that it was given by no other God but He to whom even the worshippers of many gods give the pre-eminence.

Besides those calamities that lie generally upon all, the righteous have a peculiar labor, to resist vice, and be continually in combat with dangerous temptations. The flesh is sometimes furious, sometimes remiss, but always rebellious against the spirit, and the spirit has the same sorts of conflict against the flesh: so that we cannot do as we would, or expel all concupiscence, but we strive (by the help of God) to suppress it by not consenting, and to curb it as well as we can, by a continual vigilance: lest we should be deceived by likelihoods or subtleties, or involved in errors, lest we should take good for evil and evil for good, lest fear should hold us from what we should do, and desire entice us to do what we should not: lest the sun should set upon our anger: lest enmity should make us return mischief for mischief; lest ingratitude should make us forget our benefactors; lest evil reports should molest our good conscience; lest our rash suspicion of others should deceive us, or others' false suspicion of us, deject us: lest sin should bring our bodies to obey it: lest our members should be given up as weapons to sin: lest our eye should follow our appetite; lest desire of revenge should draw us to inconvenience: lest our sight or our thought should stay too long upon a sinful delight: lest we should give willing ear to evil and indecent talk: lest our lust should become our law; and lest that we ourselves in this dangerous conflict should either hope to win the victory by our own strength, or having gotten it, should give the glory to ourselves, and not to His grace of whom St Paul says: "Thanks be unto God, who hath given us the victory through our Lord Jesus Christ:" and elsewhere: "In all these things we are more than conquerors through Him that loved us."

But yet we are to know this, that stand we never so strong against sin, or subdue it never so much: yet as long as we are mortal, we have cause every day to say: "Forgive us our trespasses." But when we ascend into that kingdom where immortality dwells, we shall neither have wars wherein to fight, nor trespasses to pray for, nor had not had any here below, if our natures had kept the gifts of their first creation. And therefore these conflicts, wherein we are endangered, and whence we desire (by a final victory) freedom, are part of those miseries wherewith the life of man is continually molested.

How great shall that felicity be, where there shall be no evil thing, where no good thing shall lie hidden, there we shall have leisure to utter forth the praises of God, which shall be all things in all! For what other thing is done, where we shall not rest with any slothfulness, nor labor for any want I know not. I am admonished also by the holy song, where I read, or hear, "Blessed are they, O Lord, which dwell in Thy house, they shall praise Thee for ever and ever." All the members and bowels of the incorruptible

body, which we now see distributed to diverse uses of necessity, because then there shall not be that necessity, but a
full, sure, secure, everlasting felicity, shall be advanced and
go forward in the praises of God. For then all the numbers
(of which I have already spoken) of the corporal harmony
shall not lie hid, which now lie hid: being disposed inwardly
and outwardly through all the members of the body, and
with other things which shall be seen there, being great and
wonderful; shall kindle the reasonable souls with delight of
such a reasonable beauty to sound forth the praises of such
a great and excellent workman. What the motions of those
bodies shall be there, I dare not rashly define, when I am
not able to dive into the depth of that mystery. Nevertheless both the motion and state, as the form of them shall
be comely and decent, whatsoever it shall be, where there
shall be nothing which shall not be comely. Truly where
the spirit will, there forthwith shall the body be: neither
will the spirit will anything, which may not beseem the
body nor the spirit. There shall be true glory, where no man
shall be praised for error or flattery. True honor, which shall
be denied unto none which is worthy, shall be given unto
none unworthy. But neither shall any unworthy person covet
after it, where none is permitted to be, but he which is
worthy. There is true peace, where no man suffers anything
which may molest him, either from himself or from any
other. He himself shall be the reward of virtue, which has
given virtue, and has promised Himself unto him, than
whom nothing can be better and greater. For what other
thing is that, which He has said by the Prophet: "I will be
their God, and they shall be My people:" but I will be
whereby they shall be satisfied: I will be whatsoever is law-
fully desired of men, life, health, food, abundance, glory,
honor, peace, and all good things? For so also is that rightly
understood, which the apostle says: "That God may be all
in all." He shall be the end of our desires, who shall be
seen without end, who shall be loved without any satiety,
and praised without any tediousness. This function, this
affection, this action verily shall be unto all as the eternal
life shall be common to all. But who is sufficient to think,

much more to utter what degrees there shall also be of the rewards for merits, of the honors and glories? But we must not doubt, but that there shall be degrees. And also that blessed city shall see that in itself, that no inferior shall envy his superior: even as now the other angels do not envy the archangels: as every one would not be which he has not received, although he be combined with a most peaceable bond of concord to him which has received, by which the finger will not be the eye in the body, when a peaceable conjunction, and knitting together of the whole flesh contains both members. Therefore one shall so have a gift less than another has, that he also has this gift, that he will have no more. Neither therefore shall they not have free will, because sins shall not delight them. For it shall be more free being freed from the delight of sinning to an undeclinable and steadfast delight of not sinning. For the first free will, which was given to man, when he was created righteous, had power not to sin, but it had also power to sin: but this last free will shall be more powerful than that, because it shall not be able to sin. But this also by the gift of God, not by the possibility of his own nature. For it is one thing to be God, another thing to be partaker of God. God cannot sin by nature, but he which is partaker of God, receiveth from Him, that he cannot sin. But there were degrees to be observed of the divine gift, that the first free will might be given, whereby man might be able not to sin: the last whereby he might not be able to sin: and the first did pertain to obtain a merit, the latter to receive a reward. But because that nature sinned, when it might sin, it is freed by a more bountiful grace, that it may be brought to that liberty, in which it cannot sin. For as the first immortality, which Adam lost by sinning, was to be able not to die. For so the will of piety and equity shall be free from being lost, as the will of felicity is free from being lost. For as by sinning we neither kept piety nor felicity: neither truly have we lost the will of felicity, felicity being lost.

Truly is God himself therefore to be denied to have free will, because He cannot sin? Therefore the free will of that city shall both be one in all, and also inseparable in every one, freed from all evil, and filled with all good, enjoying an everlasting pleasure of eternal joys, forgetful of faults, forgetful of punishments, neither therefore so forgetful of her deliverance, that she be ungrateful to her deliverer. For so much as concerns reasonable knowledge she is mindful also of her evils, which are past: but so much as concerns the experience of the senses, altogether unmindful.

For a most skillful physician also knows almost all diseases of the body, as they are known by art: but as they are felt in the body, he knows not many, which he has not suffered. As therefore there are two knowledges of evils: one, by which they are not hidden from the power of the understanding, the other, by which they are infixed to the senses of him, that feels them (for all vices are otherwise known by the doctrine of wisdom, and otherwise by the most wicked life of a foolish man) so there are two forgetfulnesses of evils. For a skillful and learned man does forget them one way, and he that has had experience and suffered them, forgets them another way. The former, if he neglect his skill, the latter, if he want misery. According to this forgetfulness which I have set down in the latter place, the saints shall not be mindful of evils past. For they shall want all evils, so that they shall be abolished utterly from their senses. Nevertheless that power of knowledge, which shall be great in them, shall not only know their own evils past, but also the everlasting misery of the damned. Otherwise, if they shall not know that they have been miserable, how, as the psalm says, "Shall they sing the mercies of the Lord for ever?" Than which song nothing verily shall be more delightful to that city, to the glory of the love of Christ, by whose blood we are delivered. There shall be perfected, "Be at rest and see, because I am God." Because there shall be the most great Sabbath having no evening, which the Lord commended unto us in the first works of the world, where it is read, "And God rested the seventh day from all His works He made, and sanctified it, because in it He rested from all His works, which God began to make." For we ourselves also be the seventh day, when we shall be replenished, and repaired with His benediction and sanctification.

There being freed from toil we shall see, because He is God, which we ourselves would have been when we fell from Him, hearing from the seducer: "Ye shall be as gods:" and departing from the true God, by whose means we should be gods by participation of Him, not by forsaking Him. For what have we done without Him, but that we have fallen from Him and gone back in His anger? Of whom we being restored and perfected with a greater grace shall rest for ever, seeing that He is God, with whom we shall be replenished, when He shall be all in all: for our good works also, although they are rather understood to be His than ours, are then imputed unto us to obtain this Sabbath: because if we shall attribute them unto ourselves, they shall be servile, when it is said of the Sabbath: "Ye shall not do any servile work in it." For which cause it is said also by the prophet Ezekiel. "And I have given my Sabbaths unto them for a sign between Me, and them, that they might know that I am the Lord, which sanctify them": Then shall we know this thing perfectly, and we shall perfectly rest and shall perfectly see, that He is God. If therefore that number of ages, as of days be accounted according to the distinctions of times, which seem to be expressed in the sacred Scriptures, that Sabbath day shall appear more evidently, because it is found to be the seventh, that the first age, as it were the first day, be from Adam unto the flood, then the second from thence unto Abraham, not by equality of times, but by number of generations. For they are found to have a tenth number. From hence now, as Matthew the Evangelist doth conclude, three ages do follow even unto the coming of Christ, every one of which is expressed by fourteen generations. From Abraham unto David is one, from thence even unto the transmigration into Babylon, is another, the third from thence unto the incarnate nativity of Christ. So all of them are made five. Now this age is the sixth, to be measured by no number, because of that which is spoken. "It is not for you to know the seasons, which the Father has placed in His own power." After this age God shall rest as in the seventh day, when God shall make that same seventh day to rest in Himself, which we shall be.

Furthermore it would take up a long time to discourse now exactly of every one of those several ages. But this seventh shall be our Sabbath, whose end shall not be the evening, but the Lord's day, as the eighth eternal day, which is sanctified and made holy by the resurrection of Christ, not only prefiguring the eternal rest of the spirit, but also of the body. There we shall rest, and see, we shall see, and love, we shall love, and we shall praise: Behold what shall be in the end without end! For what other thing is our end, but to come to that kingdom of which there is no end. I think I have discharged the debt of this great work by the help of God. Let them which think I have done too little, and they which think I have done too much, grant me a favorable pardon: But let them, which think I have performed enough, accepting it with a kind congratulation, give no thanks unto me, but "unto the Lord with me." Amen.

Suggested Additional Readings

Daniel
The Gospels of Mark, Luke, John
Romans, 1–15
St. Augustine, *Confessions*, Chap. 12

Questions for Research and Discussion

1. In the works of the Prophets, specifically Isaiah, what moral limitations in the Jews are identified as impediments to their living perfect lives? What in the sensual life does the Prophet condemn as destructive of happiness?

2. What conception of history is to be found in Isaiah? Is history the manipulations of man by God? The self-initiated actions of men alone? A cosmic scheme? A pattern of accidents? Or something else?

3. Does Isaiah think of the New Jerusalem as existing on the earth, in time, or does he hold some other conception?

4. Compare Isaiah's utopian vision with that of the Greco-Roman historians and the Greek political theorists.

5. What means does Jesus suggest to men to attain utopian happiness? Does he think of happiness in sensual terms at all? Explain.

6. In the *New Testament*, the New Jerusalem seems less and less the reestablishment of the capital city of the Jews as an earthly power and more and more a removal of the "city" to the heavens. Trace the evolution of this concept from the Gospels to Paul's epistles to the Revelations of Saint John.

7. Does St. Augustine think of the City of God as a geographical location? A physical structure? A kind of political arrangement? An emotional state in the Christian? A spiritual kingdom? A perfect human society instituted by God after history ends? Or a combination of all of these? Discuss.

8. Does Augustine emphasize faith or reason more as the means to perfection and spiritual fulfillment? Explain your answer.

9. Compare and contrast Jesus' depiction of the Heavenly City of God with Augustine's City. Are they significantly different in any way?

10. Look up materials on one of these subjects as the basis for a report:
    a. The Utopianism of Amos, Hosea, and Jeremiah
    b. The New Jerusalem and Zionism
    c. Pastoralism in the Hebrew Utopias
    d. Plato's Ideal Realm and Jesus' Heavenly Kingdom
    e. Death and the Heavenly City in the Gospels
    f. Daniel and St. John as Apocalyptics
    g. Eschatology and Paul's Epistles
    h. Allegory and the Utopian Vision
    i. Number Symbolism in Revelations and *The City of God*
    j. Augustine's View of History

V

The Middle Ages

Introduction

In the centuries between the fall of Rome and the fall of Constantinople (c. 450–1450), Augustine's spiritual and nontemporal City of God remained the dominant utopian concept of Europe. It controlled the writing of history, the principles of government, the codes of conduct among men. But it was not the only utopian vision with followers.

Despite Augustine's spiritualization of utopia, the notion persisted that some earthly realm might combine Christian virtue and sensual comforts to create a state of worldly perfection. In due course, the legend of Prester John (or Presbyter, "Elder," John) arose; and during the twelfth and thirteenth centuries it had some interesting effects. Prester John was reputed to be a Christian king of a fabulously beautiful and wealthy realm, cut off from Christian Europe by the inroads of Turks, Moslems, and Saracens. His kingdom was variously held to be Ethiopia, India, and China; the presence of Christian sects in these remote areas may have encouraged the stories of a great and pious ruler, anxious to join forces with Christian Europe to defeat the heathen in battle, restore the Holy Land to Christian rule, and establish profitable trade routes between the Occident and the Orient. Two Popes (Calixtus II, Alexander III), were supposed to have made contact with Prester John; and the Holy Crusaders were encouraged to think a strong ally stood waiting for them near Jerusalem. Generations of travelers were driven on into the depths of Asia in search of Prester John: Marco Polo thought Kublai Khan might have been the model for John. The voyages of the Spanish, Portuguese, and Dutch, looking for a passage to India, were latter-day consequences of the Prester John version of utopian thought.

While European military and political affairs were following this utopian vision, another vision was beginning to affect European religious and historical thought. Joachim of Floris (c. 1135–1202), in an attempt to clarify the historical and eschatological theories of his Christian predecessors, worked out a system of thought in which the world's history was explained in three stages, each stage corresponding to one aspect of the Trinitarian God. The earliest period, the history of the Jews, was characterized by law and fear, epitomized in the Jehovah of the Old Testament. The second period, the Christian era of grace and faith, had been ushered in by Jesus. The third and final stage, the era of the Holy Spirit, would bring the utopian state of perfect love and spirituality. Joachim thus fused the Jewish ideal of a New Jerusalem and Augustine's vision of the City of God with a belief in inevitable historical progress toward an earthly state of perfection in spirit. Joachim's deterministic optimism has been borrowed by many later thinkers; the student of Marxist-Leninist thought may be interested to find the antecedents of many Communist suppositions in this Christian writer of the twelfth century.

Just as Augustine summarized pagan and Christian beliefs of the ancient world, so Dante Alighieri (1265–1321) synthesized the prevalent beliefs of the Middle Ages. Dante's masterpiece, *The Divine Comedy*, contains many utopian elements: the search for the perfect realm, discussions of several supposed political utopias, ancient legends of Hades and Elysium, a description of the New Jerusalem and the Heavenly City of God. Divided into three parts which reflect the theories of Joachim and others, the *Comedy* shows Dante's journey through Hell (the division of the cosmos determined by the law and justice of God the Father) to Purgatory (the area of redemption established by Christ the Son from principles of Grace and Faith) to a final, apocalyptic vision of Heaven (dominated by the Holy Spirit of Love). Dante's celestial utopia is clearly located in the heavens, and it clearly is to be attained through Faith and Divine Favor: in these assertions, the *Divine Comedy* is supremely medieval and scholastic, and it represents the final embodiment of a utopian view that was about to be drastically altered.

Dante Alighieri

✠

PURGATORY

CANTO XXVIII

Now eager to search out through all its maze
    The living green of the divine forest
    Which to my eyes tempered the new sun's rays,
I left the mountain's rim, nor stayed to rest
    But took the plain by slow and slow degrees
    Where with sweet smells all the earth around is blest.
Gentle air, having no inconstancies
    Within its motion, smote upon my brow
    With no more violence than a gracious breeze;

Translated by Laurence Binyon. Reprinted by permission of The Society of Authors as the literary representative of the Estate of the late Laurence Binyon.

And trembling to the touch of it, each bough
   Was bending all its foliage toward that side
   Where the holy Mount casteth its first shadow;
Yet not so far from upright was blown wide
   But that the small birds on the topmost spray
   All their sweet art continually still plied,
And from a full throat singing loud and gay
   Welcomed the first thrills in the leaves, that bore
   A burden to the descant of their lay
Such as swells up along Chiassi's shore,
   From branch to branch of the pine-forest blown,
   When Aeolus has loosed Sirocco's roar.
Already my slow steps had borne me on
   So far within that immemorial wood
   That I could no more see whence I had gone;
And lo! a stream that stopped me where I stood;
   And at the left the ripple in its train
   Moved on the bank the grasses where it flowed.
All waters here that are most pure from stain
   Would qualified with some immixture seem
   Compared with this, which veils not the least grain,
Altho' so dark, dark goes the gliding stream
   Under the eternal shadow, that hides fast
   For ever there the sun's and the moon's beam.
With my feet halting, with my eyes I passed
   That brook, for the regaling of my sight
   With the fresh blossoms in their full contrast.
And then appeared (as in a sudden light
   Something appears which from astonishment
   Puts suddenly all other thoughts to flight)
A lady who all alone and singing went,
   And as she sang plucked flowers that numberless
   All round about her path their colors blent.
"I pray thee, O lovely Lady, if, as I guess,
   Thou warm'st thee at the radiance of Love's fire,—
   For looks are wont to be the heart's witness,—
I pray thee toward this water to draw near
   So far," said I to her, "while thou dost sing,
   That with my understanding I may hear.

Thou puttest me in remembrance of what thing
    Proserpine was, and where, when by mischance
    Her mother lost her, and she lost the spring."
Even as a lady turns round in the dance
    With feet close to each other and to the ground
    And hardly foot beyond foot doth advance,
Toward me with maiden mien she turned her round
    Upon the floor of flowers yellow and red,
    Holding the while her modest eyes earth-bound.
My supplication then she comforted,
    So near approaching, that her song divine
    Reached me with meaning to the music wed.
Soon as she came to where the grasses line
    The fair stream's bank and stand wet in its wave,
    She accorded me to lift her eyes to mine.
I think not that the light such glory gave
    Beneath the eye-lids of Venus, being hit
    So strangely by the dart her own boy drave.
Erect, she smiled from the bank opposite,
    Disposing in her hands those colors fair
    Which that land bears without seed sown in it.
Three paces the stream parted me from her;
    But Hellespont, where Xerxes bridged the strait
    That still makes human vaunt a bridle wear,
Endured not from Leander keener hate,
    'Twixt Sestos and Abydos full in foam,
    Than this from me, because it closed the gate.
"It may be," she began, "since new ye come
    And see me smiling in this place elect,
    Made for mankind to be their nest and home,
That wonder and some misgiving hold you checkt;
    But the psalm *Delectasti* beams a ray
    Which haply shall discloud your intellect.
And thou who art first and didst beseech me, say
    If there is aught that doth thy question rouse,
    Behold! I am here thy mind's thirst to allay."
"The running water," I said, "and rustling boughs
    Perplex me, appearing to serve other laws
    Than what a new belief made me espouse."

Then she: "I'll tell thee how from its own cause
   Cometh to pass what doth thy wonder tease,
   And purge away the mist that gives thee pause.
The Supreme Good, who himself alone doth please,
   Made man good, and for goodness, and this clime
   Gave him for pledge of the eternal peace.
By his default he sojourned here small time:
   By his default, for tears, labor and sweat
   He exchanged honest laughter and sweet pastime.
And lest the tumults that beneath it beat,
   From water and earth by exhalation bred,
   Which follow, far as they can rise, the heat,
Should vex the peace man here inherited,
   This mount thus far up toward the heavens rose,
   And, barred secure from storm, lifts up its head.
Now since all the air in one smooth circuit flows,
   And, save its circle is broken by some fret,
   Revolving with the primal motion goes,
Such motion, striking here, where without let
   In living air this peak upholds its height,
   Makes the wood sound, since it is thickly set,
And all the plants, so smitten, contain such might
   In them, that with their virtue the air they strew
   Which scatters it abroad in circling flight.
The rest of the earth, according to its due
   Of soil and climate doth conceive and bear
   Trees of each kind and each diverse virtue.
No marvel will it then on earth appear,
   (This known,) when some plant without seed hath struck
   Invisibly its root, to burgeon there.
Know that the blest plain whereon thou dost look
   Is pregnant of all seed beneath the skies
   And bears fruit in it no hand there doth pluck.
The water which thou seëst doth not rise
   From veins, that mist, by cold condensed, restores,
   Like rivers that now gain, now lose in size,
But issues from a spring's unfailing stores
   Which God's will, plenishing it, still re-makes
   So that on either side it freely pours.

On this side it streams virtue such as takes
   Soilure of sin out of the memory;
   On the other, memory of good deeds awakes.
On this side, Lethe, the other, Eunoë
   Its name is; nor comes healing from this well
   Unless upon both sides it tasted be.
This savor doth all savors far excel.—
   Now, though it may be all thy thirstiness
   Is quenched, even were this all that I should tell,
I give thee this corollary as a grace;
   Nor do I think my words shall less be prized
   By thee, that they exceed my promises.
They who in old time dreaming poetized
   Of the felicity of the Age of Gold
   On Helicon perchance this place agnized.
Innocent here was man's first root of old;
   Here blooms perpetual Spring, all fruits abound:
   This is the nectar whereof each hath told."
Then full upon my poets I moved me round;
   And I perceived that they with smiles had learned
   The interpretation that her discourse crowned.
To the fair lady then my face I turned.

CANTO XXIX

Singing, like to a lady in love's dream,
   She with the closing words continued on
   Blessed are they whose sins are pardoned them.
Like nymphs that used to wander, each alone,
   Amid the shadowing green from tree to tree,
   One seeking, and one hiding from, the sun,
Against the motion of the stream moved she
   Upon the bank; and I with her abreast
   Made little step with little step agree.
Not to a hundred had our steps increased
   When both the banks so curved as to compel
   My feet to turn aside unto the East.
Thus went we, and were not far when it befell

The Lady toward me turning full about
Said: "Now, my brother, look and listen well!"
And lo! a sudden splendor dazzled out
    From all sides of the forest through the trees,
    So that, if it were lightning, I made doubt.
But since the lightning, as it comes, ceases,
    And this, remaining, ever intenser grew,
    Within my thought I said: "What thing is this?"
And a sweet melody ran thrilling through
    The luminous air; which in my righteous zeal
    Made me the hardihood of Eve to rue,
Who, but a woman newly formed to feel,
    Alone, where all earth and all heaven obeyed,
    Presumed to abide not under any veil,
Beneath which had she in devotion stayed,
    I should of those ineffable delights
    Supp'd sooner, and with me longer had they delayed.
While thus I went mid the first sounds and sights
    Of the eternal pleasance, hesitant
    In joy that longed to reach yet heavenlier heights,
Before us, under the green boughs aslant,
    The air glowed as a fire glows in a blast,
    And the sweet sound was heard now as a chant.
O Virgins holy and high, if ever fast,
    And cold, and vigil, I for you endured,
    Now am I spurred to claim reward at last.
Helicon's founts for me be full out-poured,
    With all her choir Urania me uphold
    To attempt in verse things scarce to thought assured.
A little farther on seven trees of gold
    Feigned to be such by reason that the tract
    Dividing us from them the sight cajoled.
But when a nearer vision had unpacked
    The general image, which our fancies gloze,
    So that of no particular it lacked,
The power that argument for reason shows
    Perceived them candlesticks, even as they were,
    And clear the words into "Hosanna" rose.

In beauty on high the pomp was flaming there,
 Brighter by far than is the moon's mild blaze
 In her mid month through the clear midnight air.
I turned me backward filled full of amaze
 To the good Virgil, and for answer read
 No less a weight of wonder in his gaze.
Then to the things of glory again my head
 I turned, and they came moving on so slow,
 They had been passed by a bride newly wed.
The Lady cried to me: "Why dost thou glow
 To look but on the living lights in awe,
 Nor seekest what comes after them to know?"
Then saw I people in white apparel draw
 Nearer, as if one led them, rank by rank:
 Such whiteness upon earth none ever saw.
The water glittered bright on my left flank,
 And gave to me my left side, if my face
 Looked into it, like a mirror, from the bank.
When on my shore I had found such vantage-place
 That only the stream's width kept me confined,
 The better to behold, I stayed my pace.
I saw the flames come onward, and behind
 Leave the air as if by painted color sleeked
 That a brush trails, to each its tint assigned,
So that the air remained in order streaked
 With seven bands, the hues the Sun hath dyed
 His bow, and Delia her girdle freaked.
To rearward, farther than the eye descried,
 These banners streamed; as I computed it,
 Ten paces might the outermost divide.
Under so fair a sky as I have writ,
 Came four and twenty elders, two by two,
 And they wore crowns of the white lilies knit.
"Among the daughters of Adam blessed thou,
 And blessed," they continued in their song,
 "Thy beauties, the eternal ages through."
Soon as the flowers and the fresh grass along
 The other bank, opposite to my eye,
 Were cleared of those elect ones and their throng,

As star comes after star into the sky,
    Four living creatures followed in their train,
    Crowned with green leaves, slowly advancing nigh.
Each with six wings was plumed, the plumy grain
    Filled full of eyes; and even such would gleam
    The eyes of Argus, could they live again.
But further to define the forms of them,
    I spare to spend rhymes, reader, nor can aim
    At lavishness, constrained to other theme.
But read Ezekiel, who their form and frame
    Paints as he saw them, from the region cold
    Coming upon the wind in cloud and flame.
As thou upon his page dost find them scrolled,
    So were they here; but for the wings they wore,
    John is with me, and hath the difference told.
The midmost of the space between the four
    Contained a car on two wheels, triumphing,
    Which at his neck a Gryphon onward bore.
And he stretcht upward one and the other wing
    'Twixt three and three and mid band, lest he might,
    By cleaving it, to any an injury bring.
They rose so high that they were lost to sight.
    As far as he was bird, his limbs were scaled
    With gold, the rest was vermeil mixt with white.
With car so fair never was Rome regaled
    By Africanus, nor Augustus, nay,
    The Sun's own car beside it would be paled,
The Sun's own car that perished, driven astray,
    At Earth's devout prayer fallen in flames extinct,
    When Jove let justice have her secret way.
Beside the car's right wheel came dancing linked
    Three ladies in a ring; so red was one,
    That scarce in fire her form had been distinct:
The next was like as if her flesh and bone
    Were made all of an emerald; the third
    Seemed snow on which the air had newly blown.
And now the red to lead the rest appeared,
    And now the white; and from the chant which led
    They took the time, as slow or quick they heard.

By the left wheel came four with festal tread,
In purple, following in their order due
One of them, who had three eyes in her head.
After the passing of this retinue
I saw two aged men, unlike arrayed,
But like in mien, reverend and grave to view.
One showed him a familiar of that trade
Ennobled by supreme Hippocrates
Whom Nature for her dearest creatures made.
Contrary care the other seemed to please:
He bore a sword so keen and bright, its glance
Made, even across the stream, fear on me seize.
Then saw I four, of aspect humble, advance;
And behind all was an old man alone
Coming, with piercing visage, in a trance.
And all these seven had a like raiment on
With the first troop, but round about the head
A garlanding of lilies had they none,
Of roses rather, and other blossoms red.
One from short distance viewing them would swear
That over the eyes a fire upon them fed.
Now when the car came opposite me, the air
Thundered; and this folk in their solemn lines,
Seeming forbidden, did no farther dare,
Halting in that place with the van's ensigns.

Suggested Additional Readings

Dante, *Inferno* and *Purgatorio* (Ciardi translation)
"Joachim of Floris" and "Prester John" in the *Encyclopaedia
Britannica* (1965 edition)
Romance of the Rose

Questions for Discussion and Writing

1. Does Dante think of paradise as a physical location or
something else? Explain. How do you account for his use
of physical details?

2. Is Dante's Paradise a "paradise" in the earlier sense of a garden or pastoral land of perfection? How?

3. Explain the Christian symbolism in the passage from *The Divine Comedy* given above. What is the importance of numbers in Dante's description? How do you explain this?

4. Does Dante seem to depend more on the Old Testament or the New Testament for his utopian concepts? Why?

5. Is Dante at all dependent upon Saint Augustine for any of the elements in the passage given? Discuss.

6. Briefly suggest Dante's conceptions of Time and History as they are related to his utopian vision.

7. In the *Paradiso*, Dante suggests that no soul, however blessed, ever attained on earth a perfect fulfillment of the basic virtues. Does this attitude resemble or differ from those of Jesus and Augustine? How does it relate to Platonic dualism?

8. Look up Dante's theory of the several levels of allegory (in *The Banquet* or the *Letter to Con Grande*, as well as commentaries on Dante) and discuss the given selection in light of Dante's theory. Does Dante's allegory help him to deal with the utopian ideal more clearly or less clearly than, say, Plato or Augustine?

9. Research and write on one of these topics:
   a. Ethiopia and Medieval Utopias
   b. The Legend of Prester John
   c. The Orient and Utopianism
   d. The Crusades and the Search for Utopia
   e. The Passage to India
   f. Atlantis and Maritime Exploration
   g. Joachim's Theory of History (or Time or Utopia)
   h. Marco Polo and Utopia
   i. Dante's Debt to Joachimite Theory
   j. Dante and Augustine
   k. The *Inferno* and the Prophets

l. The *Purgatorio* and Aristotle
m. The *Paradiso* and Plato
n. Joachim's Theories and St. Francis of Assisi
o. Chaucer and Utopia

VI

The Renaissance

Introduction

In the period from 1400–1700, Western Europe developed the combination of social, economic, political, and aesthetic beliefs that has since been referred to as a cultural rebirth, or Renaissance. In Italy, France, and England, successively, cultural alterations resulted in new intellectual emphases; and utopian literature multiplied and developed to a vast extent. In the Humanistic shift from divine to earthly concerns, the longstanding medieval interest in the Heavenly City gave way to a reborn interest in geographical and political utopias, in historical utopias, and in utopian psychology and literature. It was during this period that the utopian myths became an integral part of "modern" (as opposed to ancient or classical) thought.

As the precursor of the Humanists, Dante had shown a typical concern of the later writers: a reawakened interest in ancient culture, especially Roman, and the desire to imitate the literary techniques of the ancient epic. Renaissance historians began to write panegyric histories of the Roman Empire, following Polybius and Livy; in time, these praise-filled accounts turned Rome into the sort of remote historical utopia that Diodorus had caused Egypt to be for the Romans themselves. Favio Biondi, Polydore Vergil, and other historians passed on to later writers a well-developed legend of the Roman Republic or the Empire as perfect political utopias.

Likewise, Dante's imitation of Virgil produced a series of imitators who deployed the utopian tales of antiquity to attract readers. Torquato Tasso's *Jerusalem Delivered* was a romantic epic, a highly colored version of the Crusades, with utopian references to shepherds and pastoral idylls, groves and guardian spirits, simplicity and moral purity. Ludovico Ariosto's *Orlando Furioso* also filled a more secular narrative with evil giants and fair maidens in distress rescued by noble heroes to live happily ever after in utopian bliss amid the fields and groves. In England, two famous Elizabethans copied the Italian romances in long narratives replete with utopian elements. Sir Philip Sidney's *Arcadia*, as its title suggests, drew upon the ancient traditions of the rural glade, the innocence of the countryside, and the life of blissful simplicity. Edmund Spenser's *The Faerie Queene* concerned itself with tales of knights honoring Gloriana, the queen of fairyland, by adventuring through the countryside into Gardens of Adonis, evil "Bowers of Bliss," and deceptive "Forests of Error." Echoes of arcadian utopia may even be found in Shakespeare's Forest of Arden (in *As You Like It*) and his wood outside Athens (*A Mid-Summer Night's Dream*) as well as Donne's lyric poem "The Ecstasy," and Marvell's "The Garden."

The explorations of the Renaissance era, which took European voyagers to the New World, also helped to revive interest in the utopia beyond the horizons. The discovery of the Incan and Mayan civilizations in South and Central America produced a full-scale cult of primitivism in Europe among worldly sophisticates like Montaigne, who reflected on the noble savages of the New World with admiration equal to that lavished by Strabo on the Scythians. Spanish explorations in Mexico, Florida, and the American West led to stories of El Dorado and the Seven Cities of Gold (also thought to be found in South America), where the inhabitants lived in luxury, plenty, and happiness. Ponce de Leon's search for the Fountain of Youth in Florida captured the European imagination once again; and adventurers among the Caribbean Islands told wondrous tales of coral reefs and innocent natives, food dropping from trees, and a paradise where work and sickness were unknown. Elizabethan travel books (Hakluyt's *Voyages*, for example) described the journeys of Dutch, French, Spanish, and English explorers, many of whom claimed to have found lands of perfection in the Indian Ocean or the South Pacific, in the jungles of America or the West Indies. Shakespeare's Othello parodies these tales in his account of how he won the lady Desdemona.

The accounts also won the interest of Renaissance political theorists who looked back to Plato and Aristotle as models for their treatises on government as man's way to collective happiness at the same time they imitated the contemporary literature of travel. Sir Thomas More's *Utopia*, the most famous and influential of the political tracts, purported to be the account of a traveler to a distant land in the Western hemisphere (perhaps California). The traveler claimed the Utopians had found a perfect state through a highly controlled system of government in which private needs were eliminated by a sharing of wealth, a strict system of justice, a program of cultural activities for all citizens, planned work for all people, rotating agricultural and urban duties, and so on. Francis Bacon took up the Platonic legend in his *New Atlantis*, a disguise for England in a more perfect state of the future; and Sir John Harrington, in the *Oceana*, similarly laid out a scheme for improving the present evils of English society, which he thought to be largely economic. Utopian political works written on the continent included Campanella's *The City of tne Sun* (a version of the El Dorado legend).

Though the emphasis on worldly utopias grew increasingly stronger during the Renaissance, the New Jerusalem was still

a popular version of the idea. One of its final appearances
—in John Bunyan's *Pilgrim's Progress*—was a clear-cut
instance of its lingering appeal among the majority of
readers, who still saw life as a pilgrimage through trials and
tests of Christian strength, with death (the River Jordan)
separating man from his spiritual home and eternal bliss.
Also, one of the ultimate masterpieces of Renaissance
thought, John Milton's *Paradise Lost*, made the Biblical
story of the Garden of Eden and man's Fall from Grace the
framework of its synthesis of classical, Humanist, and Christian thought. Like *The City of God* and *The Divine
Comedy*, *Paradise Lost* is the ideological culmination of a
cultural epoch. In many ways, it is a literary and intellectual
landmark; in the history of utopian thought, it is the last
great expression of utopian thought as it was shaped by
Christian theology.

Michel Montaigne

✠

OF CANNIBALS

When King Pyrrhus invaded Italy, having viewed and considered the order of the army the Romans sent out to meet
him; "I know not," said he, "what kind of barbarians" (for
so the Greeks called all other nations) "these may be; but
the disposition of this army, that I see, has nothing of barbarism in it." [1] As much said the Greeks of that which
Flaminius brought into their country;[2] and Philip, beholding
from an eminence the order and distribution of the Roman

From *Essays*, by Michel Montaigne. Translation by Charles Cotton.
[1] Plutarch, Life of Pyrrhus, c. 8.
[2] Idem, Life of Flaminius, c. 3.

camp formed in his kingdom by Publius Sulpicius Galba, spoke to the same effect.[3] By which it appears how cautious men ought to be of taking things upon trust from vulgar opinion, and that we are to judge by the eye of reason, and not from common report.

I long had a man in my house that lived ten or twelve years in the New World, discovered in these latter days, and in that part of it where Villegaignon landed,[4] which he called Antarctic France. This discovery of so vast a country seems to be of very great consideration. I cannot be sure, that hereafter there may not be another, so many wiser men than we having been deceived in this. I am afraid our eyes are bigger than our bellies, and that we have more curiosity than capacity; for we grasp at all, but catch nothing but wind.

Plato brings in Solon,[5] telling a story that he had heard from the priests of Sais in Egypt, that of old, and before the Deluge, there was a great island called Atlantis, situate directly at the mouth of the Straits of Gibraltar, which contained more countries than both Africa and Asia put together; and that the kings of that country, who not only possessed that isle, but extended their dominion so far into the continent that they had a country in Africa as far as Egypt, and extending in Europe to Tuscany, attempted to encroach even upon Asia, and to subjugate all the nations that border upon the Mediterranean Sea, as far as the Black Sea; and to that effect overran all Spain, the Gauls, and Italy, so far as to penetrate into Greece, where the Athenians stopped them: but that some time after, both the Athenians, and they and their island, were swallowed by the Flood.

It is very likely that this extreme irruption and inundation of water made wonderful changes and alterations in the habitations of the earth, as 'tis said that the sea then divided Sicily from Italy—

[3] Livy, History, xxxi. 34.
[4] At Brazil, in 1557.
[5] In Timaeus.

> Haec loca, vi quondam, et vasta convulsa ruina,
> Dissiluisse ferunt, quum protenus utraque tellus
> Una foret.[6]

Cyprus from Syria, the isle of Negropont from the continent of Boetia, and elsewhere united lands that were separate before, by filling up the channel betwixt them with sand and mud:

> Sterilisque diu palus, aptaque remis,
> Vicinas urbes alit, et grave sentit aratrum.[7]

But there is no great appearance that this isle was this New World so lately discovered: for that almost touched upon Spain, and it were an incredible effect of an inundation, to have tumbled back so prodigious a mass, above twelve hundred leagues: besides that our modern navigators have already almost discovered it to be no island, but *terra firma*, a continent with the East Indies on the one side, and with the lands under the two poles on the other side; or, if it be separate from them, it is by so narrow a strait and channel, that it none the more deserves the name of an island for that.

It should seem, that in this great body, there are two sorts of motions, the one natural, and the other febrific, as there are in ours. When I consider the impression that our river of Dordoigne has made in my time, on the right bank of its descent, and that in twenty years it has gained so much, and undermined the foundations of so many houses, I perceive it to be an extraordinary agitation: for had it always followed this course, or were hereafter to do it, the aspect of the world would be totally changed. But rivers alter their course, sometimes beating against the one side, and sometimes the other, and sometimes quietly keeping the channel. I do not speak

[6] "These lands, they say, once with violence and vast desolation convulsed, burst asunder, which erewhile were one."—Virgil, Aeneid, iii. 414.

[7] "That which was once a sterile marsh, and bore vessels on its bosom, now feeds neighboring cities, and admits the plough."—Horace, De Arte Poeticâ, v. 65.

of sudden inundations, the causes of which everybody under-
stands. In Medoc, by the sea-shore, the Sieur d'Arsac, my
brother, sees an estate he had there, buried under the sands
which the sea vomits before it: where the tops of some
houses are yet to be seen, and where his rents and domains
are converted into pitiful barren pasturage. The inhabitants
of this place affirm, that of late years the sea has driven so
vehemently upon them, that they have lost above four
leagues of land. These sands are her harbingers: and we
now see great heaps of moving sand, that march half a
league before her, and occupy the land.

The other testimony from antiquity, to which some would
apply this discovery of the New World, is in Aristotle; at
least, if that little book of unheard-of miracles be his. He
there tells us, that certain Carthaginians, having crossed the
Atlantic Sea without the Straits of Gibraltar, and sailed a
very long time, discovered at last a great and fruitful island,
all covered over with wood, and watered with several broad
and deep rivers; far remote from all *terra firma,* and that
they, and others after them, allured by the goodness and
fertility of the soil, went thither with their wives and children, and began to plant a colony. But the senate of Car-
thage perceiving their people by little and little to diminish,
issued out an express prohibition, that none, upon pain of
death, should transport themselves thither; and also drove
out these new inhabitants; fearing, 'tis said, lest in process of
time they should so multiply as to supplant themselves and
ruin their state. But this relation of Aristotle no more agrees
with our new-found lands than the other.

This man that I had was a plain ignorant fellow, and therefore the more likely to tell truth: for your better bred sort
of men are much more curious in their observation, 'tis true,
and discover a great deal more, but then they gloss upon it,
and to give the greater weight to what they deliver and allure
your belief, they cannot forbear a little to alter the story;
they never represent things to you simply as they are, but
rather as they appeared to them, or as they would have them
appear to you, and to gain the reputation of men of judgment, and the better to induce your faith, are willing to help

out the business with something more than is really true, of
their own invention. Now in this case, we should either
have a man of irreproachable veracity, or so simple that he
has not wherewithal to contrive, and to give a color of truth
to false relations, and who can have no ends in forging an
untruth. Such a one was mine; and besides, he has at divers
times brought to me several seamen and merchants who at
the same time went the same voyage. I shall therefore content myself with his information, without inquiring what the
cosmographers say to the business. We should have topog-
raphers to trace out to us the particular places where they
have been; but for having had this advantage over us, to have
seen the Holy Land, they would have the privilege, forsooth,
to tell us stories of all the other parts of the world besides.
I would have every one write what he knows, and as much
as he knows, but no more; and that not in this only, but in
all other subjects; for such a person may have some particular
knowledge and experience of the nature of such a river, or
such a fountain, who, as to other things, knows no more
than what everybody does, and yet to keep a clutter with
this little pittance of his, will undertake to write the whole
body of physics: a vice from which great inconveniences
derive their original.

Now, to return to my subject, I find that there is nothing
barbarous and savage in this nation, by anything that I can
gather, excepting, that every one gives the title of barbarism
to everything that is not in use in his own country. As,
indeed, we have no other level of truth and reason, than the
example and idea of the opinions and customs of the place
wherein we live: there is always the perfect religion, there
the perfect government, there the most exact and accomplished usage of all things. They are savages at the same rate
that we say fruits are wild, which nature produces of herself
and by her own ordinary progress; whereas in truth, we ought
rather to call those wild, whose natures we have changed by
our artifice, and diverted from the common order. In those,
the genuine, most useful and natural virtues and properties
are vigorous and sprightly, which we have helped to degenerate in these, by accommodating them to the pleasure of

our own corrupted palate. And yet for all this, our taste confesses a flavor and delicacy, excellent even to emulation of the best of ours, in several fruits wherein those countries abound without art or culture. Neither is it reasonable that art should gain the pre-eminence of our great and powerful mother nature. We have so surcharged her with the additional ornaments and graces we have added to the beauty and riches of her own works by our inventions, that we have almost smothered her; yet in other places, where she shines in her own purity and proper luster, she marvelously baffles and disgraces all our vain and frivolous attempts.

> Et veniunt hederae sponte sua melius;
> Surgit et in solis formosior arbutus antris;
> Et volucres nulla dulcius arte canunt.[8]

Our utmost endeavors cannot arrive at so much as to imitate the nest of the least of birds, its contexture, beauty, and convenience: not so much as the web of a poor spider.

All things, says Plato,[9] are produced either by nature, by fortune, or by art; the greatest and most beautiful by the one or the other of the former, the least and the most imperfect by the last.

These nations then seem to me to be so far barbarous, as having received but very little form and fashion from art and human invention, and consequently to be not much remote from their original simplicity. The laws of nature, however, govern them still, not as yet much vitiated with any mixture of ours: but 'tis in such purity, that I am sometimes troubled we were not sooner acquainted with these people, and that they were not discovered in those better times, when there were men much more able to judge of them than we are. I am sorry that Lycurgus and Plato had no knowledge of them; for to my apprehension, what we now see in those nations, does not only surpass all

---

[8] "The ivy grows best spontaneously; the arbutus best in shady caves; and the wild notes of birds are sweeter than art can teach." —Propertius, Elegies, i. 2, 10.

[9] Laws, 10.

the pictures with which the poets have adorned the golden
age, and all their inventions in feigning a happy state of
man, but, moreover, the fancy and even the wish and desire
of philosophy itself; so native and so pure a simplicity, as
we by experience see to be in them, could never enter into
their imagination, nor could they ever believe that human
society could have been maintained with so little artifice
and human patchwork. I should tell Plato, that it is a nation
wherein there is no manner of traffic, no knowledge of letters,
no science of numbers, no name of magistrate or political
superiority; no use of service, riches or poverty, no contracts,
no successions, no dividends, no properties, no employments,
but those of leisure, no respect of kindred, but common, no
clothing, no agriculture, no metal, no use of corn or wine;
the very words that signify lying, treachery, dissimulation,
avarice, envy, detraction, pardon, never heard of.[10] How
much would he find his imaginary Republic short of his
perfection? "Viri a diis recentes." [11]

Hos natura modos primum dedit.[12]

As to the rest, they live in a country very pleasant and
temperate, so that, as my witnesses inform me, 'tis rare to
hear of a sick person, and they moreover assure me, that
they never saw any of the natives, either paralytic, blear-
eyed, toothless, or crooked with age. The situation of their
country is along the sea-shore, enclosed on the other side
towards the land, with great and high mountains, having
about a hundred leagues in breadth between. They have
great store of fish and flesh, that have no resemblance to
those of ours: which they eat without any other cookery,
than plain boiling, roasting, and broiling. The first that rode
a horse thither, though in several other voyages he had
contracted an acquaintance and familiarity with them, put

[10] This is the famous passage which Shakespeare, through Florio's
version, 1603, or ed. 1613, p. 102, has employed in the Tempest,
ii. 1.

[11] "Men fresh from the gods."—Seneca, Epistles, 90.

[12] "These were the manners first taught by nature."—Virgil,
Georgics, ii. 20.

them into so terrible a fright, with his centaur appearance,
that they killed him with their arrows before they could
come to discover who he was. Their buildings are very long,
and of capacity to hold two or three hundred people, made
of the barks of tall trees, reared with one end upon the
ground, and leaning to and supporting one another, at the
top, like some of our barns, of which the coverings hang
down to the very ground, and serves for the side walls.
They have wood so hard, that they cut with it, and make
their swords of it, and their grills of it to broil their meat.
Their beds are of cotton, hung swinging from the roof, like
our seaman's hammocks, every man his own, for the wives
lie apart from their husbands. They rise with the sun, and
so soon as they are up, eat for all day, for they have no
more meals but that: they do not then drink, as Suidas
reports of some other people of the East that never drank
at their meals; but drink very often all day after, and sometimes to a rousing pitch. Their drink is made of a certain
root, and is of the color of our claret, and they never drink
it but lukewarm. It will not keep above two or three days;
it has a somewhat sharp, brisk taste, is nothing heady, but
very comfortable to the stomach; laxative to strangers, but
a very pleasant beverage to such as are accustomed to it.
They make use, instead of bread, of a certain white com-
pound, like Coriander comfits; I have tasted of it; the taste
is sweet and a little flat. The whole day is spent in dancing.
Their young men go a-hunting after wild beasts with bows
and arrows; one part of their women are employed in preparing their drink the while, which is their chief employment. One of their old men, in the morning before they
fall to eating, preaches to the whole family, walking from
the one end of the house to the other, and several times
repeating the same sentence, till he has finished the round,
for their houses are at least a hundred yards long. Valor
towards their enemies and love towards their wives, are the
two heads of his discourse, never failing in the close, to put
them in mind, that 'tis their wives who provide them their
drink warm and well seasoned. The fashion of their beds,
ropes, swords, and of the wooden bracelets they tie about

their wrists, when they go to fight, and of the great canes, bored hollow at one end, by the sound of which they keep the cadence of their dances, are to be seen in several places, and amongst others, at my house. They shave all over, and much more neatly than we, without other razor than one of wood or stone. They believe in the immortality of the soul, and that those who have merited well of the gods, are lodged in that part of heaven where the sun rises, and the accursed in the west.

They have I know not what kind of priests and prophets, who very rarely present themselves to the people, having their abode in the mountains. At their arrival, there is a great feast, and solemn assembly of many villages: each house, as I have described, makes a village, and they are about a French league distant from one another. This prophet declaims to them in public, exhorting them to virtue and their duty: but all their ethics are comprised in these two articles, resolution in war, and affection to their wives. He also prophesies to them events to come, and the issues they are to expect from their enterprises, and prompts them to or diverts them from war: but let him look to't; for if he fail in his divination, and anything happen otherwise than he has foretold, he is cut into a thousand pieces, if he be caught, and condemned for a false prophet: for that reason, if any of them has been mistaken, he is no more heard of.

Divination is a gift of God, and therefore to abuse it, ought to be a punishable imposture. Amongst the Scythians, where their diviners failed in the promised effect, they were laid, bound hand and foot, upon carts loaded with furze and bavins, and drawn by oxen, on which they were burned to death.[13] Such as only meddle with things subject to the conduct of human capacity, are excusable in doing the best they can: but those other fellows that come to delude us with assurances of an extraordinary faculty, beyond our understanding, ought they not to be punished, when they do not make good the effect of their promise, and for the temerity of their imposture?

[13] Herodotus, Histories, iv. 69.

They have continual war with the nations that live further within the mainland, beyond their mountains, to which they go naked, and without other arms than their bows and wooden swords, fashioned at one end like the head of our javelins. The obstinacy of their battles is wonderful, and they never end without great effusion of blood: for as to running away, they know not what it is. Every one for a trophy brings home the head of an enemy he has killed, which he fixes over the door of his house. After having a long time treated their prisoners very well, and given them all the regales they can think of, he to whom the prisoner belongs, invites a great assembly of his friends. They being come, he ties a rope to one of the arms of the prisoner, of which, at a distance, out of his reach, he holds the one end himself, and gives to the friend he loves best the other arm to hold after the same manner; which being done, they two, in the presence of all the assembly, despatch him with their swords. After that they roast him, eat him amongst them, and send some chops to their absent friends. They do not do this, as some think, for nourishment, as the Scythians anciently did, but as a representation of an extreme revenge, as will appear by this: that having observed the Portuguese, who were in league with their enemies, to inflict another sort of death upon any of them they took prisoners, which was to set them up to the girdle in the earth, to shoot at the remaining part till it was stuck full of arrows, and then to hang them, they thought those people of the other world (as being men who had sown the knowledge of a great many vices amongst their neighbors, and who were much greater masters in all sorts of mischief than they) did not exercise this sort of revenge without a meaning, and that it must needs be more painful than theirs, they began to leave their old way, and to follow this. I am not sorry that we should here take notice of the barbarous horror of so cruel an action, but that, seeing so clearly into their faults, we should be so blind to our own. I conceive there is more barbarity in eating a man alive, than when he is dead; in tearing a body limb from limb by racks and torments, that is yet in perfect sense; in roasting it by degrees; in causing it to be bitten and worried by dogs and swine (as we have not only read, but lately seen, not amongst inveterate and mortal enemies, but among neighbors and fellow-citizens, and, which is worse, under color of piety and religion), than to roast and eat him after he is dead.

Chrysippus and Zeno, the two heads of the Stoic sect, were of opinion that there was no hurt in making use of our dead carcasses, in what way soever for our necessity, and in feeding upon them too;[14] as our own ancestors, who being besieged by Caesar in the city Alexia, resolved to sustain the famine of the siege with the bodies of their old men, women, and other persons who were incapable of bearing arms.

> Vascones, ut fama est, alimentis talibus usi
> Produxere animas.[15]

And the physicians make no bones of employing it to all sorts of use, either to apply it outwardly; or to give it inwardly for the health of the patient. But there never was any opinion so irregular, as to excuse treachery, disloyalty, tyranny, and cruelty, which are our familiar vices. We may then call these people barbarous, in respect to the rules of reason: but not in respect to ourselves, who in all sorts of barbarity exceed them. Their wars are throughout noble and generous, and carry as much excuse and fair pretense, as that human malady is capable of; having with them no other foundation than the sole jealousy of valor. Their disputes are not for the conquest of new lands, for these they already possess are so fruitful by nature, as to supply them without labor or concern, with all things necessary, in such abundance that they have no need to enlarge their borders. And they are moreover, happy in this, that they only covet so much as their natural necessities require: all beyond that, is superfluous to them: men of the same age call one another generally brothers, those who are younger, children; and the old men are fathers to all. These leave to their heirs in

---

[14] Diogenes Laertius, Lives, vii. 188.
[15] " 'Tis said the Gascons with such meats appeased their hunger."—Juvenal, Satires, xv. 93.

common the full possession of goods, without any manner
of division, or other title than what nature bestows upon
her creatures, in bringing them into the world. If their
neighbors pass over the mountains to assault them, and obtain a victory, all the victors gain by it is glory only, and
the advantage of having proved themselves the better in
valor and virtue: for they never meddle with the goods of
the conquered, but presently return into their own country,
where they have no want of anything necessary, nor of this
greatest of all goods, to know happily how to enjoy their
condition and to be content. And those in turn do the same;
they demand of their prisoners no other ransom, than acknowledgment that they are overcome: but there is not one
found in an age, who will not rather choose to die than
make such a confession, or either by word or look, recede
from the entire grandeur of an invincible courage. There is
not a man amongst them who had not rather be killed and
eaten, than so much as to open his mouth to entreat he may
not. They use them with all liberality and freedom, to the
end their lives may be so much the dearer to them; but
frequently entertain them with menaces of their approaching death, of the torments they are to suffer, of the preparations making in order to it, of the mangling their limbs,
and of the feast that is to be made, where their carcass is
to be the only dish. All which they do, to no other end,
but only to extort some gentle or submissive word from
them, or to frighten them so as to make them run away,
to obtain this advantage that they were terrified, and that
their constancy was shaken; and indeed, if rightly taken, it
is in this point only that a true victory consists.

Victoria nulla est,
Quam quae confessos animo quoque subjugat hostes.[16]

The Hungarians, a very warlike people, never pretend
further than to reduce the enemy to their discretion; for
having forced this confession from them, they let them go

[16] "No victory is complete, which the conquered do not admit to
be so."—Claudius, De Sexto Consulatu Honorii, v. 248.

without injury or ransom, excepting, at the most, to make
them engage their word never to bear arms against them
again. We have sufficient advantages over our enemies that
are borrowed and not truly our own; it is the quality of a
porter, and no effect of virtue, to have stronger arms and
legs; it is a dead and corporeal quality to set in array: 'tis
a turn of fortune to make our enemy stumble, or to dazzle
him with the light of the sun; 'tis a trick of science and art,
and that may happen in a mean base fellow, to be a good
fencer. The estimate and value of a man consist in the heart
and in the will: there his true honor lies. Valor is stability,
not of legs and arms, but of the courage and the soul; it does
not lie in the goodness of our horse or our arms: but in
our own. He that falls obstinate in his courage—"Si succi-
derit, de genu pugnat" [17]—he who, for any danger of im-
minent death, abates nothing of his assurance; who, dying,
yet darts at his enemy a fierce and disdainful look, is overcome not by us, but by fortune;[18] he is killed, not conquered; the most valiant are sometimes the most unfortunate. There are defeats more triumphant than victories.
Never could those four sister victories, the fairest the sun
ever beheld, of Salamis, Plataea, Mycale, and Sicily, venture
to oppose all their united glories, to the single glory of the
discomfiture of King Leonidas and his men, at the pass of
Thermopylae. Whoever ran with a more glorious desire to
greater ambition, to the winning, than Captain Iscolas to
the certain loss of a battle?[19] Who could have found out
a more subtle invention to secure his safety, than he did
to assure his destruction? He was set to defend a certain
pass of Peloponnesus against the Arcadians, which, considering the nature of the place and the inequality of forces,
finding it utterly impossible for him to do, and seeing that
all who were presented to the enemy, must certainly be left
upon the place; and on the other side, reputing it unworthy
of his own virtue and magnanimity and of the Lacedaemo-

[17] "If his legs fail him he fights on his knees."—Seneca, De
Providentia, c. 2.
[18] Idem, De Constantia Sapientis, c. 6.
[19] Diodorus Siculus, xv. 64.

nian name to fail in any part of his duty, he chose a mean
betwixt these two extremes after this manner, the youngest
and most active of his men, he preserved for the service and
defense of their country, and sent them back; and with the
rest, whose loss would be of less consideration, he resolved
to make good the pass, and with the death of them, to make
the enemy buy their entry as dear as possibly he could; as
it fell out, for being presently environed on all sides by the
Arcadians, after having made a great slaughter of the enemy,
he and his were all cut in pieces. Is there any trophy dedicated to the conquerors, which was not much more due to
these who were overcome? The part that true conquering
is to play, lies in the encounter, not in the coming off; and
the honor of valor consists in fighting, not in subduing.

But to return to my story: these prisoners are so far from
discovering the least weakness, for all the terrors that can
be represented to them that, on the contrary, during the
two or three months they are kept, they always appear with
a cheerful countenance; importune their masters to make
haste to bring them to the test, defy, rail at them, and reproach them with cowardice, and the number of battles they
have lost against those of their country. I have a song made
by one of these prisoners, wherein he bids them "come all,
and dine upon him, and welcome, for they shall withal eat
their own fathers and grandfathers, whose flesh has served
to feed and nourish him. These muscles," says he, "this
flesh and these veins, are your own: poor silly souls as you
are, you little think that the substance of your ancestors'
limbs is here yet; notice what you eat, and you will find in
it the taste of your own flesh": in which song there is to be
observed an invention that nothing relishes of the barbarian.
Those that paint these people dying after this manner, represent the prisoner spitting in the faces of his executioners
and making wry mouths at them. And 'tis most certain, that
to the very last gasp, they never cease to brave and defy them
both in word and gesture. In plain truth, these men are very
savage in comparison of us; of necessity, they must either be
absolutely so or else we are savages; for there is a vast difference betwixt their manners and ours.

The men there have several wives, and so much the greater number, by how much they have the greater reputation for valor. And it is one very remarkable feature in their marriages, that the same jealousy our wives have to hinder and divert us from the friendship and familiarity of other women, those employ to promote their husbands' desires, and to procure them many spouses; for being above all things solicitous of their hubands' honor, 'tis their chiefest care to seek out, and to bring in the most companions they can, forasmuch as it is a testimony of the husband's virtue. Most of our ladies will cry out, that 'tis monstrous; whereas in truth, it is not so; but a truly matrimonial virtue, and of the highest form. In the Bible, Sarah, with Leah and Rachel, the two wives of Jacob, gave the most beautiful of their handmaids to their husbands; Livia preferred the passions of Augustus to her own interest;[20] and the wife of King Deiotarus, Stratonice, did not only give up a fair young maid that served her to her husband's embraces, but moreover carefully brought up the children he had by her, and assisted them in the succession to their father's crown.

And that it may not be supposed, that all this is done by a simple and servile obligation to their common practice, or by any authoritative impression of their ancient custom, without judgment or reasoning and from having a soul so stupid, that it cannot contrive what else to do, I must here give you some touches of their sufficiency in point of understanding. Besides what I repeated to you before, which was one of their songs of war, I have another, a love-song, that begins thus: "Stay, adder, stay, that by thy pattern my sister may draw the fashion and work of a rich ribbon, that I may present to my beloved, by which means thy beauty and the excellent order of thy scales shall for ever be preferred before all other serpents." Wherein the first couplet, "Stay, adder," &c., makes the burden of the song. Now I have conversed enough with poetry to judge thus much: that not only, there is nothing of barbarous in this invention, but, moreover, that it is perfectly Anacreontic. To which may

[20] Suetonius, Life of Augustus, c. 71.

be added, that their language is soft, of a pleasing accent, and something bordering upon the Greek terminations.

Three of these people, not foreseeing how dear their knowledge of the corruptions of this part of the world will one day cost their happiness and repose, and that the effect of this commerce will be their ruin, as I presuppose it is in a very fair way (miserable men to suffer themselves to be deluded with desire of novelty and to have left the serenity of their own heaven, to come so far to gaze at ours!) were at Rouen at the time that the late King Charles IX was there. The king himself talked to them a good while, and they were made to see our fashions, our pomp, and the form of a great city. After which, some one asked their opinion, and would know of them, what of all the things they had seen, they found most to be admired? To which they made answer, three things, of which I have forgotten the third, and am troubled at it, but two I yet remember. They said, that in the first place they thought it very strange, that so many tall men wearing beards, strong, and well armed, who were about the king ('tis like they meant the Swiss of his guard) should submit to obey a child, and that they did not rather choose out one amongst themselves to command. Secondly (they have a way of speaking in their language, to call men the half of one another), that they had observed, that there were amongst us men full and crammed with all manner of commodities, whilst, in the meantime, their halves were begging at their doors, lean, and half-starved with hunger and poverty; and they thought it strange that these necessitous halves were able to suffer so great an inequality and injustice, and that they did not take the others by the throats, or set fire to their houses.

I talked to one of them a great while together, but I had so ill an interpreter, and one who was so perplexed by his own ignorance to apprehend my meaning, that I could get nothing out of him of any moment. Asking him, what advantage he reaped from the superiority he had amongst his own people (for he was a captain, and our mariners called him king), he told me; to march at the head of them to war. Demanding of him further, how many men he had to follow him? he showed me a space of ground, to signify as many as could march in such a compass, which might be four or five thousand men; and putting the question to him, whether or no his authority expired with the war? he told me this remained: that when he went to visit the villages of his dependence, they plained him paths through the thick of their woods, by which he might pass at his ease. All this does not sound very ill, and the last was not at all amiss, for they wear no breeches.

Sir Thomas More

✻

UTOPIA

The island of Utopia is in the middle two hundred miles broad, and holds almost at the same breadth over a great part of it; but it grows narrower towards both ends. Its figure is not unlike a crescent: between its horns, the sea comes in eleven miles broad, and spreads itself into a great bay, which is environed with land to the compass of about five hundred miles, and is well secured from winds. In this bay there is no great current, the whole coast is, as it were, one continued harbor, which gives all that live in the island great convenience for mutual commerce; but the entry into the bay, occasioned by rocks on the one hand, and shallows on the other, is very dangerous. In the middle of it there is one single rock which appears above water, and may therefore be easily avoided, and on the top of it there is a tower in which a garrison is kept, the other rocks lie under water, and are very dangerous. The channel is known only to the natives, so that if any stranger should enter into the bay, without one of their pilots, he would run great danger of shipwreck; for even they themselves could not pass it safe

From *Utopia*, by Sir Thomas More. First published in 1516.

if some marks that are on the coast did not direct their way; and if these should be but a little shifted, any fleet that might come against them, how great soever it were, would be certainly lost. On the other side of the island there are likewise many harbors; and the coast is so fortified, both by nature and art, that a small number of men can hinder the descent of a great army. But they report (and there remains good marks of it to make it credible) that this was no island at first, but a part of the continent. Utopus that conquered it (whose name it still carries, for Abraxa was its first name) brought the rude and uncivilized inhabitants into such a good government, and to that measure of politeness, that they now far excel all the rest of mankind; having soon subdued them, he designed to separate them from the continent, and to bring the sea quite round them. To accomplish this, he ordered a deep channel to be dug fifteen miles long; and that the natives might not think he treated them like slaves, he not only forced the inhabitants, but also his own soldiers, to labor in carrying it on. As he set a vast number of men to work, he beyond all men's expectations brought it to a speedy conclusion. And his neighbors who at first laughed at the folly of the undertaking, no sooner saw it brought to perfection, than they were struck with admiration and terror.

There are fifty-four cities in the island, all large and well built: the manners, customs, and laws of which are the same, and they are all contrived as near in the same manner as the ground on which they stand will allow. The nearest lie at least twenty-four miles distance from one another, and the most remote are not so far distant, but that a man can go on foot in one day from it, to that which lies next it. Every city sends three of their wisest senators once a year to Amaurot, to consult about their common concerns; for that is chief town of the island, being situated near the center of it, so that it is the most convenient place for their assemblies. The jurisdiction of every city extends at least twenty miles: and where the towns lie wider, they have much more ground: no town desires to enlarge its bounds, for the people consider themselves rather as tenants than landlords. They have built over all the country, farmhouses for husbandmen, which are well contrived, and are furnished with all things necessary for country labor. Inhabitants are sent by turns from the cities to dwell in them; no country family has fewer than forty men and women in it, besides two slaves. There is a master and a mistress set over every family; and over thirty families there is a magistrate. Every year twenty of this family come back to the town, after they have stayed two years in the country; and in their room there are other twenty sent from the town, that they may learn country work ·from those that have been already one year in the country, as they must teach those that come to them the next from the town. By this means such as dwell in those country farms are never ignorant of agriculture, and so commit no errors, which might otherwise be fatal, and bring them under a scarcity of corn. But though there is every year such a shifting of the husbandmen, to prevent any man being forced against his will to follow that hard course of life too long; yet many among them take such pleasure in it, that they desire leave to continue in it many years. These husbandmen till the ground, breed cattle, hew wood, and convey it to the towns, either by land or water, as is most convenient. They breed an infinite multitude of chickens in a very curious manner; for the hens do not sit and hatch them, but vast number of eggs are laid in a gentle and equal heat, in order to be hatched, and they are no sooner out of the shell, and able to stir about, but they seem to consider those that feed them as their mothers, and follow them as other chickens do the hen that hatched them. They breed very few horses, but those they have are full of mettle, and are kept only for exercising their youth in the art of sitting and riding them; for they do not put them to any work, either of ploughing or carriage, in which they employ oxen; for though their horses are stronger, yet they find oxen can hold out longer; and as they are not subject to so many diseases, so they are kept upon a less charge, and with less trouble; and even when they are so worn out, that they are no more fit for labor, they are good meat at last. They sow no corn, but that which is to be their bread;

for they drink either wine, cider, or perry, and often water, sometimes boiled with honey or licorice, with which they abound; and though they know exactly how much corn will serve every town and all that tract of country which belongs to it, yet they sow much more, and breed more cattle than are necessary for their consumption; and they give that over-plus of which they make no use to their neighbors. When they want anything in the country which it does not pro-duce, they fetch that from the town, without carrying any-thing in exchange for it. And the magistrates of the town take care to see it given them; for they meet generally in the town once a month, upon a festival day. When the time of harvest comes, the magistrates in the country send to those in the towns, and let them know how many hands they will need for reaping the harvest; and the number they call for being sent to them, they commonly despatch it all in one day.

Of Their Towns,
Particularly of Amaurot

He that knows one of their towns, knows them all, they are so like one another, except where the situation makes some difference. I shall therefore describe one of them; and none is so proper as Amaurot; for as none is more eminent, all the rest yielding in precedence to this, because it is the seat of their supreme council; so there was none of them better known to me, I having lived five years altogether in it.

It lies upon the side of a hill, or rather a rising ground: its figure is almost square, for from the one side of it, which shoots up almost to the top of the hill, it runs down in a descent for two miles to the river Anider; but it is a little broader the other way that runs along by the bank of that river. The Anider rises about eighty miles above Amaurot, in a small spring at first; but other brooks falling into it, of which two are more considerable than the rest. As it runs by Amaurot, it is grown half a mile broad; but it still grows larger and larger, till after sixty miles course below it, it is lost in the ocean, between the town and the sea, and for some miles above the town, it ebbs and flows every six hours, with a strong current. The tide comes up for about thirty miles so full, that there is nothing but salt water in the river, the fresh water being driven back with its force; and above that, for some miles, the water is brackish; but a little higher, as it runs by the town, it is quite fresh; and when the tide ebbs, it continues fresh all along to the sea. There is a bridge cast over the river, not of timber, but of fair stone, consisting of many stately arches; it lies at that part of the town which is farthest from the sea, so that ships without any hindrance lie all along the side of the town. There is likewise another river that runs by it, which though it is not great, yet it runs pleasantly, for it rises out of the same hill on which the town stands, and so runs down through it, and falls into the Anider. The inhabitants have fortified the fountain-head of this river, which springs a little without the towns; that so if they should happen to be besieged, the enemy might not be able to stop or divert the course of the water, nor poison it; from thence it is carried in earthen pipes to the lower streets; and for those places of the town to which the water of that small river cannot be conveyed, they have great cisterns for receiving the rain-water, which supplies the want of the other. The town is compassed with a high and thick wall, in which there are many towers and forts; there is also a broad and deep dry ditch, set thick with thorns, cast round three sides of the town, and the river is instead of a ditch on the fourth side. The streets are very convenient for all carriage, and are well sheltered from the winds. Their buildings are good, and are so uniform, that a whole side of a street looks like one house. The streets are twenty feet broad; there lie gardens behind all their houses; these are large but enclosed with buildings, that on all hands face the streets; so that every house has both a door to the street, and a back door to the garden. Their doors have all two leaves, which, as they are easily opened, so they shut of their own accord; and there being no property among them, every man may freely enter into any house whatsoever. At every ten years end they shift their houses by lots. They cultivate their gardens with great care, so that they have both vines, fruits, herbs, and flowers in them; and all is so well ordered, and so finely kept, that I never saw gardens anywhere that were both so fruitful and so beautiful as theirs. And this humor of ordering their gardens so well, is not only kept up by the pleasure they find in it, but also by an emulation between the inhabitants of the several streets, who vie with each other; and there is indeed nothing belonging to the whole town that is both more useful and more pleasant. So that he who founded the town, seems to have taken care of nothing more than of their gardens; for they say, the whole scheme of the town was designed at first by Utopus, but he left all that belonged to the ornament and improvement of it, to be added by those that should come after him, that being too much for one man to bring to perfection. Their records, that contain the history of their town and state, are preserved with an exact care, and run backwards 1,760 years. From these it appears that their houses were at first low and mean, like cottages, made of any sort of timber, and were built with mud walls and thatched with straw. But now their houses are three stories high: the fronts of them are faced either with stone, plastering, or brick; and between the facings of their walls they throw in their rubbish. Their roofs are flat, and on them they lay a sort of plaster, which costs very little, and yet is so tempered that it is not apt to take fire, and yet resists the weather more than lead. They have great quantities of glass among them, with which they glaze their windows. They use also in their windows a thin linen cloth, that is so oiled or gummed that it both keeps out the wind and gives free admission to the light.

Of Their Magistrates

Thirty families choose every year a magistrate, who was anciently called the Syphogrant, but is now called the Philarch; and over every ten Syphogrants, with the families subject to them, there is another magistrate, who was anciently called the Tranibor, but of late the Archphilarch. All the Syphogrants, who are in number 200, choose the

Prince out of a list of four, who are named by the people of the four divisions of the city; but they take an oath before they proceed to an election, that they will choose him whom they think most fit for the office. They give their voices secretly, so that it is not known for whom every one gives his suffrage. The Prince is for life, unless he is removed upon suspicion of some design to enslave the people. The Tranibors are new chosen every year, but yet they are for the most part continued. All their other magistrates are only annual. The Tranibors meet every third day, and oftener if necessary, and consult with the Prince, either concerning the affairs of the state in general, or such private differences as may arise sometimes among the people; though that falls out but seldom. There are always two Syphogrants called into the council-chamber, and these are changed every day. It is a fundamental rule of their government, that no conclusion can be made in anything that relates to the public, till it has been first debated three several days in their council. It is death for any to meet and consult concerning the state, unless it be either in their ordinary council, or in the assembly of the whole body of the people.

These things have been so provided among them, that the Prince and the Tranibors may not conspire together to change the government, and enslave the people; and therefore when anything of great importance is set on foot, it is sent to the Syphogrants; who after they have communicated it to the families that belong to their divisions, and have considered it among themselves, make report to the senate; and upon great occasions, the matter is referred to the council of the whole island. One rule observed in their council, is, never to debate a thing on the same day in which it is first proposed; for that is always referred to the next meeting, that so men may not rashly, and in the heat of discourse, engage themselves too soon, which might bias them so much, that instead of consulting the good of the public, they might rather study to support their first opinions, and by a perverse and preposterous sort of shame, hazard their country rather than endanger their own reputation, or venture the being suspected to have wanted foresight in the expedients that they at first proposed. And therefore to prevent this, they take care that they may rather be deliberate than sudden in their motions.

OF THEIR TRADES, AND MANNER OF LIFE

Agriculture is that which is so universally understood among them, that no person, either man or woman, is ignorant of it; they are instructed in it from their childhood, partly by what they learn at school, and partly by practice; they being led out often into the fields, about the town, where they not only see others at work, but are likewise exercised in it themselves. Besides agriculture, which is so common to them all, every man has some peculiar trade to which he applies himself, such as the manufacture of wool, or flax, masonry, smith's work, or carpenter's work; for there is no sort of trade that is in great esteem among them. Throughout the island they wear the same sort of clothes without any other distinction, except what is necessary to distinguish the two sexes, and the married and unmarried. The fashion never alters; and as it is neither disagreeable nor uneasy, so it is suited to the climate, and calculated both for their summers and winters. Every family makes their own clothes; but all among them, women as well as men, learn one or other of the trades formerly mentioned. Women, for the most part, deal in wool and flax, which suit best with their weakness, leaving the ruder trades to the men. The same trade generally passes down from father to son, inclinations often following descent; but if any man's genius lies another way, he is by adoption translated into a family that deals in the trade to which he is inclined: and when that is to be done, care is taken not only by his father, but by the magistrate, that he may be put to a discreet and good man. And if after a person has learned one trade, he desires to acquire another, that is also allowed, and is managed in the same manner as the former. When he has learned both, he follows that which he likes best, unless the public has more occasion for the other.

The chief, and almost the only business of the Syphogrants, is to take care that no man may live idle, but that every one may follow his trade diligently: yet they do not wear themselves out with perpetual toil, from morning to night, as if they were beasts of burden, which as it is indeed a heavy slavery, so it is everywhere the common course of life amongst all mechanics except the Utopians; but they dividing the day and night into twenty-four hours, appoint six of these for work; three of which are before dinner; and three after. They then sup, and at eight o'clock, counting from noon, go to bed and sleep eight hours. The rest of their time besides that taken up in work, eating and sleeping, is left to every man's discretion; yet they are not to abuse that interval to luxury and idleness, but must employ it in some proper exercise according to their various inclinations, which is for the most part reading. It is ordinary to have public lectures every morning before daybreak; at which none are obliged to appear but those who are marked out for literature; yet a great many, both men and women of all ranks, go to hear lectures of one sort or other, according to their inclinations. But if others, that are not made for contemplation, choose rather to employ themselves at that time in their trades, as many of them do, they are not hindered, but are rather commended, as men that take care to serve their country. After supper, they spend an hour in some diversion, in summer in their gardens, and in winter in the halls where they eat; where they entertain each other, either with music or discourse. They do not so much as know dice, or any such foolish and mischievous games: they have, however, two sorts of games not unlike our chess; the one is between several numbers, in which one number, as it were, consumes another: the other resembles a battle between the virtues and the vices, in which the enmity in the vices among themselves, and their agreement against virtue, is not unpleasantly represented; together with the special oppositions between the particular virtues and vices; as also the methods by which vice either openly assaults or secretly undermines virtue; and virtue on the other hand resists it. But the time appointed for labor is to be narrowly examined, otherwise you may imagine, that since there are only six hours appointed for work, they may fall under a scarcity of necessary provisions. But it is so far from being true, that this time is not sufficient for supplying them with plenty of all things, either necessary or convenient; that it is rather too much; and this you will easily apprehend, if you consider how great a part of all other nations is quite idle. First, women generally do little, who are the half of mankind; and if some few women are diligent, their husbands are idle: then consider the great company of idle priests, and of those that are called religious men; add to these all rich men, chiefly those that have estates in land, who are called noblemen and gentlemen, together with their families, made up of idle persons, that are kept more for show than use; add to these, all those strong and lusty beggars, that go about pretending some disease, in excuse for their begging; and upon the whole account you will find that the number of those by whose labors mankind is supplied, is much less than you perhaps imagined. Then consider how few of those that work are employed in labors that are of real service; for we who measure all things by money, give rise to many trades that are both vain and superfluous, and serve only to support riot and luxury. For if those who work were employed only in such things as the conveniences of life require, there would be such an abundance of them, that the prices of them would so sink, that tradesmen could not be maintained by their gains; if all those who labor about useless things, were set to more profitable employments, and if all they that languish out their lives in sloth and idleness, every one of whom consumes as much as any two of the men that are at work, were forced to labor, you may easily imagine that a small proportion of time would serve for doing all that is either necessary, profitable, or pleasant to mankind, especially while pleasure is kept within its due bounds. This appears very plainly in Utopia, for there, in a great city, and in all the territory that lies round it, you can scarce find five hundred, either men or women, by their age and strength, are capable of labor, that are not engaged in it; even the Syphogrants, though excused by the law, yet do not excuse themselves, but work, that by their examples they may excite the industry of the rest of the people. The like exemption is allowed to those, who being recommended to the people by the priests, are by the secret suffrages of the Syphogrants privileged from labor, that they may apply themselves wholly to study; and if any of these fall short of those hopes that they seemed at first to give, they are obliged to return to work. And sometimes a mechanic, that so employs his leisure hours, as to make a considerable advancement in learning, is eased from being a tradesman, and ranked among their learned men. Out of these they choose their ambassadors, their priests, their Tranibors, and the Prince himself; anciently called their Barzenes, but is called of late their Ademus.

And thus from the great numbers among them that are neither suffered to be idle, not to be employed in any fruitless labor, you may easily make the estimate how much may be done in those few hours in which they are obliged to labor. But besides all that has been already said, it is to be considered that the needful arts among them are managed with less labor than anywhere else. The building or the repairing of houses among us employ many hands, because often a thriftless heir suffers a house that his father built to fall into decay, so that his successor must, at a great cost, repair that which he might have kept up with a small charge: it frequently happens, that the same house which one person built at a vast expense, is neglected by another, who thinks he has a more delicate sense of the beauties of architecture; and he suffering it to fall to ruin, builds another at no less charge. But among the Utopians, all things are so regulated that men very seldom build upon a new piece of ground; and are not only very quick in repairing their houses, but show their foresight in preventing their decay: so that their buildings are preserved very long, with but little labor; and thus the builders to whom that care belongs are often without employment, except the hewing of timber, and the squaring of stones, that the materials may be in readiness for raising a building very suddenly, when there is any occasion for it. As to their clothes, observe how little work is spent in them: while they are at labor, they are clothed with leather and skins, cast carelessly about them, which will last seven years; and when they appear in public they put on an upper garment, which hides the other; and these are all of one color, and that is the natural color of the wool. As they need less woolen cloth than is used anywhere else, so that which they make use of is much less costly. They use linen cloth more; but that is prepared with less labor, and they value cloth only by the whiteness of the linen, or the cleanness of the wool, without much regard to the fineness of the thread: while in other places, four or five upper garments of woolen cloth, of different colors, and as many vests of silk, will scarce serve one man; and while those that are nicer think ten too few, every man there is content with one, which very often serves him two years. Nor is there anything that can tempt a man to desire more; for if he had them, he would neither be the warmer, nor would he make one jot the better appearance for it. And thus, since they are all employed in some useful labor, and since they content themselves with fewer things, it falls out that there is a great abundance of all things among them: so that it frequently happens, that, for want of other work, vast numbers are sent out to mend the highways. But when no public undertaking is to be performed, the hours of working are lessened. The magistrates never engage the people in unnecessary labor, since the chief end of the constitution is to regulate labor by the necessities of the public, and to allow all the people as much time as is necessary for the improvement of their minds, in which they think the happiness of life consists.

Francis Bacon

✠

ATLANTIS

The next day, the same governor came again to us, immediately after dinner, and excused himself, saying, "That the day before he was called from us somewhat abruptly, but now he would make us amends, and spend time with us, if we held his company and conference agreeable." We answered, that we held it so agreeable and pleasing to us, as we forgot both dangers past, and fears to come, for the time we heard him speak; and that we thought an hour spent with him was worth years of our former life. He bowed himself a little to us, and after we were set again, he said, "Well, the questions are on your part." One of our number said, after a little pause, that there was a matter we were no less desirous to know than fearful to ask, lest we might presume too far. But encouraged by his rare humanity towards us (that could scarce think ourselves strangers, being his vowed and professed servants), we would take the hardness to propound it; humbly beseeching him, if he thought it not fit to be answered, that he would pardon it, though he rejected it. We said, we well observed those his words, which he formerly spake, that this happy island, where we now stood, was known to few, and yet knew most of the nations of the world, which we found to be true, considering they had the languages of Europe, and knew much of our state and business; and yet we in Europe (notwithstanding all the remote discoveries and navigations of this last age) never heard any of the least inkling or glimpse of this island. This we found wonderful strange; for that all nations have interknowledge one of another, either by voyage into foreign parts, or by strangers that come to them;

From *The New Atlantis*, by Francis Bacon. First published in 1629.

and though the traveler into a foreign country doth commonly know more by the eye than he that stayeth at home can by relation of the traveler; yet both ways suffice to make a mutual knowledge, in some degree, on both parts. But for this island, we never heard tell of any ship of theirs, that had been seen to arrive upon any shore of Europe; no, nor of either the East or West Indies, nor yet of any ship of any part of the world, that had made return for them. And yet the marvel rested not in this. For the situation of it (as his lordship said) in the secret conclave of such a vast sea might cause it. But then, that they should have knowledge of the languages, books, affairs, of those that lie such a distance from them, it was a thing we could not tell what to make of; for that it seemed to us a condition and propriety of divine powers and beings, to be hidden and unseen to others, and yet to have others open, and as in a light to them. At this speech the governor gave a gracious smile and said, that we did well to ask pardon for this question we now asked, for that it imported, as if we thought this land a land of magicians, that sent forth spirits of the air into all parts, to bring them news and intelligence of other countries. It was answered by us all, in all possible humbleness, but yet with a countenance taking knowledge, that we knew that he spake it but merrily. That we were apt enough to think, there was somewhat supernatural in this island, but yet rather as angelical than magical. But to let his lordship know truly what it was that made us tender and doubtful to ask this question, it was not any such conceit, but because we remembered he had given a touch in his former speech, that this land had laws of secrecy touching strangers. To this he said, "You remember it aright; and therefore in that I shall say to you, I must reserve some particulars, which it is not lawful for me to reveal, but there will be enough left to give you satisfaction.

"You shall understand (that which perhaps you will scarce think credible) that about three thousand years ago, or somewhat more, the navigation of the world (especially for remote voyages) was greater than at this day. Do not think with yourselves, that I know not how much it is increased with you, within these threescore years; I know it well, and yet I say, greater then than now; whether it was, that the example of the ark, that saved the remnant of men from the universal deluge, gave men confidence to adventure upon the waters, or what it was; but such is the truth. The Phoenicians, and especially the Tyrians, had great fleets; so had the Carthaginians their colony, which is yet farther west. Toward the east the shipping of Egypt, and of Palestine, was likewise great. China also, and the great Atlantis (that you call America), which have now but junks and canoes, abounded then in tall ships. This island (as appeareth by faithful registers of those times) had then fifteen hundred strong ships, of great content. Of all this there is with you sparing memory, or none; but we have large knowledge thereof.

"At that time, this land was known and frequented by the ships and vessels of all the nations before named. And (as it cometh to pass) they had many times men of other countries, that were no sailors, that came with them; as Persians, Chaldeans, Arabians, so as almost all nations of might and fame resorted hither; of whom we have some stirps and little tribes with us at this day. And for our own ships, they went sundry voyages, as well to your straits, which you call the Pillars of Hercules, as to other parts in the Atlantic and Mediterranean Seas; as to Paguin (which is the same with Cambalaine) and Quinzy, upon the Oriental Seas, as far as to the borders of the East Tartary.

"At the same time, and an age after or more, the inhabitants of the great Atlantis did flourish. For though the narration and description which is made by a great man with you, that the descendants of Neptune planted there, and of the magnificent temple, palace, city and hill; and the manifold streams of goodly navigable rivers, which as so many chains environed the same site and temple; and the several degrees of ascent, whereby men did climb up to the same, as if it had been a Scala Coeli; be all poetical and fabulous; yet so much is true, that the said country of Atlantis, as well that of Peru, then called Coya, as that of Mexico, then named Tyrambel, were mighty and proud kingdoms, in arms, shipping, and riches; so mighty, as at one time, or at least within the space of ten years, they both made two great expeditions; they of Tyrambel through the Atlantic to the Mediterranean Sea; and they of Coya, through the South Sea upon this our island; and for the former of these, which was into Europe, the same author amongst you, as it seemeth, had some relation from the Egyptian priest, whom he citeth. For assuredly, such a thing there was. But whether it were the ancient Athenians that had the glory of the repulse and resistance of those forces, I can say nothing; but certain it is there never came back either ship or man from that voyage. Neither had the other voyage of those of Coya upon us had better fortune, if they had not met with enemies of greater clemency. For the king of this island, by name Altabin, a wise man and a great warrior, knowing well both his own strength and that of his enemies, handled the matter so, as he cut off their land forces from their ships, and entoiled both their navy and their camp with a greater power than theirs, both by sea and land; and compelled them to render themselves without striking a stroke; and after they were at his mercy, contenting himself only with their oath, that they should no more bear arms against him, dismissed them all in safety. But the divine revenge overtook not long after those proud enterprises. For within less than the space of one hundred years the Great Atlantis was utterly lost and destroyed; not by a great earthquake, as your man saith, for that whole tract is little subject to earthquakes, but by a particular deluge, or inundation; those countries having at this day far greater rivers, and far higher mountains to pour down waters, than any part of the old world. But it is true that the same inundation was not deep, not past forty foot, in most places, from the ground, so that although it destroyed man and beast generally, yet some few wild inhabitants of the wood escaped. Birds also were saved by flying to the high trees and woods. For as for men, although they had buildings in many places higher than the depth of the water, yet that inundation, though it were shallow, had a long continuance, whereby they of the vale that were not drowned perished for want of food, and other things necessary. So as marvel you not at the thin population of America, nor at the rudeness and ignorance of the people; for you must account your inhabitants of America as a young people, younger a thousand years at the least than the rest of the world, for that there was so much time between the universal flood and their particular inundation. For the poor remnant of human seed which remained in their mountains, peopled the country again slowly, by little and little, and being simple and a savage people (not like Noah and his sons, which was the chief family of the earth), they were not able to leave letters, arts, and civility to their posterity; and having likewise in their mountainous habitations been used, in respect of the extreme cold of those regions, to clothe themselves with the skins of tigers, bears, and great hairy goats, that they have in those parts; when after they came down into the valley, and found the intolerable heats which are there, and knew no means of lighter apparel, they were forced to begin the custom of going naked, which continueth at this day. Only they take great pride and delight in the feathers of birds, and this also they took from those their ancestors of the mountains, who were invited unto it, by the infinite flight of birds, that came up to the high grounds, while the waters stood below. So you see, by this main accident of time, we lost our traffic with the Americans, with whom of all others, in regard they lay nearest to us, we had most commerce. As for the other parts of the world, it is most manifest that in the ages following (whether it were in respect of wars, or by a natural revolution of time) navigation did everywhere greatly decay, and specially far voyages (the rather by the use of galleys, and such vessels as could hardly brook the ocean) were altogether left and omitted. So then, that part of intercourse which could be from other nations, to sail to us, you see how it hath long since ceased; except it were by some rare accident, as this of yours. But now of the cessation of that other part of intercourse, which might be by our sailing to other nations, I must yield you some other cause. For I cannot say, if I shall say truly, but our shipping, for number, strength, mariners, pilots, and all things that appertain to navigation, is as great as ever; and therefore why we should sit at home, I shall now give you an account by itself; and it will draw nearer, to give you satisfaction, to your principal question.

"There reigned in this island, about 1,900 years ago, a king, whose memory of all others we most adore; not superstitiously, but as a divine instrument, though a mortal man: his name was Salomona; and we esteem him as the lawgiver of our nation. This king had a large heart, inscrutable for good; and was wholly bent to make his kingdom and people happy. He therefore taking into consideration how sufficient and substantive this land was, to maintain itself without any aid at all of the foreigner; being 5,000 miles in circuit, and of rare fertility of soil, in the greatest part thereof; and finding also the shipping of this country might be plentifully set on work, both by fishing and by transportations from port to port, and likewise by sailing unto some small islands that are not far from us, and are under the crown and laws of this state; and recalling into his memory the happy and flourishing estate wherein this land then was, so as it might be a thousand ways altered to the worse, but scarce any one way to the better; though nothing wanted to his noble and heroical intentions, but only (as far as human foresight might reach) to give perpetuity to that which was in his time so happily established, therefore amongst his other fundamental laws of this kingdom he did ordain the interdicts and prohibitions which we have touching entrance of strangers; which at that time (though it was after the calamity of America) was frequent; doubting novelties and commixture of manners. It is true, the like law against the admission of strangers without license is an ancient law in the kingdom of China, and yet continued in use. But there it is a poor thing; and hath made them a curious, ignorant, fearful foolish nation. But our lawgiver made his law of another temper. For first, he hath preserved all points of humanity, in taking order and making provision for the relief of strangers distressed; whereof you have tasted." At which speech (as reason was) we all rose up, and bowed ourselves. He went on: "That king also still desiring to join humanity and policy together; and thinking it against humanity, to detain strangers here against their wills; and against policy, that they should return, and discover their knowledge of this estate, he took this course; he did ordain, that of the strangers that should be permitted to land, as many at all times might depart as many as would; but as many as would stay, should have very good conditions, and means to live from the state. Wherein he saw so far, that now in so many ages since the prohibition, we have memory not of one ship that ever returned, and but of thirteen persons only, at several times, that chose to return in our bottoms. What those few that returned may have reported abroad, I know not. But you must think, whatsoever they have said, could be taken where they came but for a dream. Now for our traveling from hence into parts abroad, our lawgiver thought fit altogether to restrain it. So is it not in China. For the Chinese sail where they will, or can; which showeth, that their law of keeping out strangers is a law of pusillanimity and fear. But this restraint of ours hath one only exception, which is admirable; preserving the good which cometh by communicating with strangers, and avoiding the hurt: and I will now open it to you. And here I shall seem a little to digress, but you will by-and-by find it pertinent. Ye shall understand, my dear friends, that amongst the excellent acts of that king, one above all hath the preeminence. It was the erection and institution of an order, or society, which we call Salomon's House; the noblest foundation, as we think, that ever was upon the earth, and the lantern of this kingdom. It is dedicated to the study of the works and creatures of God. Some think it beareth the founder's name a little corrupted, as if it should be Solomon's House. But the records write it as it is spoken. So as I take it to be denominate of the king of the Hebrews, which is famous with you, and no strangers to us; for we have some parts of his works which with you are lost; namely, that natural history which he wrote of all plants, from the cedar of Libanus to the moss that groweth out of the wall; and of all things that have life and motion. This maketh me think that our king finding himself to symbolize, in many things, with that king of the Hebrews, which lived many years before him, honored him with the title of this foundation. And I am the rather induced to be of this opinion, for that I find in ancient records, this order or society is sometimes called Solomon's House, and sometimes the College of the Six Days' Works; whereby I am satisfied that our excellent king had learned from the Hebrews that God had created the world, and all that therein is, within six days: and therefore he instituted that house, for the finding out of the true nature of all things, whereby God might have the more glory in the workmanship of them, and men the more fruit in their use of them, did give it also that second name. But now to come to our present purpose. When the king had forbidden to all his people navigation into any part that was not under his crown, he made nevertheless this ordinance; that every twelve years there should be set forth out of this kingdom, two ships, appointed to several voyages; that in either of these ships there should be a mission of three of the fellows or brethren of Salomon's House, whose errand was only to give us knowledge of the affairs and state of those countries to which they were designed; and especially of the sciences, arts, manufactures, and inventions of all the world; and withal to bring unto us books, instruments, and patterns in every kind: that the ships, after they had landed the brethren, should return; and that the brethren should stay abroad till the new mission, the ships are not otherwise fraught than with store of victuals, and good quantity of treasure to remain with the brethren, for the buying of such things, and rewarding of such persons, as they should think fit. Now for me to tell you how the vulgar sort of mariners are contained from being discovered at land, and how they that must be put on shore for any time, color themselves under the names of other nations, and to what places these voyages have been designed; and what places of rendezvous are appointed for the new missions, and the like circumstances of the practice, I may not do it, neither is it much to your desire. But thus you see we maintain a trade, not for gold, silver, or jewels, nor for silks, nor for spices, nor any other commodity of matter; but only for God's first creature, which was light;

to have light, I say, of the growth of all parts of the world."
And when he had said this, he was silent, and so were we
all; for indeed we were all astonished to hear so strange
things so probably told. And he perceiving that we were
willing to say somewhat, but had it not ready, in great
courtesy took us off, and descended to ask us questions of
our voyage and fortunes, and in the end concluded that we
might do well to think with ourselves, what time of stay we
would demand of the state, and bade us not to scant ourselves; for he would procure such time as we desired. Whereupon we all rose up and presented ourselves to kiss the
skirt of his tippet, but he would not suffer us, and so took
his leave. But when it came once amongst our people, that
the state used to offer conditions to strangers that would
stay, we had work enough to get any of our men to look to
our ship, and to keep them from going presently to the
governor, to crave conditions; but with much ado we re-
strained them, till we might agree what course to take.

Thomas Campanella

✖

THE CITY OF THE SUN

G. M. Tell me about their children.
Capt. When their women have brought forth children, they
suckle and rear them in temples set apart for all. They give
milk for two years or more as the physician orders. After
that time the weaned child is given into the charge of the
mistresses, if it is a female, and to the masters, if it is a
male. And then with other young children they are pleasantly
instructed in the alphabet, and in the knowledge of the
pictures, and in running, walking and wrestling; also in the

From *The City of the Sun*, by Thomas Campanella. First published in 1623.

historical drawings, and in languages; and they are adorned with a suitable garment of different colors. After their sixth year they are taught natural science, and then the mechanical sciences. The men who are weak in intellect are sent to farms, and when they have become more proficient some of them are received into the state. And those of the same age and born under the same constellation are especially like one another in strength and in appearance, and hence arises much lasting concord in the state, these men honoring one another with mutual love and help. Names are given to them by Metaphysicus, and that not by chance but designedly, and according to each one's peculiarity, as was the custom among the ancient Romans. Wherefore one is called Beautiful (*Pulcher*), another the Big-nosed (*Naso*), another the Fat-legged (*Cranipes*), another Crooked (*Torvus*), another Lean (*Macer*), and so on. But when they have become very skilled in their professions and done any great deed in war or in time of peace, a cognomen from art is given to them, such as Beautiful, the great painter (*Pulcher, Pictor Magnus*), the golden one (*Aureus*), the excellent one (*Excellens*), or the strong (*Strenuus*); or from their deeds, such as Naso the Brave (*Nason Fortis*), or the cunning, or the great, or very great conqueror; or from the enemy any one has overcome, Africanus, Asiaticus, Etruscus; or if any one has overcome Manfred or Tortelius, he is called Macer Manfred or Tortelius, and so on. All these cognomens are added by the higher magistrates, and very often with a crown suitable to the deed or art, and with the flourish of music. For gold and silver is reckoned of little value among them except as material for their vessels and ornaments, which are common to all.

G. M. Tell me, I pray you, is there no jealousy among them or disappointment to that one who has not been elected to a magistracy, or to any other dignity to which he aspires?

Capt. Certainly not. For no one wants either necessaries or luxuries. Moreover, the race is managed for the good of the commonwealth and not of private individuals, and the magistrates must be obeyed. They deny what we hold—viz., that it is natural to man to recognize his offspring and to educate them, and to use his wife and house and children as his own. For they say that children are bred for the preservation of the species and not for individual pleasure, as St. Thomas also asserts. Therefore the breeding of children has reference to the commonwealth and not to individuals, except in so far as they are constituents of the commonwealth. And since individuals for the most part bring forth children wrongly and educate them wrongly, they consider that they remove destruction from the state, and therefore, for this reason, with most sacred fear, they commit the education of the children, who as it were are the element of the republic, to the care of magistrates; for the safety of the community is not that of a few. And thus they distribute male and female breeders of the best natures according to philosophical rules. Plato thinks that this distribution ought to be made by lot, lest some men seeing that they are kept away from the beautiful women, should rise up with anger and hatred agianst the magistrates; and he thinks further that those who do not deserve cohabitation with the more beautiful women, should be deceived whilst the lots are being led out of the city by the magistrates, so that at all times the women who are suitable should fall to their lot, not those whom they desire. This shrewdness, however, is not necessary among the inhabitants of the City of the Sun. For with them deformity is unknown. When the women are exercised they get a clear complexion, and become strong of limb, tall and agile, and with them beauty consists in tallness and strength. Therefore, if any woman dyes her face, so that it may become beautiful, or uses high-heeled boots so that she may appear tall, or garments with trains to cover her wooden shoes, she is condemned to capital punishment. But if the women should even desire them, they have no facility for doing these things. For who indeed would give them this facility? Further, they assert that among us abuses of this kind arise from the leisure and sloth of women. By these means they lose their color and have pale complexions, and become feeble and small. For this reason they are without proper complexions, use high sandals, and become beautiful not from strength, but from slothful tenderness. And thus they ruin their own tempers and natures, and consequently those of their off-spring. Furthermore, if at any time a man is taken captive with ardent love for a certain woman, the two are allowed to converse and joke together, and to give one another garlands of flowers or leaves, and to make verses. But if the race is endangered, by no means is further union between them permitted. Moreover, the love born of eager desire is not known among them; only that born of friendship.

Domestic affairs and partnerships are of little account, because, excepting the sign of honor, each one receives what he is in need of. To the heroes and heroines of the republic, it is customary to give the pleasing gifts of honor, beautiful wreaths, sweet food or splendid clothes, while they are feasting. In the daytime all use white garments within the city, but at night or outside the city they use red garments either of wool or silk. They hate black as they do dung, and therefore they dislike the Japanese, who are fond of black. Pride they consider the most execrable vice, and one who acts proudly is chastised with the most ruthless correction. Wherefore no one thinks it lowering to wait at table or to work in the kitchen or fields. All work they call discipline, and thus they say that it is honorable to go on foot, to do any act of nature, to see with the eye, and to speak with the tongue; and when there is need, they distinguish philosophically between tears and spittle.

Every man who, when he is told off to work, does his duty, is considered very honorable. It is not the custom to keep slaves. For they are enough, and more than enough, for themselves. But with us, alas! it is not so. In Naples there exists seventy thousand souls, and out of these scarcely ten or fifteen thousand do any work, and they are always lean from overwork and are getting weaker every day. The rest become a prey to idleness, avarice, ill-health, lasciviousness, usury and other vices, and contaminate and corrupt very many families by holding them in servitude for their own use, by keeping them in poverty and slavishness, and by imparting to them their own vices. Therefore public slavery

ruins them; useful works, in the field, in military service and
in arts, except those which are debasing, are not cultivated,
the few who do practice them doing so with much aversion.
But in the City of the Sun, while duty and work is distributed among all, it only falls to each one to work for
about four hours every day. The remaining hours are spent
in learning joyously, in debating, in reading, in reciting, in
writing, in walking, in exercising the mind and body, and
with play. They allow no game which is played while sitting,
neither the single die nor dice, nor chess, nor others like
these. But they play with the ball, with the sack, with the
hoop, with wrestling, with hurling at the stake. They say,
moreover, that grinding poverty renders men worthless,
cunning, sulky, thievish, insidious, vagabonds, liars, false
witnesses, &c.; and that wealth makes them insolent, proud,
ignorant, traitors, assumers of what they know not, deceivers,
boasters, wanting in affection, slanderers, &c. But with them
all the rich and poor together make up the community. They
are rich because they want nothing, poor because they possess nothing; and consequently they are not slaves to circumstances, but circumstances serve them. And on this point
they strongly recommend the religion of the Christians, and
especially the life of the Apostles.

G. M. This seems excellent and sacred, but the community of women is a thing too difficult to attain. The holy
Roman Clement says that wives ought to be common in
accordance with the apostolic institution, and praises Plato
and Socrates, who thus teach, but the Glossary interprets
this community with regard to obedience. And Tertullian
agrees with the Glossary, that the first Christians had everything in common except wives.

Capt. These things I know little of. But this I saw among
the inhabitants of the City of the Sun that they did not
make this exception. And they defend themselves by the
opinion of Socrates, of Cato, of Plato, and of St. Clement,
but, as you say, they misunderstand the opinions of these
thinkers. And the inhabitants of the solar city ascribe this to
their want of education, since they are by no means learned
in philosophy. Nevertheless, they send abroad to discover

the customs of nations, and the best of these they always adopt. Practice makes the women suitable for war and other duties. Thus they agree with Plato, in whom I have read these same things. The reasoning of our Cajetan does not convince me, and least of all that of Aristotle. This thing, however, existing among them is excellent and worthy of imitation—viz., that no physical defect renders a man incapable of being serviceable except the decrepitude of old age, since even the deformed are useful for consultation. The lame serve as guards, watching with the eyes which they possess. The blind card wool with their hands, separating the down from the hairs, with which latter they stuff the couches and sofas; those who are without the use of eyes and hands give the use of their ears or their voice for the convenience of the state, and if one has only one sense, he uses it in the farms. And these cripples are well treated, and some become spies, telling the officers of the state what they have heard.

G. M. Tell me now, I pray you, of their military affairs. Then you may explain their arts, ways of life and sciences, and lastly their religion.

Capt. The triumvir, Power, has under him all the magistrates of arms, of artillery, of cavalry, of foot-soldiers, of architects, and of strategists, and the masters and many of the most excellent workmen obey the magistrates, the men of each are paying allegiance to their respective chiefs. Moreover, Power is at the head of all the professors of gymnastics, who teach military exercise, and who are prudent generals, advanced in age. By these the boys are trained after their twelfth year. Before this age, however, they have been accustomed to wrestling, running, throwing the weight and other minor exercises, under inferior masters. But at twelve they are taught how to strike at the enemy, at horses and elephants, to handle the spear, the sword, the arrow and the sling; to manage the horse; to advance and to retreat; to remain in order of battle; to help a comrade in arms; to anticipate the enemy by cunning; and to conquer.

The women also are taught these arts under their own magistrates and mistresses, so that they may be able if need be to render assistance to the males in battles near the city. They are taught to watch the fortifications lest at some time a hasty attack should suddenly be made. In this respect they praise the Spartans and Amazons. The women know well also how to let fly fiery balls, and how to make them from lead; how to throw stones from pinnacles and to go in the way of an attack. They are accustomed also to give up wine unmixed altogether, and that one is punished most severely who shows any fear.

The inhabitants of the City of the Sun do not fear death, because they all believe that the soul is immortal, and that when it has left the body it is associated with other spirits, wicked or good, according to the merits of this present life. Although they are partly followers of Bramah and Pythagoras, they do not believe in the transmigration of souls, except in some cases, by a distinct decree of God. They do not abstain from injuring an enemy of the republic and of religion, who is unworthy of pity. During the second month the army is reviewed, and every day there is practice of arms, either in the cavalry plain or within the walls. Nor are they ever without lectures on the science of war. They take care that the accounts of Moses, of Joshua, of David, of Judas Maccabeus, of Caesar, of Alexander, of Scipio, of Hannibal, and other great soldiers should be read. And then each one gives his own opinion as to whether these generals acted well or ill, usefully or honorably, and then the teacher answers and says who are right.

G. M. With whom do they wage war, and for what reasons, since they are so prosperous?

Capt. Wars might never occur, nevertheless they are exercised in military tactics and in hunting, lest perchance they should become effeminate and unprepared for any emergency. Besides there are four kingdoms in the island, which are very envious of their prosperity, for this reason that the people desire to live after the manner of the inhabitants of the City of the Sun, and to be under their rule rather than that of their own kings. Wherefore the state often makes war upon these because, being neighbors, they are usurpers and live impiously, since they have not an object of worship and do not observe the religion of other nations or of the Brahmins. And other nations of India, to which formerly they were subject, rise up as it were in rebellion, as also do the Taprobanese, whom they wanted to join them at first. The warriors of the City of the Sun, however, are always the victors. As soon as they suffered from insult or disgrace or plunder, or when their allies have been harassed, or a people have been oppressed by a tyrant of the state (for they are always the advocates of liberty), they go immediately to the council for deliberation. After they have knelt in the presence of God that He might inspire their consultation, they proceed to examine the merits of the business, and thus war is decided on. Immediately after a priest, whom they call Forensic, is sent away. He demands from the enemy the restitution of the plunder, asks that the allies should be freed from oppression, or that the tyrant should be deposed. If they deny these things war is declared by invoking the vengeance of God—the God of Sabboth—for destruction of those who maintain an unjust cause. But if the enemy refuse to reply, the priest gives him the space of one hour for his answer, if he is a king, but three if it is a republic, so that they cannot escape giving a response. And in this manner is war undertaken against the insolent enemies of natural rights and of religion. When war has been declared, the deputy of Power performs everything, but Power, like the Roman dictator, plans and wills everything, so that hurtful tardiness may be avoided. And when anything of great moment arises he consults Hoh and Wisdom and Love.

Before this, however, the occasion of war and the justice of making an expedition is declared by a herald in the great council. All from twenty years and upwards are admitted to this council, and thus the necessaries are agreed upon. All kinds of weapons stand in the armories, and these they use often in sham fights. The exterior walls of each ring are full of guns prepared by their labors, and they have other engines for hurling which are called cannons, and which they take into battle upon mules and asses and carriages. When they have arrived in an open plain they enclose in the middle the provisions, engines of war, chariots, ladders and machines and all fight courageously. Then each one returns to the standards, and the enemy thinking that they are giving and preparing to flee, are deceived and relax their order: then the warriors of the City of the Sun, wheeling into wings and columns on each side, regain their breath and strength, and ordering the artillery to discharge their bullets they resume the fight against a disorganized host. And they observe many ruses of this kind. They overcome all mortals with their stratagems and engines. Their camp is fortified after the manner of the Romans. They pitch their tents and fortify with wall and ditch with wonderful quickness. The masters of works, of engines and hurling machines, stand ready, and the soldiers understand the use of the spade and the axe.

Five, eight, or ten leaders learned in the order of battle and in strategy consult together concerning the business of war, and command their bands after consultation. It is their wont to take out with them a body of boys, armed and on horses, so that they may learn to fight, just as the whelps of lions and wolves are accustomed to blood. And these in time of danger betake themselves to a place of safety, along with many armed women. After the battle the women and boys soothe and relieve the pain of the warriors, and wait upon them and encourage them with embraces and pleasant words. How wonderful a help is this! For the soldiers, in order that they may acquit themselves as sturdy men in the eyes of their wives and offspring, endure hardships, and so love makes them conquerors. He who in the fight first scales the enemy's walls receives after the battle a crown of grass, as a token of honor, and at the presentation the women and boys applaud loudly; that one who affords aid to an ally gets a civic crown of oak-leaves; he who kills a tyrant dedicates his arms in the temple and receives from Hoh the cognomen of his deed, and other warriors obtain other kinds of crowns.

Andrew Marvell

✱

THE GARDEN

How vainly men themselves amaze
To win the Palm, the Oke, or Bayes;
And their uncessant Labours see
Crown'd from some single Herb or Tree.
Whose short and narrow verged Shade
Does prudently their Toyles upbraid;
While all Flow'rs and all Trees do close
To weave the Garlands of repose.

Fair quiet, have I found thee here,
And Innocence thy Sister dear!
Mistaken long, I sought you then
In busie Companies of Men.
Your sacred Plants, if here below,
Only among the Plants will grow.
Society is all but rude,
To this delicious Solitude.

No white nor red was ever seen
So am'rous as this lovely green.
Fond Lovers, cruel as their Flame,
Cut in these Trees their Mistress name.
Little, Alas, they know, or heed,
How far these Beauties Hers exceed!
Fair Trees! where s'eer your barkes I wound,
No Name shall but your own be found.

When we have run our Passions heat,
Love hither makes his best retreat.
The *Gods*, that mortal Beauty chase,
Still in a Tree did end their race.

First published in 1681.

Apollo hunted *Daphne* so,
Only that She might Laurel grow.
And *Pan* did after *Syrinx* speed,
Not as a Nymph, but for a Reed.

What wond'rous Life is this I lead!
Ripe Apples drop about my head;
The Lucious Clusters of the Vine
Upon my Mouth do crush their Wine;
The Nectaren, and curious Peach,
Into my hands themselves do reach;
Stumbling on Melons, as I pass,
Insnar'd with Flow'rs, I fall on Grass.

Mean while the Mind, from pleasure less,
Withdraws into its happiness:
The Mind, that Ocean where each kind
Does streight its own resemblance find;
Yet it creates, transcending these,
Far other Worlds, and other Seas;
Annihilating all that's made
To a green Thought in a green Shade.

Here at the Fountains sliding foot,
Or at some Fruit-trees mossy root,
Casting the Bodies Vest aside,
My Soul into the boughs does glide:
There like a Bird it sits, and sings,
Then whets, and combs its silver Wings;
And, till prepar'd for longer flight,
Waves in its Plumes the various Light.

Such was that happy Garden-state,
While Man there walk'd without a Mate:
After a Place so pure, and sweet,
What other Help could yet be meet!
But 'twas beyond a Mortal's share
To wander solitary there:
Two Paradises 'twere in one
To live in Paradise alone.

How well the skilful Gardner drew
Of flow'rs and herbes this Dial new;
Where from above the milder Sun
Does through a fragrant Zodiack run;
And, as it works, th'industrious Bee
Computes its time as well as we.
How could such sweet and wholsome Hours
Be reckon'd but with herbs and flow'rs!

John Milton

✠

ADAM IN EDEN

For Man to tell how human Life began
Is hard; for who himself beginning knew?
Desire with thee still longer to converse
Induc'd me. As new wak't from soundest sleep
Soft on the flow'ry herb I found me laid
In Balmy Sweat, which with his Beams the Sun
Soon dri'd, and on the reeking moisture fed.
Straight toward Heav'n my wond'ring Eyes I turn'd,
And gaz'd a while the ample Sky, till rais'd
By quick instinctive motion up I sprung,
As thitherward endeavoring, and upright
Stood on my feet; about me round I saw
Hill, Dale, and shady Woods, and sunny Plains,
And liquid Lapse of murmuring Streams; by these,
Creatures that liv'd, and mov'd, and walk'd, or flew,
Birds on the branches warbling; all things smil'd,
With fragrance and with joy my heart o'erflow'd.
Myself I then perus'd, and Limb by Limb
Survey'd, and sometimes went, and sometimes ran

From *Paradise Lost*, VIII. 250–523. First published in 1674.

With supple joints, as lively vigor led:
But who I was, or where, or from what cause,
Knew not; to speak I tri'd, and forthwith spake,
My tongue obey'd and readily could name
Whate'er I saw. Thou Sun, said I, fair Light,
And thou enlight'n'd Earth, so fresh and gay,
Ye Hills and Dales, ye Rivers, Woods, and Plains
And ye that live and move, fair Creatures, tell,
Tell, if ye saw, how came I thus, how here?
Not of myself; by some great Maker then,
In goodness and in power preëminent;
Tell me, how may I know him, how adore,
From whom I have that thus I move and live,
And feel that I am happier than I know.
While thus I call'd, and stray'd I knew not whither,
From where I first drew Air, and first beheld
This happy Light, when answer none return'd,
On a green shady Bank profuse of Flow'rs
Pensive I sat me down; there gentle sleep
First found me, and with soft oppression seiz'd
My drowsed sense, untroubl'd, though I thought
I then was passing to my former state
Insensible, and forthwith to dissolve:
When suddenly stood at my Head a dream,
Whose inward apparition gently mov'd
My fancy to believe I yet had being,
And liv'd: One came, methought, of shape Divine,
And said, thy Mansion wants thee, *Adam*, rise,
First Man, of Men innumerable ordain'd
First Father, call'd by thee I come thy Guide
To the Garden of bliss thy seat prepar'd.
So saying, by the hand he took me rais'd,
And over Fields and Waters, as in Air
Smooth sliding without step, last led me up
A woody Mountain; whose high top was plain,
A Circuit wide, enclos'd, with goodliest Trees
Planted, with Walks, and Bowers, that what I saw
Of Earth before scarce pleasant seem'd. Each Tree
Load'n with fairest Fruit, that hung to the Eye

Tempting, stirr'd in me sudden appetite
To pluck and eat; whereat I wak'd, and found
Before mine Eyes all real, as the dream
Had lively shadow'd: Here had new begun
My wand'ring, had not he who was my Guide
Up hither, from among the Trees appear'd,
Presence Divine. Rejoicing, but with awe,
In adoration at his feet I fell
Submiss: he rear'd me, and Whom thou sought'st I am,
Said mildly, Author of all this thou seest
Above, or round about thee or beneath.
This Paradise I give thee, count it thine
To Till and keep, and of the Fruit to eat:
Of every Tree that in the Garden grows
Eat freely with glad heart; fear here no dearth:
But of the Tree whose operation brings
Knowledge of good and ill, which I have set
The Pledge of thy Obedience and thy Faith,
Amid the Garden by the Tree of Life,
Remember what I warn thee, shun to taste,
And shun the bitter consequence: for know,
The day thou eat'st thereof, my sole command
Transgrest, inevitably thou shalt die;
From that day mortal, and this happy State
Shalt lose, expell'd from hence into a World
Of woe and sorrow. Sternly he pronounc'd
The rigid interdiction, which resounds
Yet dreadful in mine ear, though in my choice
Not to incur; but soon his clear aspect
Return'd and gracious purpose thus renew'd.
Not only these fair bounds, but all the Earth
To thee and to thy Race I give; as Lords
Possess it, and all things that therein live,
Or live in Sea, or Air, Beast, Fish, and Fowl.
In sign whereof each Bird and Beast behold
After thir kinds; I bring them to receive
From thee thir Names, and pay thee fealty
With low subjection; understand the same
Of Fish within thir wat'ry residence,

Not hither summon'd, since they cannot change
Thir Element to draw the thinner Air.
As thus he spake, each Bird and Beast behold
Approaching two and two, These cow'ring low
With blandishment, each Bird stoop'd on his wing.
I nam'd them, as they pass'd, and understood
Thir Nature, with such knowledge God endu'd
My sudden apprehension: but in these
I found not what methought I wanted still;
And to the Heav'nly vision thus presum'd.

  O by what Name, for thou above all these,
Above mankind, or aught than mankind higher,
Surpassest far my naming, how may I
Adore thee, Author of this Universe,
And all this good to man, for whose well being
So amply, and with hands so liberal
Thou hast provided all things: but with mee
I see not who partakes. In solitude
What happiness, who can enjoy alone,
Or all enjoying, what contentment find?
Thus I presumptuous; and the vision bright,
As with a smile more bright'n'd, thus repli'd.

  What call'st thou solitude? is not the Earth
With various living creatures, and the Air
Replenisht, and all these at thy command
To come and play before thee; know'st thou not
Thir language and thir ways? They also know,
And reason not contemptibly; with these
Find pastime, and bear rule; thy Realm is large.
So spake the Universal Lord, and seem'd
So ordering. I with leave of speech implor'd,
And humble deprecation thus repli'd.

  Let not my words offend thee, Heav'nly Power,
My Maker, be propitious while I speak.
Hast thou not made me here thy substitute,
And these inferior far beneath me set?
Among unequals what society
Can sort, what harmony or true delight?
Which must be mutual, in proportion due

Giv'n and receiv'd; but in disparity
The one intense, the other still remiss
Cannot well suit with either, but soon prove
Tedious alike: Of fellowship I speak
Such as I seek, fit to participate
All rational delight, wherein the brute
Cannot be human consort; they rejoice
Each with thir kind, Lion with Lioness;
So fitly them in pairs thou hast combin'd;
Much less can Bird with Beast, or Fish with Fowl
So well converse, nor with the Ox the Ape;
Worse then can Man With Beast, and least of all.
    Whereto th' Almighty answer'd, not displeas'd.
A nice and subtle happiness I see
Thou to thyself proposest, in the choice
Of thy Associates, *Adam*, and wilt taste
No pleasure, though in pleasure, solitary.
What think'st thou then of mee, and this my State,
Seem I to thee sufficiently possest
Of happiness, or not? who am alone
From all Eternity, for none I know
Second to mee or like, equal much less.
How have I then with whom to hold converse
Save with the Creatures which I made, and those
To me inferior, infinite descents
Beneath what other Creatures are to thee?
    He ceas'd, I lowly answer'd. To attain
The highth and depth of thy Eternal ways
All human thoughts come short, Supreme of things;
Thou in thyself are perfet, and in thee
Is no deficience found; not so is Man,
But in degree, the cause of his desire
By conversation with his like to help,
Or solace his defects. No need that thou
Shouldst propagate, already infinite;
And through all numbers absolute, though One;
But Man by number is to manifest
His single imperfection, and beget
Like of his like, his Image multipli'd,

In unity defective, which requires
Collateral love, and dearest amity.
Thou in thy secrecy although alone,
Best with thyself accompanied, seek'st not
Social communication, yet so pleas'd,
Canst raise thy Creature to what highth thou wilt
Of Union or Communion, deifi'd;
I by conversing cannot these erect
From prone, nor in thir ways complacence find.
Thus I embold'n'd spake, and freedom us'd
Permissive, and acceptance found, which gain'd
This answer from the gracious voice Divine.

   Thus far to try thee, *Adam*, I was pleas'd,
And find thee knowing not of Beasts alone,
Which thou hast rightly nam'd, but of thyself,
Expressing well the spirit within thee free,
My Image, not imparted to the Brute,
Whose fellowship therefore unmeet for thee
Good reason was thou freely shouldst dislike,
And be so minded still; I, ere thou spak'st,
Knew it not good for Man to be alone,
And no such company as then thou saw'st
Intended thee, for trial only brought,
To see how thou couldst judge of fit and meet:
What next I bring shall please thee, be assur'd,
Thy likeness, thy fit help, thy other self,
Thy wish, exactly to thy heart's desire.

   Hee ended, or I heard no more, for now
My earthly by his Heav'nly overpower'd,
Which it had long stood under, strain'd to the highth
In that celestial Colloquy sublime,
As with an object that excels the sense,
Dazzl'd and spent, sunk down, and sought repair
Of sleep, which instantly fell on me, call'd
By Nature as in aid, and clos'd mine eyes.
Mine eyes he clos'd, but op'n left the Cell
Of Fancy my internal sight, by which
Abstract as in a trance methought I saw,
Though sleeping where I lay, and saw the shape

Still glorious before whom awake I stood;
Who stooping op'n'd my left side, and took
From thence a Rib, with cordial spirits warm,
And Life-blood streaming fresh; wide was the wound,
But suddenly with flesh fill'd up and heal'd:
The Rib he form'd and fashion'd with his hands;
Under his forming hands a Creature grew,
Manlike, but different sex, so lovely fair,
That what seem'd fair in all the World, seem'd now
Mean, or in her summ'd up, in her contain'd
And in her looks, which from that time infus'd
Sweetness into my heart, unfelt before,
And into all things from her Air inspir'd
The spirit of love and amorous delight.
She disappear'd, and left me dark, I wak'd
To find her, or for ever to deplore
Her loss, and other pleasures all abjure:
When out of hope, behold her, not far off,
Such as I saw her in my dream, adorn'd
With what all Earth or Heaven could bestow
To make her amiable: On she came,
Led by her Heav'nly Maker, though unseen,
And guided by his voice, nor uninform'd
Of nuptial Sanctity and marriage Rites:
Grace was in all her steps, Heav'n in her Eye,
In every gesture dignity and love.
I overjoy'd could not forbear aloud.
    This turn hath made amends; thou hast fulfill'd
Thy words, Creator bounteous and benign,
Giver of all things fair, but fairest this
Of all thy gifts, nor enviest. I now see
Bone of my Bone, Flesh of my Flesh, my Self
Before me; Woman is her Name, of Man
Extracted; for this cause he shall forgo
Father and Mother, and to his Wife adhere;
And they shall be one Flesh, one Heart, one Soul.
    She heard me thus, and though divinely brought,
Yet Innocence and Virgin Modesty,
Her virtue and the conscience of her worth,

That would be woo'd, and not unsought be won,
Not obvious, not obtrusive, but retir'd,
The more desirable, or to say all,
Nature herself, though pure of sinful thought,
Wrought in her so, that seeing me, she turn'd;
I follow'd her, she what was Honor knew,
And with obsequious Majesty approv'd
My pleaded reason. To the Nuptial Bow'r
I led her blushing like the Morn: all Heav'n,
And happy Constellations on that hour
Shed thir selectest influence; the Earth
Gave sign of gratulation, and each Hill;
Joyous the Birds; fresh Gales and gentle Airs
Whisper'd it to the Woods, and from thir wings
Flung Rose, flung Odors from the spicy Shrub,
Disporting, till the amorous Bird of Night
Sung Spousal, and bid haste the Ev'ning Star
On his Hill top, to light the bridal Lamp.
Thus I have told thee all my State, and brought
My Story to the sum of earthly bliss
Which I enjoy.

Suggested Additional Readings

John Donne, *The Ecstasy*
Harrington, *Oceana*
Rabelais, *Gargantua* and *Pantagruel*
Shakespeare, *The Tempest*
Sidney, *Arcadia*
Spenser, *The Faerie Queene*, I, II

Questions for Research and Discussion

1. Why does Montaigne title his essay, "Of Cannibals"?
Trace the appearance of cannibals in the utopian selections
in previous chapters. How do you explain the connection
between utopian literature and the interest in cannibalism?

2. How accurate a picture of the Brazilian natives does Montaigne have? What were the sources of his information? Is he tied closely to these sources?

3. Discuss Montaigne's use of classical and medieval lore concerning utopia. Does he accept it uncritically or not? Does he modify it in any important way?

4. To what extent does More's *Utopia* seem to depend on Plato's *Republic*? What are the obvious similarities? Differences? What do the differences indicate about the classical and Renaissance ideals of perfection?

5. What is More's fundamental attitude toward human nature? Is it like or unlike Montaigne's? Is it appropriate to the Humanistic philosophy or not?

6. More is one of the first utopian writers to treat in any detail a program of cultural activity for the Utopians' leisure time. How do you account for the previous lack of interest in this subject and for More's concern with it?

7. In what ways does Bacon's *New Atlantis* depend on Plato? Is Bacon's idea of political utopia significantly different from More's?

8. To which of the ancient utopian writers does Campanella seem most indebted? Explain. Read the remaining portions of *The City of the Sun* and discuss its debt to medieval symbolists (like Dante) and to the new travel books of Campanella's own time.

9. Compare Marvell's treatment of life in the garden paradise with that in Genesis (p. 5–8 above) and Milton's *Paradise Lost*.

10. Many readers find Milton's picture of life in Eden unappealing. What is your response to the Miltonic conception of perfection and happiness? How do you explain this reaction? Do you prefer Plato's Republic to Milton's Eden?

11. In what ways do More and Milton reflect a different attitude toward work and leisure time from that of Herodotus, Plato, Plutarch, and other ancient authors? Are they more or less like twentieth-century thinkers in their attitude?

12. Are Milton's Adam and Eve, as beings in a state of Grace and perfection, understandable or sympathetic characters? Explain. Are they substantially different from the Utopians? The El Doradans?

13. During the Renaissance, the ancient notion that kings rule by God's favor (that is, Divine Right) was under attack. Is this political issue reflected in any of the utopian selections here?

14. Would you say that the examples of Renaissance utopias given here tend to romanticize the pastoral life or not? Can this fact be accounted for by the discovery of primitive peoples in the new world? By the move to urban centers by more and more people? By disgust with commercialism and urbanization? By deep-seated Christian beliefs? By admiration for ancient literature? Or something else?

15. Research one of these topics for written or oral presentation:
    a. The Noble Savage in Shakespeare's Dramas
    b. Montaigne's Primitivism
    c. God in the Renaissance Utopia
    d. The Island as Utopian Symbol
    e. Puritanism and the New Jerusalem
    f. Milton's Utopianism in His Education Tracts
    g. Utopianism and Reform (Social, Religious, or Political) in the Renaissance
    h. Spenser and Utopian Morality
    i. Sidney's *Arcadia* and Spenser's *Faerie Queene*
    j. The *Arcadia* and Greek Myths
    k. Spenser and Dante (or Milton)
    l. Utopia and Time in the Renaissance
    m. The Legend of El Dorado

VII

The
Eighteenth Century

Introduction

Although there were exceptions, in general the Humanist writers of the Renaissance era were optimistic in their conception of human nature. They emphasized man's potential for achievement, for intellectual and emotional fulfillment; and most of the utopian literature of the time postulated this fulfillment as attending social, political, and economic improvements. The Humanists—Bacon, More, Milton—thought that by examining human experience and identifying its faults, better systems might be conceived by which the human lot could be improved. Utopia was both "no place" and "good place" (from the Greek, *ou* and *eu*); increasingly, the Humanists came to emphasize the desirability of systems and institutions as the means of establishing utopia in the here and now.

As intellectual successors to Humanism, the Neo-Classicists ("new" classicists) of the eighteenth century were generally disillusioned with human nature; in fact, most of the writers of the Neo-Classical movement, in France as well as in England, were skeptical or even cynical about the race of men. Such sixteenth- and seventeenth-century phenomena as the Reformation and Counter-Reformation, the nationalistic wars of France and Sweden, the vicious commercial rivalries, and the bloody Cromwell era in England convinced the later writers that all schemes for perfecting a basically depraved human race were visionary and hopeless. The Neo-Classicists stressed institutions as the way to curb the madness, foolishness, and selfishness of mankind; instead of hoping for perfection, they settled for workable improvements.

Though many Neo-Classicists repudiated Thomas Hobbes' *Leviathan*, they often shared its assumption that human life is nasty, brutish, and short. This being the case, a strong tide of anti-utopian thought is to be found in eighteenth-century writing. Jonathan Swift's great satire, *Gulliver's Travels*, is a striking example of such thought. Swift certainly wished to reform his readers, but it is doubtful that he truly expected to do much more than reprimand them. *Gulliver's Travels* shows the optimistically ignorant Gulliver visiting several "foreign" countries (often islands), which are sometimes disguises for England and France. In Lilliput, he sees a tiny race that is handsome to behold and that lives according to many Platonic precepts. There is a three-class society; the laws reflect *The Republic*; but the tiny people nonetheless miss having a utopia because of their pettiness, jealousy, envy, and cruelty. Their tiny size symbolizes the smallness of the human spirit. In Brobdingnag, Gulliver encounters a tribe of giants, ruled by a wise, compassionate Philosopher-King. But the giants are gross physically; their bodies, being mortal and animal, prevent their happiness. As his climactic adventure, Gulliver goes to a pastoral land very like the Sparta of Plutarch. Here there are two groups: the Houyhnhnms (horses whose wants are few and who rule by horse-sense) and Yahoos (vile creatures that are caricatures of people). Swift follows Plato by dividing human nature into the Mind and Body, or Reason and Passion, symbolized by Houyhnhnms and Yahoos. Houyhnhnmland is utopia but it is unattainable since men cannot suppress their passions as the horses do. Gulliver is cast out at last, much as Adam and Eve were driven out of Eden.

Bernard Mandeville, a witty cynic, also espoused the view that human nature was too depraved to permit a moral utopia; but he argued by the use of an animal allegory (like Swift's Houyhnhnm fable) that human vice could be the foundation for a collective, material good. "Private vices are public benefits" was the theme of his *The Fable of the Bees*, which used Plato's favorites to insist that economic prosperity can be purchased only by encouraging such personal faults as vanity, pride, greed, and so forth. To substitute moral perfection for material fulfillment, argued Mandeville, was unrealistic; as for utopia, who wanted it if it meant changing human nature? This view was also to be found in Alexander Pope's *Epistles*, James Boswell's *The Life of Samuel Johnson*, and Oliver Goldsmith's *Asem, An Eastern Tale*.

Rasselas, Prince of Abyssinia, by Samuel Johnson, was a Neo-Classical example of anti-utopian thought that drew directly from many longstanding utopian legends. Abyssinia was, of course, Ethiopia. Johnson equipped it with a "Happy Valley," much like Eden in its pastoral and physical qualities. And he showed that the perfect state of human happiness is a delusion and a snare. Rasselas, the prince, travels through the world searching for the life of happiness and finally concludes that human existence is everywhere a state in which much is to be endured and little is to be enjoyed. Voltaire's *Candide*, published in the same month as *Rasselas*, similarly shows a foolishly optimistic youth searching for perfect happiness. Candide even gets to the utopian land of El Dorado, where the inhabitants indeed are completely wealthy, virtuous, and happy. But Candide is miserable because he is vain, selfish, and competitive—the things the El Doradans are not—and he leaves the utopia rather than become different. You can't change human nature, say Voltaire and Johnson alike, and that means that utopia can never exist.

Finally, Edward Gibbon's *History of the Decline and Fall of the Roman Empire* needs to be mentioned as a peculiar

variety of Neo-Classical anti-utopian thought. Gibbon's
History was the culmination of the enduring legend of Rome
as a working utopia that was so popular during the Renaissance. Gibbon found much in Rome to admire; but like the
other Neo-Classicists, he stressed the necessity for strong institutions as checks to human frailties, both individual and
collective. Gibbon saw Rome as a pattern of all human cultures: doomed from the start, no matter how glorious they
became, because they were composed of men. To Gibbon,
Rome was as close to utopia as men had ever come, but it
was far from perfect and it inevitably collapsed.

Though the eighteenth-century emphasis on the imperfection of individual man and the authority of institutions
came under attack in the following century, the Neo-Classical literature of the utopian tradition left an important
bequest. In hearkening back to the classical emphasis on
reason (*nous*) as the way to truth, in stressing the necessity
of founding plans for improvement in human nature as it
is, and in making workability (or functionalism) the criterion
for truth, the Neo-Classicists prepared the way for the social
and scientific modifications of utopian thought that pervaded
nineteenth-century literature.

Jonathan Swift

✠

THE LILLIPUTIANS

OF THE INHABITANTS OF LILLIPUT

Although I intend to leave the Description of this Empire
to a particular Treatise, yet in the mean time I am content
to gratify the curious Reader with some general Ideas. As
the common Size of the Natives is somewhat under six

From *Gulliver's Travels*, I, by Jonathan Swift. First published in
1726.

Inches, so there is an exact Proportion in all other Animals, as well as Plants and Trees: For Instance, the tallest Horses and Oxen are between four and five Inches in Height, the Sheep an Inch and a half, more or less; their Geese about the Bigness of a Sparrow; and so the several Gradations downwards, till you come to the smallest, which, to my Sight, were almost invisible; but Nature hath adapted the Eyes of the *Lilliputians* to all Objects proper for their View: They see with great Exactness, but at no great Distance. And to show the Sharpness of their Sight towards Objects that are near, I have been much pleased with observing a Cook pulling a Lark, which was not so large as a common Fly; and a young Girl threading an invisible Needle with invisible Silk. Their tallest Trees are about seven Foot high; I mean some of those in the great Royal Park, the Tops whereof I could but just reach with my Fist clinched. The other Vegetables are in the same Proportion: But this I leave to the Reader's Imagination.

THEIR LEARNING, LAWS, AND CUSTOMS

I shall say but little at present of their Learning, which for many Ages hath flourished in all its Branches among them: But their Manner of Writing is very peculiar; being neither from the Left to the Right, like the *Europeans*; nor from the Right to the Left, like the *Arabians*; nor from up to down, like the *Chinese*; nor from down to up, like the *Cascagians*; but aslant from one Corner of the Paper to the other, like Ladies in *England*.

They bury their Dead with their Heads directly downwards; because they hold an Opinion, that in eleven Thousand Moons they are all to rise again; in which Period, the Earth (which they conceive to be flat) will turn upside down, and by this Means they shall, at their Resurrection, be found ready standing on their Feet. The Learned among them confess the Absurdity of this Doctrine; but the Practice still continues, in Compliance to the Vulgar.

There are some Laws and Customs in this Empire very peculiar; and if they were not so directly contrary to those of my own dear Country, I should be tempted to say a little in their Justification. It is only to be wished, that they were as well executed. The first I shall mention, relateth to Informers. All Crimes against the State, are punished here with the utmost Severity; but if the Person accused make his Innocence plainly to appear upon his Tryal, the Accuser is immediately put to an ignominious Death; and out of his Goods or Lands, the innocent Person is quadruply recompensed for the Loss of his Time, for the Danger he underwent, for the Hardship of his Imprisonment, and for all the Charges he hath been at in making his Defense. Or, if that Fund be deficient, it is largely supplyed by the Crown. The Emperor doth also confer on him some publick Mark of his Favor; and Proclamation is made of his Innocence through the whole City.

They look upon Fraud as a greater Crime than Theft, and therefore seldom fail to punish it with Death: For they allege, that Care and Vigilance, with a very common Understanding, may preserve a Man's Goods from Thieves; but Honesty hath no Fence against superior Cunning: And since it is necessary that there should be a perpetual Intercourse of buying and selling, and dealing upon Credit; where Fraud is permitted or connived at, or hath no Law to punish it, the honest Dealer is always undone, and the Knave gets the Advantage. I remember when I was once interceeding with the King for a Criminal who had wronged his Master of a great Sum of Money, which he had received by Order, and ran away with; and happening to tell his Majesty, by way of Extenuation, that it was only a Breach of Trust; the Emperor thought it monstrous in me to offer, as a Defense, the greatest Aggravation of the Crime: And truly, I had little to say in Return, farther than the common Answer, that different Nations had different Customs; for, I confess, I was heartily ashamed.

Although we usually call Reward and Punishment, the two Hinges upon which all Government turns; yet I could never observe this Maxim to be put in Practice by any Nation, except that of *Lilliput*. Whoever can there bring sufficient Proof that he hath strictly observed the Laws of his

Country for Seventy-three Moons, hath a Claim to certain Privileges, according to his Quality and Condition of Life, with a proportionable Sum of Money out of a Fund appropriated for that Use: He likewise acquires the Title of *Snilpall*, or *Legal*, which is added to his Name, but doth not descend to his Posterity. And these People thought it a prodigious Defect of Policy among us, when I told them that our Laws were enforced only by Penalties, without any Mention of Reward. It is upon this account that the Image of Justice, in their Courts of Judicature, is formed with six Eyes, two before, as many behind, and on each Side one, to signify Circumspection; with a Bag of Gold open in her right Hand, and a Sword sheathed in her left, to shew she is more disposed to reward than to punish.

In chusing Persons for all Employments, they have more Regard to good Morals than to great Abilities: For, since Government is necessary to Mankind, they believe that the common Size of human Understandings, is fitted to some Station or other; and that Providence never intended to make the Management of publick Affairs a Mystery, to be comprehended only by a few Persons of sublime Genius, of which there seldom are three born in an Age: But, they suppose Truth, Justice, Temperance, and the like, to be in every Man's Power; the Practice of which Virtues, assisted by Experience and a good Intention, would qualify any Man for the Service of his Country, except where a Course of Study is required. But they thought the Want of Moral Virtues was so far from being supplied by superior Endowments of the Mind, that Employments could never be put into such dangerous Hands as those of Persons so qualified; and at least, that the Mistakes committed by Ignorance in a virtuous Disposition, would never be of such fatal Consequence to the Publick Weal, as the Practices of a Man, whose Inclinations led him to be corrupt, and had great Abilities to manage, to multiply, and defend his Corruptions.

In like Manner, the Disbelief of a Divine Providence renders a Man uncapable of holding any publick Station: For, since Kings avow themselves to be the Deputies of

Providence, the *Lilliputians* think nothing can be more absurd than for a Prince to employ such Men as disown the Authority under which he acteth.

In relating these and the following Laws, I would only be understood to mean the original Institutions, and not the most scandalous Corruptions into which these People are fallen by the degenerate Nature of Man. For as to that infamous Practice of acquiring great Employment by dancing on the Ropes, or Badges of Favor and Distinction by leaping over Sticks, and creeping under them; the Reader is to observe, that they were first introduced by the Grandfather of the Emperor now reigning; and grew to the present Height, by the gradual Increase of Party and Faction.

Ingratitude is among them a capital Crime, as we read it to have been in some other Countries: For they reason thus; that whoever makes ill Returns to his Benefactor, must needs be a common Enemy to the rest of Mankind, from whom he hath received no Obligation; and therefore such a Man is not fit to live.

THE MANNER OF EDUCATING THEIR CHILDREN

Their Notions relating to the Duties of Parents and Children differ extremely from ours. For, since the Conjunction of Male and Female is founded upon the great Law of Nature, in order to propagate and continue the Species; the *Lilliputians* will needs have it, that Men and Women are joined together like other Animals, by the Motives of Concupiscence; and that their Tenderness towards their Young, proceedeth from the like natural Principle: For which Reason they will never allow, that a Child is under any Obligation to his Father for begetting him, or to his Mother for bringing him into the World; which, considering the Miseries of human Life, was neither a Benefit in itself, nor intended so by his Parents, whose Thoughts in their Love-encounters were otherwise employed. Upon these, and the like Reasonings, their Opinion is, that Parents are the last of all others to be trusted with the Education of their own Children: And therefore they have in every Town publick

Nurseries, where all Parents, except Cottagers and Laborers, are obliged to send their Infants of both Sexes to be reared and educated when they come to the Age of twenty Moons; at which Time they are supposed to have some Rudiments of Docility. These Schools are of several Kinds, suited to different Qualities, and to both Sexes. They have certain Professors well skilled in preparing Children for such a Condition of Life as befits the Rank of their Parents, and their own Capacities as well as Inclinations. I shall first say something of the Male Nurseries, and then of the Female.

The Nurseries for Males of Noble or Eminent Birth, are provided with grave and learned Professors, and their several Deputies. The Clothes and Food of the Children are plain and simple. They are bred up in the Principles of Honor, Justice, Courage, Modesty, Clemency, Religion, and Love of their Country: They are always employed in some Business, except in the Times of eating and sleeping, which are very short, and two Hours for Diversions, consisting of bodily Exercises. They are dressed by Men until four Years of Age, and then are obliged to dress themselves, although their Quality be ever so great; and the Women Attendants, who are aged proportionably to ours at fifty, perform only the most menial Offices. They are never suffered to converse with Servants, but go together in small or greater Numbers to take their Diversions, and always in the Presence of a Professor, or one of his Deputies; whereby they avoid those early bad Impressions of Folly and Vice to which our Children are subject. Their Parents are suffered to see them only twice a Year; the Visit is not to last above an Hour; they are allowed to kiss the Child at Meeting and Parting; but a Professor, who always standeth by on those Occasions, will not suffer them to whisper, or use any fondling Expressions, or bring any Presents of Toys, Sweet-meats, and the like.

The Pension from each Family for the Education and Entertainment of a Child, upon Failure of due Payment, is levied by the Emperor's Officers.

The Nurseries for Children of ordinary Gentlemen, Merchants, Traders, and Handicrafts, are managed proportionably after the same Manner; only those designed for Trades, are put out Apprentices at seven Years old; whereas those of Persons of Quality continue in their Exercises until Fifteen, which answers to One and Twenty with us: But the Confinement is gradually lessened for the last three Years.

In the Female Nurseries, the young Girls of Quality are educated much like the Males, only they are dressed by orderly Servants of their own Sex, but always in the Presence of a Professor or Deputy, until they come to dress themselves, which is at five Years old. And if it be found that these Nurses ever presume to entertain the Girls with frightful or foolish Stories, or the common Follies practiced by Chamber-Maids among us; they are publickly whipped thrice about the City, imprisoned for a Year, and banished for Life to the most desolate Parts of the Country. Thus the young Ladies there are as much ashamed of being Cowards and Fools, as the Men; and despise all personal Ornaments beyond Decency and Cleanliness; neither did I perceive any Difference in their Education, made by their Difference of Sex, only that the Exercises of the Females were not altogether so robust; and that some Rules were given them relating to domestick Life, and a smaller Compass of Learning was enjoyned them: For, their Maxim is, that among People of Quality, a Wife should be always a reasonable and agreeable Companion, because she cannot always be young. When the Girls are twelve Years old, which among them is the marriageable Age, their Parents or Guardians take them home, with great Expressions of Gratitude to the Professors, and seldom without Tears of the young Lady and her Companions.

In the Nurseries of Females of the meaner Sort, the Children are instructed in all Kinds of Works proper for their Sex, and their several Degrees: Those intended for Apprentices are dismissed at seven Years old, the rest are kept to eleven.

The meaner Families who have Children at these Nurseries, are obliged, besides their annual Pension, which is as low as possible, to return to the Steward of the Nursery a small Monthly Share of their Gettings, to be a Portion for the Child; and therefore all Parents are limited in their Expenses by the Law. For the *Lilliputians* think nothing can be more unjust, than that People, in Subservience to their own Appetites, should bring Children into the World, and leave the Burthen of supporting them on the Publick. As to Persons of Quality, they give Security to appropriate a certain Sum for each Child, suitable to their Condition; and these Funds are always managed with good Husbandry, and the most exact Justice.

The Cottagers and Laborers keep their Children at home, their Business being only to till and cultivate the Earth; and therefore their Education is of little Consequence to the Publick; but the Old and Diseased among them are supported by Hospitals: For begging is a Trade unknown in this Empire.

Samuel Johnson

THE HAPPY VALLEY

Ye who listen with credulity to the whispers of fancy, and pursue with eagerness the phantoms of hope; who expect that age will perform the promises of youth, and that the deficiencies of the present day will be supplied by the morrow; attend to the history of Rasselas, prince of Abyssinia.

Rasselas was the fourth son of the mighty emperor, in whose dominions the Father of waters begins his course; whose bounty pours down the streams of plenty, and scatters over half the world the harvests of Egypt.

According to the custom which has descended from age to age among the monarchs of the torrid zone, he was confined in a private palace, with the other sons and daughters of Abyssinian royalty, till the order of succession should call him to the throne.

From *Rasselas, Prince of Abyssinia,* Chapters 1–4, by Samuel Johnson. First published in 1759.

The place, which the wisdom or policy of antiquity had destined for the residence of the Abyssinian princes, was a spacious valley in the kingdom of Amhara, surrounded on every side by mountains, of which the summits overhang the middle part. The only passage, by which it could be entered, was a cavern that passed under a rock, of which it has long been disputed whether it was the work of nature or of human industry. The outlet of the cavern was concealed by a thick wood, and the mouth which opened into the valley was closed with gates of iron, forged by the artificers of ancient days, so massy that no man could, without the help of engines, open or shut them.

From the mountains on every side, rivulets descended that filled all the valley with verdure and fertility, and formed a lake in the middle inhabited by fish of every species, and frequented by every fowl whom nature has taught to dip the wing in water. This lake discharged its superfluities by a stream which entered a dark cleft of the mountain on the northern side, and fell with dreadful noise from precipice to precipice till it was heard no more.

The sides of the mountains were covered with trees; the banks of the brooks were diversified with flowers; every blast shook spices from the rocks, and every month dropped fruits upon the ground. All animals that bite the grass, or browse the shrub, whether wild or tame, wandered in this extensive circuit, secured from beasts of prey by the mountains which confined them. On one part were flocks and herds feeding in the pastures, on another all the beasts of chase frisking in the lawns; the spritely kid was bounding on the rocks, the subtle monkey frolicking in the trees, and the solemn elephant reposing in the shade. All the diversities of the world were brought together, the blessings of nature were collected, and its evils extracted and excluded.

The valley, wide and fruitful, supplied its inhabitants with the necessaries of life, and all delights and superfluities were added at the annual visit which the emperor paid his children, when the iron gate was opened to the sound of musick; and during eight days every one that resided in the valley was required to propose whatever might contribute to make seclusion pleasant, to fill up the vacancies of attention, and lessen the tediousness of time. Every desire was immediately granted. All the artificers of pleasure were called to gladden the festivity; the musicians exerted the power of harmony, and the dancers shewed their activity before the princes, in hope that they should pass their lives in this blissful captivity, to which these only were admitted whose performance was thought able to add novelty to luxury. Such was the appearance of security and delight which this retirement afforded, that they to whom it was new always desired that it might be perpetual; and as those, on whom the iron gate had once closed, were never suffered to return, the effect of longer experience could not be known. Thus every year produced new schemes of delight, and new competitors for imprisonment.

The palace stood on an eminence raised about thirty paces above the surface of the lake. It was divided into many squares or courts, built with greater or less magnificence according to the rank of those for whom they were designed. The roofs were turned into arches of massy stone joined with a cement that grew harder by time, and the building stood from century to century, deriding the solstitial rains and equinoctial hurricanes, without need of reparation.

This house, which was so large as to be fully known to none but some ancient officers who successively inherited the secrets of the place, was built as if suspicion herself had dictated the plan. To every room there was an open and secret passage, every square had a communication with the rest, either from the upper stories by private galleries, or by subterranean passages from the lower apartments. Many of the columns had unsuspected cavities, in which successive monarchs reposited their treasures. They then closed up the opening with marble, which was never to be removed but in the utmost exigencies of the kingdom; and recorded their accumulations in a book which was itself concealed in a tower not entered but by the emperor, attended by the prince who stood next in succession.

THE DISCONTENT OF RASSELAS
IN THE HAPPY VALLEY

Here the sons and daughters of Abyssinia lived only to know the soft vicissitudes of pleasure and repose, attended by all that were skillful to delight, and gratified with whatever the senses can enjoy. They wandered in gardens of fragrance, and slept in the fortresses of security. Every art was practiced to make them pleased with their own condition. The sages who instructed them, told them of nothing but the miseries of publick life, and described all beyond the mountains as regions of calamity, where discord was always raging, and where man preyed upon man.

To heighten their opinion of their own felicity, they were daily entertained with songs, the subject of which was the *happy valley*. Their appetites were excited by frequent enumerations of different enjoyments, and revelry and merriment was the business of every hour from the dawn of morning to the close of even.

These methods were generally successful; few of the princes had ever wished to enlarge their bounds, but passed their lives in full conviction that they had all within their reach that art or nature could bestow, and pitied those whom fate had excluded from this seat of tranquility, as the sport of chance, and the slaves of misery.

Thus they rose in the morning, and lay down at night, pleased with each other and with themselves, all but Rasselas, who, in the twenty-sixth year of his age, began to withdraw himself from their pastimes and assemblies, and to delight in solitary walks and silent meditation. He often sat before tables covered with luxury, and forgot to taste the dainties that were placed before him: he rose abruptly in the midst of the song, and hastily retired beyond the sound of musick. His attendants observed the change and endeavored to renew his love of pleasure: he neglected their endeavors, repulsed their invitations, and spent day after day on the banks of rivulets sheltered with trees, where he sometimes listened to the birds in the branches, sometimes observed the fish playing in the stream, and anon cast his eyes upon the pastures and mountains filled with animals, of which some were biting the herbage, and some sleeping among the bushes.

This singularity of his humor made him much observed. One of the Sages, in whose conversation he had formerly delighted, followed him secretly, in hope of discovering the cause of his disquiet. Rasselas, who knew not that any one was near him, having for some time fixed his eyes upon the goats that were brousing among the rocks, began to compare their condition with his own.

"What," said he, "makes the difference between man and all the rest of the animal creation? Every beast that strays beside me has the same corporal necessities with myself; he is hungry and crops the grass, he is thirsty and drinks the stream, his thirst and hunger are appeased, he is satisfied and sleeps; he rises again and is hungry, he is again fed and is at rest. I am hungry and thirsty like him, but when thirst and hunger cease I am not at rest; I am, like him, pained with want, but am not, like him, satisfied with fullness. The intermediate hours are tedious and gloomy; I long again to be hungry that I may again quicken my attention. The birds peck the berries or the corn, and fly away to the groves where they sit in seeming happiness on the branches, and waste their lives in tuning one unvaried series of sounds. I likewise can call the lutanist and the singer, but the sounds that pleased me yesterday weary me to day, and will grow yet more wearisome to morrow. I can discover within me no power of perception which is not glutted with its proper pleasure, yet I do not feel myself delighted. Man has surely some latent sense for which this place affords no gratification, or he has some desires distinct from sense which must be satisfied before he can be happy."

After this he lifted up his head, and seeing the moon rising, walked towards the palace. As he passed through the fields, and saw the animals around him, "Ye," said he, "are happy, and need not envy me that walk thus among you, burthened with myself; nor do I, ye gentle beings, envy your felicity; for it is not the felicity of man. I have many distresses from which ye are free; I fear pain when I do not feel it; I sometimes shrink at evils recollected, and sometimes start at evils anticipated: surely the equity of providence has balanced peculiar sufferings with peculiar enjoyments."

With observations like these the prince amused himself as he returned, uttering them with a plaintive voice, yet with a look that discovered him to feel some complacence in his own perspicacity, and to receive some solace of the miseries of life, from consciousness of the delicacy with which he felt, and the eloquence with which he bewailed them. He mingled cheerfully in the diversions of the evening, and all rejoiced to find that his heart was lightened.

The Wants of Him That Wants Nothing

On the next day his old instructor, imagining that he had now made himself acquainted with his disease of mind, was in hope of curing it by counsel, and officiously sought an opportunity of conference, which the prince, having long considered him as one whose intellects were exhausted, was not very willing to afford: "Why," said he, "does this man thus intrude upon me; shall I be never suffered to forget those lectures which pleased only while they were new, and to become new again must be forgotten?" He then walked into the wood, and composed himself to his usual meditations; when, before his thoughts had taken any settled form, he perceived his pursuer at his side, and was at first prompted by his impatience to go hastily away; but, being unwilling to offend a man whom he had once reverenced and still loved, he invited him to sit down with him on the bank.

The old man, thus encouraged, began to lament the change which had been lately observed in the prince, and to enquire why he so often retired from the pleasures of the palace, to loneliness and silence. "I fly from pleasure," said the prince, "because pleasure has ceased to please; I am lonely because I am miserable, and am unwilling to cloud with my presence the happiness of others." "You, Sir," said the sage, "are the first who has complained of misery in the *happy valley*. I hope to convince you that your complaints have no real cause. You are here in full possession of all that

the emperor of Abyssinia can bestow; here is neither labor
to be endured nor danger to be dreaded, yet here is all that
labor or danger can procure. Look around and tell me which
of your wants is without supply: if you want nothing, how
are you unhappy?"

"That I want nothing," said the prince, "or that I know
not what I want, is the cause of my complaint; if I had any
known want, I should have a certain wish; that wish would
excite endeavor, and I should not then repine to see the sun
move so slowly towards the western mountain, or lament
when the day breaks and sleep will no longer hide me from
myself. When I see the kids and the lambs chasing one another, I fancy that I should be happy if I had something to
pursue. But, possessing all that I can want, I find one day
and one hour exactly like another, except that the latter is
still more tedious than the former. Let your experience inform me how the day may now seem as short as in my
childhood, while nature was yet fresh, and every moment
shewed me what I never had observed before. I have already
enjoyed too much; give me something to desire."

The old man was surprised at this new species of affliction,
and knew not what to reply, yet was unwilling to be silent.
"Sir," said he, "if you had seen the miseries of the world,
you would know how to value your present state." "Now,"
said the prince, "you have given me something to desire; I
shall long to see the miseries of the world, since the sight
of them is necessary to happiness."

The Prince Continues
to Grieve and Muse

At this time the sound of musick proclaimed the hour of
repast, and the conversation was concluded. The old man
went away sufficiently discontented to find that his reasonings had produced the only conclusion which they were
intended to prevent. But in the decline of life shame and
grief are of short duration; whether it be that we bear easily
what we have born long, or that, finding ourselves in age
less regarded, we less regard others; or, that we look with

slight regard upon afflictions, to which we know that the hand of death is about to put an end.

The prince, whose views were extended to a wider space, could not speedily quiet his emotions. He had been before terrified at the length of life which nature promised him, because he considered that in a long time much must be endured; he now rejoiced in his youth, because in many years much might be done.

This first beam of hope, that had been ever darted into his mind, rekindled youth in his cheeks, and doubled the luster of his eyes. He was fired with the desire of doing something, though he knew not yet with distinctness, either end or means.

He was now no longer gloomy and unsocial; but, considering himself as master of a secret stock of happiness, which he could enjoy only by concealing it, he affected to be busy in all schemes of diversion, and endeavored to make others pleased with the state of which he himself was weary. But pleasures never can be so multiplied or continued, as not to leave much of life unemployed; there were many hours, both of the night and day, which he could spend without suspicion in solitary thought. The load of life was much lightened: he went eagerly into the assemblies, because he supposed the frequency of his presence necessary to the success of his purposes; he retired gladly to privacy, because he had now a subject of thought.

His chief amusement was to picture to himself that world which he had never seen; to place himself in various conditions; to be entangled in imaginary difficulties, and to be engaged in wild adventures: but his benevolence always terminated his projects in the relief of distress, the detection of fraud, the defeat of oppression, and the diffusion of happiness.

Thus passed twenty months of the life of Rasselas. He busied himself so intensely in visionary bustle, that he forgot his real solitude; and, amidst hourly preparations for the various incidents of human affairs, neglected to consider by what means he should mingle with mankind.

One day, as he was sitting on a bank, he feigned to him-

self an orphan virgin robbed of her little portion by a treach-
erous lover, and crying after him for restitution and redress.
So strongly was the image impressed upon his mind, that
he started up in the maid's defense, and run forward to
seize the plunderer with all the eagerness of real pursuit.
Fear naturally quickens the flight of guilt. Rasselas could
not catch the fugitive with his utmost efforts; but, resolving
to weary, by perseverance, him whom he could not surpass
in speed, he pressed on till the foot of the mountain stopped
his course.

Here he recollected himself, and smiled at his own useless impetuosity. Then raising his eyes to the mountain,
"This," said he, "is the fatal obstacle that hinders at once
the enjoyment of pleasure, and the exercise of virtue. How
long is it that my hopes and wishes have flown beyond this
boundary of my life, which yet I never have attempted to
surmount!"

Struck with this reflection, he sat down to muse, and remembered, that since he first resolved to escape from his
confinement, the sun had passed twice over him in his annual course. He now felt a degree of regret with which he
had never been before acquainted. He considered how much
might have been done in the time which had passed, and
left nothing real behind it. He compared twenty months
with the life of man. "In life," said he, "is not to be counted
the ignorance of infancy, or imbecility of age. We are long
before we are able to think, and we soon cease from the
power of acting. The true period of human existence may
be reasonably estimated as forty years, of which I have mused
away the four and twentieth part. What I have lost was
certain, for I have certainly possessed it; but of twenty
months to come who can assure me?"

The consciousness of his own folly pierced him deeply,
and he was long before he could be reconciled to himself.
"The rest of my time," said he, "has been lost by the crime
or folly of my ancestors, and the absurd institutions of my
country; I remember it with disgust, but without remorse:
but the months that have passed since new light darted into
my soul, since I formed a scheme of reasonable felicity,

have been squandered by my own fault. I have lost that which can never be restored: I have seen the sun rise and set for twenty months, an idle gazer on the light of heaven: In this time the birds have left the nest of their mother, and committed themselves to the woods and to the skies: the kid has forsaken the teat, and learned by degrees to climb the rocks in quest of independent sustenance. I only have made no advances, but am still helpless and ignorant. The moon, by more than twenty changes, admonished me of the flux of life; the stream that rolled before my feet upbraided my inactivity. I sat feasting on intellectual luxury, regardless alike of the examples of the earth, and the instructions of the planets. Twenty months are past, who shall restore them!"

These sorrowful meditations fastened upon his mind; he past four months in resolving to lose no more time in idle resolves, and was awakened to more vigorous exertion by hearing a maid, who had broken a porcelain cup, remark, that what cannot be repaired is not to be regretted.

This was obvious; and Rasselas reproached himself that he had not discovered it, having not known, or not considered, how many useful hints are obtained by chance, and how often the mind, hurried by her own ardor to distant views, neglects the truths that lie open before her. He, for a few hours, regretted his regret, and from that time bent his whole mind upon the means of escaping from the valley of happiness.

Oliver Goldsmith

✖

ASEM, AN EASTERN TALE

Where Tauris lifts its head above the storm, and presents nothing to the sight of the distant traveler but a prospect

From *The Bee*, by Oliver Goldsmith. First published in 1759.

of nodding rocks, falling torrents, and all the variety of tremendous nature; on the bleak bosom of this frightful mountain, secluded from society, and detesting the ways of men, lived Asem the Man-hater.

Asem had spent his youth with men, had shared in their amusements, and had been taught to love his fellow-creatures with the most ardent affection; but from the tenderness of his disposition, he exhausted all his fortune in relieving the wants of the distressed. The petitioner never sued in vain; the weary traveler never passed his door; he only desisted from doing good when he had no longer the power of relieving.

For a fortune thus spent in benevolence, he expected a grateful return from those he had formerly relieved; and made his application with confidence of redress: the ungrateful world soon grew weary of his importunity; for pity is but a short-lived passion. He soon, therefore, began to view mankind in a very different light from that in which he had before beheld them; he perceived a thousand vices he had never before suspected to exist; wherever he turned, ingratitude, dissimulation, and treachery, contributed to increase his detestation of them. Resolved, therefore, to continue no longer in a world which he hated, and which repaid his detestation with contempt, he retired to this region of sterility, in order to brood over his resentment in solitude, and converse with the only honest heart he knew,—namely, with his own.

A cave was his only shelter from the inclemency of the weather; fruits, gathered with difficulty from the mountain's side, his only food; and his drink was fetched, with danger and toil, from the headlong torrent. In this manner he lived, sequestered from society, passing the hours in meditation, and sometimes exulting that he was able to live independent of his fellow-creatures.

At the foot of the mountain, an extensive lake displayed its glassy bosom, reflecting on its broad surface the impending horrors of the mountain. To this capacious mirror he would sometimes descend, and, reclining on its steep banks, cast an eager look on the smooth expanse that lay before him. "How beautiful," he often cried, "is Nature! how lovely even in her wildest scenes! How finely contrasted is the level plain that lies beneath me, with yon awful pile that hides its tremendous head in clouds! But the beauty of these scenes is no way comparable with their utility: from hence a hundred rivers are supplied, which distribute health and verdure to the various countries through which they flow. Every part of the universe is beautiful, just, and wise; but man, vile man, is a solecism in nature; the only monster in the creation. Tempests and whirlwinds have their use; but vicious, ungrateful man, is a blot in the fair page of universal beauty. Why was I born of that detested species, whose vices are almost a reproach to the wisdom of the divine Creator? Were men entirely free from vice, all would be uniformity, harmony, and order. A world of moral rectitude should be the result of a perfect moral agent. Why, why then, O Allah! must I be thus confined in darkness, doubt, and despair?"

Just as he uttered the word despair, he was going to plunge into the lake beneath him, at once to satisfy his doubts, and put a period to his anxiety, when he perceived a most majestic being walking on the surface of the water, and approaching the bank on which he stood. So unexpected an object at once checked his purpose; he stopped, contemplated, and fancied he saw something awful and divine in his aspect.

"Son of Adam," cried the Genius, "stop thy rash purpose; the Father of the Faithful has seen thy justice, thy integrity, thy miseries, and hath sent me to afford and administer relief. Give me thine hand, and follow without trembling wherever I shall lead: in me behold the Genius of Conviction, kept by the Great Prophet, to turn from their errors those who go astray, not from curiosity, but a rectitude of intention. Follow me, and be wise."

Asem immediately descended upon the lake, and his guide conducted him along the surface of the water; till, coming near the center of the lake, they both began to sink; the waters closed over their heads; they descended several hundred fathoms, till Asem, just ready to give up his life as inevitably lost, found himself, with his celestial guide, in another world, at the bottom of the waters, where human foot had never trod before. His astonishment was beyond description, when he saw a sun like that he had left, a serene sky over his head, and blooming verdure under his feet.

"I plainly perceive your amazement," said the Genius; "but suspend it for a while. This world was formed by Allah, at the request, and under the inspection, of our great Prophet; who once entertained the same doubts which filled your mind when I found you, and from the consequence of which you were so lately rescued. The rational inhabitants of this world are formed agreeable to your own ideas; they are absolutely without vice. In other respects, it resembles your earth, but differs from it in being wholly inhabited by men who never do wrong. If you find this world more agreeable than that you so lately left, you have free permission to spend the remainder of your days in it; but permit me for some time to attend you, that I may silence your doubts, and make you better acquainted with your company and your new habitation."

"A world without vice! Rational beings without immorality!" cried Asem, in a rapture; "I thank thee, O Allah! who hast at length heard my petitions: this, this indeed will produce happiness, ecstasy, and ease. O, for an immortality, to spend it among men who are incapable of ingratitude, injustice, fraud, violence, and a thousand other crimes that render society miserable!"

"Cease thine exclamations," replied the Genius. "Look around thee: reflect on every object and action before us, and communicate to me the result of thine observations. Lead wherever you think proper, I shall be your attendant and instructor." Asem and his companion traveled on in silence for some time, the former being entirely lost in astonishment; but at last recovering his former serenity, he could not help observing, that the face of the country bore a near resemblance to that he had left, except that this subterranean world still seemed to retain its primeval wildness.

"Here," cried Asem, "I perceive animals of prey, and

others that seem only designed for their subsistence; it is the very same in the world over our heads. But had I been permitted to instruct our Prophet, I would have removed this defect, and formed no voracious or destructive animals, which only prey on the other parts of the creation."—"Your tenderness for inferior animals is, I find, remarkable," said the Genius, smiling. "But, with regard to meaner creatures, this world exactly resembles the other, and, indeed, for obvious reasons; for the earth can support a more considerable number of animals, by their thus becoming food for each other, than if they had lived entirely on the vegetable productions. So that animals of different natures thus formed, instead of lessening their multitude, subsist in the greatest number possible. But let us hasten on to the inhabited country before us, and see what that offers for instruction."

They soon gained the utmost verge of the forest, and entered the country inhabited by men without vice; and Asem anticipated in idea the rational delight he hoped to experience in such an innocent society. But they had scarce left the confines of the wood, when they beheld one of the inhabitants flying with hasty steps, and terror in his countenance, from an army of squirrels, that closely pursued him. "Heavens!" cried Asem, "why does he fly? What can he fear from animals so contemptible?" He had scarce spoken, when he perceived two dogs pursuing another of the human species, who with equal terror and haste attempted to avoid them. "This," cried Asem to his guide, "is truly surprising; nor can I conceive the reason for so strange an action."—"Every species of animals," replied the Genius, "has of late grown very powerful in this country; for the inhabitants, at first, thinking it unjust to use either fraud or force in destroying them, they have insensibly increased, and now frequently ravage their harmless frontiers."—"But they should have been destroyed," cried Asem; "you see the consequence of such neglect."—"Where is, then, that tenderness you so lately expressed for subordinate animals?" replied the Genius, smiling; "you seem to have forgot that branch of justice."—"I must acknowledge my mistake," returned Asem; "I am now convinced that we must be guilty of tyranny and injustice to the brute creation, if we would enjoy the world ourselves. But let us no longer observe the duty of man to these irrational creatures, but survey their connections with one another."

As they walked farther up the country, the more he was surprised to see no vestiges of handsome houses, no cities, nor any mark of elegant design. His conductor, perceiving his surprise, observed, that the inhabitants of this new world were perfectly content with their ancient simplicity; each had a house, which, though homely, was sufficient to lodge his little family; they were too good to build houses, which could only increase their own pride, and the envy of the spectator: what they built was for convenience, and not for show. "At least, then," said Asem, "they have neither architects, painters, nor statuaries, in their society; but these are idle arts, and may be spared. However, before I spend much more time here, you should have my thanks for introducing me into the society of some of their wisest men: there is scarce any pleasure to me equal to a refined conversation; there is nothing of which I am so enamored as wisdom." "Wisdom!" replied his instructor, "how ridiculous! We have no wisdom here, for we have no occasion for it; true wisdom is only a knowledge of our own duty, and the duty of others to us; but of what use is such wisdom here? each intuitively performs what is right in himself, and expects the same from others. If by wisdom you should mean vain curiosity, and empty speculation, as such pleasures have their origin in vanity, luxury, or avarice, we are too good to pursue them." "All this may be right," says Asem; "but methinks I observe a solitary disposition prevail among the people; each family keeps separately within their own precincts, without society, or without intercourse." "That indeed is true," replied the other; "here is no established society; nor should there be any: all societies are made either through fear or friendship; the people we are among are too good to fear each other; and there are no motives to private friendship, where all are equally meritorious." "Well, then," said the sceptic, "as I am to spend my time here, if I am to have neither the polite arts, nor wisdom, nor friendship, in such a world, I should be glad, at least, of an easy companion, who may tell me his thoughts, and to whom I may communicate mine." "And to what purpose should either do this?" says the Genius: "flattery or curiosity are vicious motives, and never allowed of here; and wisdom is out of the question."

"Still, however," said Asem, "the inhabitants must be happy; each is contented with his own possessions, nor avariciously endeavors to heap up more than is necessary for his own subsistence; each has therefore leisure for pitying those that stand in need of his compassion." He had scarcely spoken, when his ears were assaulted with the lamentations of a wretch who sat by the way-side, and in the most deplorable distress seemed gently to murmur at his own misery. Asem immediately ran to his relief, and found him in the last stage of a consumption. "Strange," cried the son of Adam, "that men who are free from vice should thus suffer so much misery without relief!" "Be not surprised," said the wretch who was dying: "would it not be the utmost injustice for beings, who have only just sufficient to support themselves, and are content with a bare subsistence, to take it from their own mouths to put it into mine? They never are possessed of a single meal more than is necessary; and what is barely necessary cannot be dispensed with." "They should have been supplied with more than is necessary," cried Asem—"and yet I contradict my own opinion but a moment before;—all is doubt, perplexity, and confusion. Even the want of ingratitude is no virtue here, since they never received a favor. They have, however, another excellence yet behind; the love of their country is still, I hope, one of their darling virtues." "Peace, Asem," replied the Guardian, with a countenance not less severe than beautiful, "nor forfeit all thy pretensions to wisdom: the same selfish motives by which we prefer our own interest to that of others, induce us to regard our country preferably to that of another. Nothing less than universal benevolence is free from vice, and that you see is practiced here." "Strange!" cries the disappointed pilgrim, in an agony of distress; "what sort of a world am I now introduced to? There is scarce a single virtue, but that of temperance, which they practice; and in that they are no way superior to the very brute creation. There is scarce an amusement which they enjoy; fortitude, liberality, friendship, wisdom, conversation, and love of country, all are virtues entirely unknown here: thus it seems that to be unacquainted with vice is not to know virtue. Take me, O my Genius, back to that very world which I have despised: a world which has Allah for its contriver, is much more wisely formed than that which has been projected by Mahomet. Ingratitude, contempt, and hatred, I can now suffer, for perhaps I have deserved them. When I arraigned the wisdom of Providence, I only showed my own ignorance; henceforth let me keep from vice myself, and pity it in others."

He had scarce ended, when the Genius, assuming an air of terrible complacency, called all his thunders around him, and vanished in a whirlwind. Asem astonished at the terror of the scene, looked for his imaginary world; when, casting his eyes around, he perceived himself in the very situation, and in the very place, where he first began to repine and despair; his right foot had been just advanced to take the fatal plunge, nor had it been yet withdrawn; so instantly did Providence strike the series of truths just imprinted on his soul. He now departed from the water side in tranquility; and leaving his horrid mansion, traveled to Segestan, his native city; where he diligently applied himself to commerce, and put in practice that wisdom he had learned in solitude. The frugality of a few years soon produced opulence; the number of his domestics increased; his friends came to him from every part of the city; nor did he receive them with disdain: and a youth of misery was concluded with an old age of elegance, affluence, and ease.

Suggested Additional Readings

Edward Gibbon, *The Decline and Fall of the Roman Empire*, Chaps. 1–3
Thomas Hobbes, *Leviathan*

Bernard Mandeville, *The Fable of the Bees*
Alexander Pope, *An Essay on Man*
Jonathan Swift, *Gulliver's Travels*, IV
Voltaire, *Candide*

Questions for Research and Discussion

1. Read Swift's account of Houyhnhnmland in Book IV of *Gulliver's Travels*, and compare it with Plato's Republic, Plutarch's Sparta, More's Utopia or Milton's Eden.

2. Plato's Republic has been accused of being a concealed totalitarian state. Can the same be said of Lilliput? Why or why not?

3. What do the Lilliputians' laws and customs indicate about Swift's ideal of human behavior?

4. Summarize Johnson's criticism of the hedonistic, sensual utopia. What does Johnson suppose to be the essentials of human nature?

5. Compare and contrast the views of mankind held by Swift and Johnson. Are they different in any basic way?

6. If Johnson attacks the sensual utopia, may Goldsmith be said to attack the moral utopia? Discuss.

7. Both *Asem* and *Rasselas* wear the trappings of the Oriental romance. How does the tradition of utopian literature help to explain this fact?

8. The Neo-Classicists in general held that only through his ability to think sensibly and practically ("reasonably") could man hope to improve himself and his world. The three works given above are all examples of a reasoning or common-sense estimate of human life. How do they contradict each other? What does this contradiction show about using Reason as the way to establishing utopia?

9. Do the writers included here think it possible to alter human nature? Defend your answer.

10. Investigate fully one of these topics:
    a. Utopia and the Animal Fable in Neo-Classical Literature
    b. The Bee (in the works of Mandeville, Pope, Swift, and John Gay)
    c. Carl Becker's *The Heavenly City of the Eighteenth Century Philosophers*
    d. Stoicism and Utopia in Eighteenth-Century Thought
    e. The Neo-Classical Attack on Pastoralism
    f. Swift and Primitivism
    g. Gay's *Polly* and the Noble Savage
    h. Robinson Crusoe's Island Paradise
    i. Gibbon and Rome as Utopia
    j. Voltaire's Version of El Dorado

VIII

The
Nineteenth Century

Introduction

In the four thousand years of recorded utopian thought, there is no period in which its consequences are more obvious than in the nineteenth century A.D. The utopian vision colored men's lives more positively than ever before; the emerging sciences of the period borrowed utopian assumptions that continue today as the determinants of much modern thought.

There are many reasons for the explosion of utopianism during the last century. The American and French Revolutions had seemed to promise that the accumulated political and social injustices of centuries might be swept away and real, working utopian systems substituted in place of worn-out tyrannies. The Neo-Classicist's Christian, pessimistic view of man's base, sinful nature was replaced by a Romantic version of Renaissance optimism: men were essentially good until they became corrupted by wrongful institutions and erroneous social teaching. Continued explorations disclosed new lands and peoples whose seemingly simple, happy lives showed alternatives to the un-utopian existence of the European. A rapidly developing "science" indicated that men could systematize knowledge in ways that would unerringly lead to future betterment for the individual and society. In these and other ways, the intellectual climate of the nineteenth century permitted a full flowering of utopian thought.

In some ways, utopianism continued to follow the patterns set up in the past. Explorations of traders, whalers, and missionaries provided still more legendary happy islands of plenty and happiness, Edens of primitive joy. Tahiti, Hawaii, Bali, Samoa—all were glorified by artists like Gauguin, who fled there to escape the crowded, commercial ugliness of civilized life, and by writers like Herman Melville and Robert Louis Stevenson, who saw within the noble Polynesian savage the virtues the white man had lost. In Europe itself, the age-old folk tales of lost paradise or never-never lands where the miserable wretch marries the prince and lives happily forever after were collected by the folklorists—the Grimm Brothers among them. These stories were imitated by Hans Christian Andersen, Oscar Wilde, and others; tales of *The Garden of Paradise* and *The Selfish Giant* were thus the nineteenth-century version of literary escapism which utopian desires had often taken in the past.

But there were new forms of utopianism—not escapist but pragmatic—which maintained that men could work in the here and now, on the earth, to bring into being the happy life. Chief among these were such religious cults as the Mormons, the Menonites, the Shakers, and the Dukhobors, which variously preached the need for polygamy, celibacy, nudity, hard work, prayer, poverty, or something else as the means to happiness. All of the nineteenth-century religious groups had in common the belief that God blessed those men who lived and worked together, sharing their goods and the faith as God expressly revealed it through some chosen agent, a Joseph Smith or a "Mother" Ann Lee. Literally hundreds of agrarian religious communities were built and flourished during the 1800's—in Utah, New York, Pennsylvania, Tennessee, Canada, Siberia. Some of them were perhaps as close to functioning social utopias as man has ever come.

There were, moreover, other communities set up on utopian lines but without a theological emphasis. One of the most famous of these, the Pantisocracy planned by Coleridge, Leigh Hunt, and other English Romantics, never got beyond the planning stage. But Brook Farm, another community of ethical- and social-minded intellectuals, was actually founded in Massachusetts in the last half of the century and it worked surprisingly well. Emerson, Hawthorne, and other Transcendental philosophers were interested in Brook Farm, which promised to provide a laboring, thinking community of men and women living in accordance with the principles of reason, work, and economic sharing. Everyone was required to do all sorts of work, manual as well as mental, much in the style of More's Utopians; this led to dissatisfaction on the part of Hawthorne, for instance, who lacked the talent for hoeing potatoes. After a series of fires and quarrels, Brook Farm finally went the way of the other agrarian utopian communities of the era.

Though some visionaries tried to rush utopia into being right away, others took a more gradual view, attempting to foresee the consequences of such obviously significant new conditions as the improved technology of the so-called Industrial Revolution, the growth of cities along with industry, the increase in population, and such new scientific theories as evolution. The theories of such precedent thinkers as Adam Smith and Thomas Malthus about economic principles, food supply, and population growth led to further views that affected later utopianists. The opinion that "happiness" and "good" must be communal underlay the Utilitarianism of Jeremy Bentham and J. S. Mill, which insisted on the social and economic principle of "The greatest good for the greatest number."

Within this context, the utopian thought of Karl Marx was formulated in his extended treatise, *Das Kapital*. Marx's views, though visionary and utopian throughout, were curiously traditional in some ways, despite their reputation for radical and innovational thought. Marx followed certain eighteenth-century historians in believing that history, the record of past events, could yield a sure and certain science of human behavior that would enable one to predict the future. Like Joachim of Floris, Marx thought that human events moved from stage to stage, each representing a drastic alteration of the previous one, with the end product a utopian state of perfect happiness for all here on earth. Marx dispensed with traditional theology; but he was confident that the capitalist phase of history was about to end with the overthrow of the rich by the multitude of workers, who would then live in a classless, communistic society where all men worked and shared and lived in peace, prosperity, and happiness. *Das Kapital* harkens back to apocalyptic visions of the *Old Testament* but it substitutes the ·nineteenth-century notions of man's natural goodness and economic determinism for Jehovah's magnanimity and Providential plan.

Marx's historical optimism was matched by the biological optimism of those thinkers who accepted the Darwinian theory of evolution as it was reflected in the thought of de Lamarck and T. H. Huxley. No matter how much the theories of survival of the fittest and natural selection disturbed Christian apologists, they seemed to indicate that the human race must in time evolve into some still higher and more glorious form, which would make possible at last a practicable utopia. Such higher beings were shown in William Dean Howells' *A Traveler from Altruria*, which sharply pointed out that America had not yet evolved into a utopia; but Edward Bellamy's *Looking Backward* showed the lofty society of Boston in the year 2000 A.D., enjoying the blessings of technology and prosperity and a higher morality. George Bernard Shaw's *Back to Methuselah* most specifically spelled out the way the human race could develop from an aboriginal Garden of Eden to a society with social and biological shortcomings to a culture in which death was overcome and injustice governmentally eliminated. According to Shaw, by the simple process of inevitable development, men must eventually wind up as pure, reasonable, eternal spirits—in short as divine. Darwinism was nowhere more ingeniously adapted to the utopian dream than in Shaw's play.

To be sure, there were those who seriously questioned the propositions that technology could produce happiness, that money was the answer to human misery, and that goodness was to be attained only through collective enterprise. Probably the most appealing of those who stood in deliberate opposition to the "social" utopianists of the nineteenth century was Henry David Thoreau. Thoreau's *Walden* must be placed within the broad category of utopian literature, partly because of its description of the Eden-like existence that Thoreau scrupulously led on the banks of Walden Pond, doing without the social and economic benefits so highly stressed by other thinkers of his day. Perfect happiness, Thoreau at last decided, was not possible and was irrelevant anyway. But a man might still find a utopian state within himself, in his own mind, not simply by running away from the world but by refusing to be misled by it into mistaking the perceptions of others for his own and thus slowly losing his own values and identity. Thoreau concluded that one need not live always alone in the woods in order to be fully alive. Among crowds of men, one can still find in himself the blissful state of complete awareness which is Thoreau's conception of utopian life. Not by flight to Tahiti nor by merging oneself into the indistinguishable mass of the greatest number will one find satisfaction, but by being oneself even in the mass can a man find his utopia. Thoreau's idea of the self is very like Melville's metaphor of the isle in the shark-filled ocean.

William Dean Howells

✠

AN ALTRURIAN
IN AMERICA

We left the hotel, and I began to walk my friend across the meadow toward the lake. I wished him to see the reflection of the afterglow in its still waters, with the noble lines of the mountain range that glassed itself there; the effect is one of the greatest charms of that lovely region, the sojourn of the sweetest summer in the world, and I am always impatient to show it to strangers.

We climbed the meadow wall and passed through a stretch of woods, to a path leading down to the shore, and, as we loitered along in the tender gloom of the forest, the music of the hermit-thrushes rang all round us, like crystal bells, like silver flutes, like the drip of fountains, like the choiring of still-eyed cherubim. We stopped from time to time and listened, while the shy birds sang unseen in their covert of shadows; but we did not speak till we emerged from the trees, and suddenly stood upon the naked knoll overlooking the lake.

Then I explained: "The woods used to come down to the shore here, and we had their mystery and music to the water's edge; but last winter the owner cut the timber off. It looks rather ragged now." I had to recognize the fact, for I saw the Altrurian staring about him over the clearing, in a kind of horror. It was a squalid ruin, a graceless desolation, which not even the pitying twilight could soften. The stumps showed their hideous mutilation everywhere; the brush had been burned, and the fires had scorched and blackened the lean soil of the hill slope, and blasted it with

From *A Traveler from Altruria*, by William Dean Howells. First published in 1872.

sterility. A few weak saplings, withered by the flames, drooped and straggled about; it would be a century before the forces of nature could repair the waste.

"You say the owner did this," said the Altrurian. "Who is the owner?"

"Well, it does seem too bad," I answered evasively. "There has been a good deal of feeling about it. The neighbors tried to buy him off before he began the destruction, for they knew the value of the woods as an attraction to summer boarders; the city cottagers, of course, wanted to save them, and, together, they offered for the land pretty nearly as much as the timber was worth. But he had got it into his head that the land here by the lake would sell for building lots if it was cleared, and he could make money on that as well as on the trees; and so they had to go. Of course, one might say that he was deficient in public spirit, but I don't blame him, altogether."

"No," the Altrurian assented, somewhat to my surprise, I confess.

I resumed: "There was no one else to look after his interests, and it was not only his right but his duty to get the most he could for himself and his own, according to his best light. That is what I tell people when they fall foul of him for his want of public spirit."

"The trouble seems to be, then, in the system that obliges each man to be the guardian of his own interests. Is that what you blame?"

"No, I consider it a very perfect system. It is based upon individuality, and we believe that individuality is the principle that differences civilized men from savages, from the lower animals, and makes us a nation instead of a tribe or a herd. There isn't one of us, no matter how much he censured this man's want of public spirit, but would resent the slightest interference with his property rights. The woods were his; he had the right to do what he pleased with his own."

"Do I understand you that, in America, a man may do what is wrong with his own?"

"He may do anything with his own."

"To the injury of others?"

"Well, not in person or property. But he may hurt them in taste and sentiment as much as he likes. Can't a man do what he pleases with his own in Altruria?"

"No, he can only do right with his own."

"And if he tries to do wrong, or what the community thinks is wrong?"

"Then the community takes his own from him." Before I could think of anything to say to this he went on: "But I wish you would explain to me why it was left to this man's neighbors to try and get him to sell his portion of the landscape?"

"Why, bless my soul!" I exclaimed, "who else was there? You wouldn't have expected to take up a collection among the summer boarders?"

"That wouldn't have been so unreasonable; but I didn't mean that. Was there no provision for such an exigency in your laws? Wasn't the state empowered to buy him off at the full value of his timber and his land?"

"Certainly not," I replied. "That would be rank paternalism."

It began to get dark, and I suggested that we had better be going back to the hotel. The talk seemed already to have taken us away from all pleasure in the prospect; I said, as we found our way through the rich, balsam-scented twilight of the woods, where one joy-haunted thrush was still singing, "You know that in America the law is careful not to meddle with a man's private affairs, and we don't attempt to legislate personal virtue."

"But marriage," he said, "surely you have the institution of marriage?"

I was really annoyed at this. I returned sarcastically, "Yes, I am glad to say that there we can meet your expectation; we have marriage, not only consecrated by the Church, but established and defended by the State. What has that to do with the question?"

"And you consider marriage," he pursued, "the citadel of morality, the fountain of all that is pure and good in your private life, the source of home and the image of heaven?"

"There are some marriages," I said, with a touch of our national humor, "that do not quite fill the bill, but that is certainly our ideal of marriage."

"Then why do you say that you have not legislated personal virtue in America?" he asked. "You have laws, I believe, against theft and murder and slander and incest and perjury and drunkenness?"

"Why, certainly."

"Then it appears to me that you have legislated honesty, regard for human life, regard for character, abhorrence of unnatural vice, good faith and sobriety. I was told on the train coming up, by a gentleman who was shocked at the sight of a man beating his horse, that you even had laws against cruelty to animals."

"Yes, and I am happy to say that they are enforced to such a degree that a man cannot kill a cat cruelly without being punished for it." The Altrurian did not follow up his advantage, and I resolved not to be outdone in magnanimity. "Come, I will own that you have the best of me on those points. I must say you've trapped me very neatly, too; I can enjoy a thing of that kind when it's well done, and I frankly knock under. But I had in mind something altogether different when I spoke. I was thinking of those idealists who want to bind us hand and foot, and render us the slaves of a state where the most intimate relations of life shall be penetrated by legislation, and the very hearthstone shall be a tablet of laws."

"Isn't marriage a rather intimate relation of life?" asked the Altrurian. "And I understood that gentleman on the train to say that you had laws against cruelty to children and societies established to see them enforced. You don't consider such laws an invasion of the home, do you, or a violation of its immunities? I imagine," he went on, "that the difference between your civilization and ours is only one of degree, after all, and that America and Altruria are really one at heart."

I thought his compliment a bit hyperbolical, but I saw that it was honestly meant, and as we Americans are first of all patriots, and vain for our country before we are vain for ourselves, I was not proof against the flattery it conveyed to me civically if not personally.

Edward Bellamy

LOOKING BACKWARD

Mr. Barton's Sermon

We have had among us, during the past week, a critic from the nineteenth century, a living representative of the epoch of our great-grandparents. It would be strange if a fact so extraordinary had not somewhat strongly affected our imaginations. Perhaps most of us have been stimulated to some effort to realize the society of a century ago, and figure to ourselves what it must have been like to live then. In inviting you now to consider certain reflections upon this subject which have occurred to me, I presume that I shall rather follow than divert the course of your own thoughts."

Edith whispered something to her father at this point, to which he nodded assent and turned to me.

"Mr. West," he said, "Edith suggests that you may find it slightly embarrassing to listen to a discourse on the lines Mr. Barton is laying down, and if so, you need not be cheated out of a sermon. She will connect us with Mr. Sweetser's speaking room if you say so, and I can still promise you a very good discourse."

"No, no," I said. "Believe me, I would much rather hear what Mr. Barton has to say."

"As you please," replied my host.

When her father spoke to me Edith had touched a screw, and the voice of Mr. Barton had ceased abruptly. Now at another touch the room was once more filled with the

From *Looking Backward, 2000–1887*, by Edward Bellamy. First published in 1887.

earnest sympathetic tones which had already impressed me most favorably.

"I venture to assume that one effect has been common with us as a result of this effort at retrospection, and that it has been to leave us more than ever amazed at the stupendous change which one brief century has made in the material and moral conditions of humanity.

"Still, as regards the contrast between the poverty of the nation and the world in the nineteenth century and their wealth now, it is not greater, possibly, than had been before seen in human history, perhaps not greater, for example, than that between the poverty of this country during the earliest colonial period of the seventeenth century and the relatively great wealth it had attained at the close of the nineteenth, or between the England of William the Conqueror and that of Victoria. Although the aggregate riches of a nation did not then, as now, afford any accurate criterion of the masses of its people, yet instances like these afford partial parallels for the merely material side of the contrast between the nineteenth and the twentieth centuries. It is when we contemplate the moral aspect of that contrast that we find ourselves in the presence of a phenomenon for which history offers no precedent, however far back we may cast our eye. One might almost be excused who should exclaim, 'Here, surely, is something like a miracle!' Nevertheless, when we give over idle wonder, and begin to examine the seeming prodigy critically, we find it no prodigy at all, much less a miracle. It is not necessary to suppose a moral new birth of humanity, or a wholesale destruction of the wicked and survival of the good, to account for the fact before us. It finds its simple and obvious explanation in the reaction of a changed environment upon human nature. It means merely that a form of society which was founded on the pseudo self-interest of selfishness, and appealed solely to the anti-social and brutal side of human nature, has been replaced by institutions based on the true self-interest of a rational unselfishness, and appealing to the social and generous instincts of men.

"My friends, if you would see men again the beasts of

prey they seemed in the nineteenth century, all you have to do is to restore the old social and industrial system, which taught them to view their natural prey in their fellow-men, and find their gain in the loss of others. No doubt it seems to you that no necessity, however dire, would have tempted you to subsist on what superior skill or strength enabled you to wrest from others equally needy. But suppose it were not merely your own life that you were responsible for. I know well that there must have been many a man among our ancestors who, if it had been merely a question of his own life, would sooner have given it up than nourished it by bread snatched from others. But this he was not permitted to do. He had dear lives dependent on him. Men loved women in those days, as now. God knows how they dared be fathers, but they had babies as sweet, no doubt, to them as ours to us, whom they must feed, clothe, educate. The gentlest creatures are fierce when they have young to provide for, and in that wolfish society the struggle for bread borrowed a peculiar desperation from the tenderest sentiments. For the sake of those dependent on him, a man might not choose, but must plunge into the foul fight,— cheat, overreach, supplant, defraud, buy below worth and sell above, break down the business by which his neighbor fed his young ones, tempt men to buy what they ought not and to sell what they should not, grind his laborers, sweat his debtors, cozen his creditors. Though a man sought it carefully with tears, it was hard to find a way in which he could earn a living and provide for his family except by pressing in before some weaker rival and taking the food from his mouth. Even the ministers of religion were not exempt from this cruel necessity. While they warned their flocks against the love of money, regard for their families compelled them to keep an outlook for the pecuniary prizes of their calling. Poor fellows, theirs was indeed a trying business, preaching to men a generosity and unselfishness which they and everybody knew would, in the existing state of the world, reduce to poverty those who should practice them, laying down laws of conduct which the law of self-preservation compelled men to break. Looking on the inhuman spectacle of society, these worthy men bitterly bemoaned the depravity of human nature; as if angelic nature would not have been debauched in such a devil's school! Ah, my friends, believe me, it is not now in this happy age that humanity is proving the divinity within it. It was rather in those evil days when not even the fight for life with one another, the struggle for mere existence, in which mercy was folly, could wholly banish generosity and kindness from the earth.

"It is not hard to understand the desperation with which men and women, who under other conditions would have been full of gentleness and ruth, fought and tore each other in the scramble for gold, when we realize what it meant to miss it, what poverty was in that day. For the body it was hunger and thirst, torment by heat and frost, in sickness neglect, in health unremitting toil; for the moral nature it meant oppression, contempt, and the patient endurance of indignity, brutish associations from infancy, the loss of all the innocence of childhood, the grace of womanhood, the dignity of manhood; for the mind it meant the death of ignorance, the torpor of all those faculties which distinguish us from brutes, the reduction of life to a round of bodily functions.

"Ah, my friends, if such a fate as this were offered you and your children as the only alternative of success in the accumulation of wealth, how long do you fancy would you be in sinking to the moral level of your ancestors?

"Some two or three centuries ago an act of barbarity was committed in India, which, though the number of lives destroyed was but a few score, was attended by such peculiar horrors that its memory is likely to be perpetual. A number of English prisoners were shut up in a room containing not enough air to supply one-tenth their number. The unfortunates were gallant men, devoted comrades in service, but, as the agonies of suffocation began to take hold on them, they forgot all else, and became involved in a hideous struggle, each one for himself, and against all others, to force a way to one of the small apertures of the prison at which alone it was possible to get a breath of air. It was a struggle in which men became beasts, and the recital of its horrors by the few survivors so shocked our forefathers that for a century later we find it a stock reference in their literature as a typical illustration of the extreme possibilities of human misery, as shocking in its moral as its physical aspect. They could scarcely have anticipated that to us the Black Hole of Calcutta, with its press of maddened men tearing and trampling one another in the struggle to win a place at the breathing holes, would seem a striking type of the society of their age. It lacked something of being a complete type, however, for in the Calcutta Black Hole there were no tender women, no little children and old men and women, no cripples. They were at least all men, strong to bear, who suffered.

"When we reflect that the ancient order of which I have been speaking was prevalent up to the end of the nineteenth century, while to us the new order which succeeded it already seems antique, even our parents having known no other, we cannot fail to be astounded at the suddenness with which a transition so profound beyond all previous experience of the race must have been effected. Some observation of the state of men's minds during the last quarter of the nineteenth century will, however, in great measure, dissipate this astonishment. Though general intelligence in the modern sense could not be said to exist in any community at that time, yet, as compared with previous generations, the one then on the stage was intelligent. The inevitable consequence of even this comparative degree of intelligence had been a perception of the evils of society, such as had never before been general. It is quite true that these evils had been even worse, much worse, in previous ages. It was the increased intelligence of the masses which made the difference, as the dawn reveals the squalor of surroundings which in the darkness may have seemed tolerable. The keynote of the literature of the period was one of compassion for the poor and unfortunate, and indignant outcry against the failure of the social machinery to ameliorate the miseries of men. It is plain from these outbursts that the moral hideousness of the spectacle about them was, at least by flashes, fully realized by the best of the men of that time, and that the lives of some of the more sensitive and generous hearted of them were rendered well-nigh unendurable by the intensity of their sympathies.

"Although the idea of the vital unity of the family of mankind, the reality of human brotherhood, was very far from being apprehended by them as the moral axiom it seems to us, yet it is a mistake to suppose that there was no feeling at all corresponding to it. I could read you passages of great beauty from some of their writers which show that the conception was clearly attained by a few, and no doubt vaguely by many more. Moreover, it must not be forgotten that the nineteenth century was in name Christian, and the fact that the entire commercial and industrial frame of society was the embodiment of the anti-Christian spirit must have had some weight, though I admit it was strangely little, with the nominal followers of Jesus Christ.

"When we inquire why it did not have more, why, in general, long after a vast majority of men had agreed as to the crying abuses of the existing social arrangement, they still tolerated it, or contented themselves with talking of petty reforms in it, we come upon an extraordinary fact. It was the sincere belief of even the best of men at that epoch that the only stable elements in human nature, on which a social system could be safely founded, were its worst propensities. They had been taught and believed that greed and self-seeking were all that held mankind together, and that all human associations would fall to pieces if anything were done to blunt the edge of these motives or curb their operation. In a word, they believed—even those who longed to believe otherwise—the exact reverse of what seems to us self-evident; they believed, that is, that the anti-social qualities of men, and not their social qualities, were what furnished the cohesive force of society. It seemed reasonable to them that men lived together solely for the purpose of overreaching and oppressing one another, and of being overreached and oppressed, and that while a society that gave full scope to these propensities could stand, there would be little chance for one based on the idea of cooperation for the benefit of all. It seems absurd to expect any one to believe that convictions like these were ever seriously entertained by men; but that they were not only entertained by our great-grandfathers, but were responsible for the long delay in doing away with the ancient order, after a conviction of its intolerable abuses had become general, is as well established as any fact in history can be. Just here you will find the explanation of the profound pessimism of the literature of the last quarter of the nineteenth century, the note of melancholy in its poetry, and the cynicism of its humor.

"Feeling that the condition of the race was unendurable, they had no clear hope of anything better. They believed that the evolution of humanity had resulted in leading it into a *cul de sac*, and that there was no way of getting forward. The frame of men's minds at this time is strikingly illustrated by treatises which have come down to us, and may even now be consulted in our libraries by the curious, in which laborious arguments are pursued to prove that despite the evil plight of men, life was still, by some slight preponderance of considerations, probably better worth living than leaving. Despising themselves, they despised their Creator. There was a general decay of religious belief. Pale and watery gleams, from skies thickly veiled by doubt and dread, alone lighted up the chaos of earth. That men should doubt Him whose breath is in their nostrils, or dread the hands that molded them, seems to us indeed a pitiable insanity; but we must remember that children who are brave by day have sometimes foolish fears at night. The dawn has come since then. It is very easy to believe in the fatherhood of God in the twentieth century.

"Briefly, as must needs be in a discourse of this character, I have adverted to some of the causes which had prepared men's minds for the change from the old to the new order, as well as some causes of the conservatism of despair which for a while held it back after the time was ripe. To wonder at the rapidity with which the change was completed after its possibility was first entertained is to forget the intoxicating effect of hope upon minds long accustomed to despair. The sunburst, after so long and dark a night, must needs have had a dazzling effect. From the moment men allowed themselves to believe that humanity after all had not been meant for a dwarf, that its squat stature was not the measure of its possible growth, but that it stood upon the verge of an avatar of limitless development, the reaction must needs have been overwhelming. It is evident that nothing was able to stand against the enthusiasm which the new faith inspired.

"Here, at last, men must have felt, was a cause compared with which the grandest of historic causes had been trivial. It was doubtless because it could have commanded millions of martyrs, that none were needed. The change of a dynasty in a petty kingdom of the old world often cost more lives than did the revolution which set the feet of the human race at last in the right way.

"Doubtless it ill beseems one to whom the boon of life in our resplendent age has been vouchsafed to wish his destiny other, and yet I have often thought that I would fain exchange my share in this serene and golden day for a place in that stormy epoch of transition, when heroes burst the barred gate of the future and revealed to the kindling gaze of a hopeless race, in place of the blank wall that had closed its path, a vista of progress whose end, for very excess of light, still dazzles us. Ah, my friends! who will say that to have lived then, when the weakest influence was a lever to whose touch the centuries trembled, was not worth a share even in this era of fruition?

"You know the story of that last, greatest, and most bloodless of revolutions. In the time of one generation men laid aside the social traditions and practices of barbarians, and assumed a social order worthy of rational and human beings. Ceasing to be predatory in their habits, they became co-workers, and found in fraternity, at once, the science of wealth and happiness. 'What shall I eat and drink, and wherewithal shall I be clothed?' stated as a problem beginning and ending in self, had been an anxious and an endless one. But when once it was conceived, not from the individual, but the fraternal standpoint, 'What shall we eat and drink, and wherewithal shall we be clothed?'—its difficulties vanished.

"Poverty with servitude had been the result, for the mass of humanity, of attempting to solve the problem of maintenance from the individual standpoint, but no sooner had the nation become the sole capitalist and employer than not alone did plenty replace poverty, but the last vestige of the serfdom of man to man disappeared from earth. Human slavery, so often vainly scotched, at last was killed. The means of subsistence no longer doled out by men to women, by employer to employed, by rich to poor, was distributed from a common stock as among children at the father's table. It was impossible for a man any longer to use his fellow-men as tools for his own profit. His esteem was the only sort of gain he could thenceforth make out of him. There was no more either arrogance or servility in the relations of human beings to one another. For the first time since the creation every man stood up straight before God. The fear of want and the lust of gain became extinct motives when abundance was assured to all and immoderate possessions made impossible of attainment. There were no more beggars nor almoners. Equity left charity without an occupation. The ten commandments became well-nigh obsolete in a world where there was no temptation to theft, no occasion to lie either for fear or favor, no room for envy where all were equal, and little provocation to violence where men were disarmed of power to injure one another. Humanity's ancient dream of liberty, equality, fraternity, mocked by so many ages, at last was realized.

"As in the old society the generous, the just, the tender-hearted had been placed at a disadvantage by the possession of those qualities, so in the new society the coldhearted, the greedy, and self-seeking found themselves out of joint with the world. Now that the conditions of life for the first time ceased to operate as a forcing process to develop the brutal qualities of human nature, and the premium which had heretofore encouraged selfishness was not only removed, but placed upon unselfishness, it was for the first time possible to see what unperverted human nature really was like. The depraved tendencies, which had previously overgrown and obscured the better to so large an extent, now withered like cellar fungi in the open air, and the nobler qualities showed a sudden luxuriance which turned cynics into panegyrists and for the first time in human history tempted mankind to fall in love with itself. Soon was fully revealed, what the divines and philosophers of the old world never would have believed, that human nature in its essential qualities is good, not bad, that men by their natural intention and structure are generous, not selfish, pitiful, not cruel, sympathetic, not arrogant, godlike in aspirations, instinct with divinest impulses of tenderness and self-sacrifice, images of God indeed, not the travesties upon Him they had seemed. The constant pressure, through numberless generations, of conditions of life which might have perverted angels, had not been able to essentially alter the natural nobility of the stock, and these conditions once removed, like a bent tree, it had sprung back to its normal uprightness.

"To put the whole matter in the nutshell of a parable, let me compare humanity in the olden time to a rosebush planted in a swamp, watered with black bog-water, breathing miasmatic fogs by day, and chilled with poison dews at night. Innumerable generations of gardeners had done their best to make it bloom, but beyond an occasional half-opened bud with a worm at the heart, their efforts had been unsuccessful. Many, indeed, claimed that the bush was no rosebush at all, but a noxious shrub, fit only to be uprooted and burned. The gardeners, for the most part, however, held that the bush belonged to the rose family, but had some ineradicable taint about it, which prevented the buds from coming out, and accounted for its generally sickly condition. There were a few, indeed, who maintained that the stock was good enough, that the trouble was in the bog, and that under more favorable conditions the plant might be expected to do better. But these persons were not regular gardeners, and being condemned by the latter as mere theorists and day dreamers, were, for the most part, so regarded by the people. Moreover, urged some eminent moral philosophers, even conceding for the sake of the argument that the bush might possibly do better elsewhere, it was a more valuable discipline for the buds to try to bloom in a bog than it would be under

more favorable conditions. The buds that succeeded in opening might indeed be very rare, and the flowers pale and scent-
less, but they represented far more moral effort than if they
had bloomed spontaneously in a garden.

"The regular gardeners and the moral philosophers had
their way. The bush remained rooted in the bog, and the
old course of treatment went on. Continually new varieties of
forcing mixtures were applied to the roots, and more recipes
than could be numbered, each declared by its advocates the
best and only suitable preparation, were used to kill the
vermin and remove the mildew. This went on a very long
time. Occasionally some one claimed to observe a slight improvement in the appearance of the bush, but there were
quite as many who declared that it did not look so well as it
used to. On the whole there could not be said to be any
marked change. Finally, during a period of general despond-
ency as to the prospects of the bush where it was, the idea
of transplanting it was again mooted, and this time found
favor. 'Let us try it,' was the general voice. 'Perhaps it may
thrive better elsewhere, and here it is certainly doubtful if it
be worth cultivating longer.' So it came about that the rosebush of humanity was transplanted, and set in sweet, warm,
dry earth, where the sun bathed it, the stars wooed it, and
the south wind caressed it. Then it appeared that it was indeed a rosebush. The vermin and the mildew disappeared,
and the bush was covered with most beautiful red roses,
whose fragrance filled the world.

"It is a pledge of the destiny appointed for us that the
Creator has set in our hearts an infinite standard of achievement, judged by which our past attainments seem always insignificant, and the goal never nearer. Had our forefathers
conceived a state of society in which men should live together like brethren dwelling in unity, without strifes or
envying, violence or overreaching, and where, at the price of
a degree of labor not greater than health demands, in their
chosen occupations, they should be wholly freed from care
for the morrow and left with no more concern for their liveli-
hood than trees which are watered by unfailing streams,—
had they conceived such a condition, I say, it would have

seemed to them nothing less than paradise. They would have confounded it with their idea of heaven, nor dreamed that there could possibly lie further beyond anything to be desired or striven for.

"But how is it with us who stand on this height which they gazed up to? Already we have well-nigh forgotten, except when it is especially called to our minds by some occasion like the present, that it was not always with men as it is now. It is a strain on our imaginations to conceive the social arrangements of our immediate ancestors. We find them grotesque. The solution of the problem of physical maintenance so as to banish care and crime, so far from seeming to us an ultimate attainment, appears but as a preliminary to anything like real human progress. We have but relieved ourselves of an impertinent and needless harassment which hindered our ancestors from undertaking the real ends of existence. We are merely stripped for the race; no more. We are like a child which has just learned to stand upright and to walk. It is a great event, from the child's point of view, when he first walks. Perhaps he fancies that there can be little beyond that achievement, but a year later he has forgotten that he could not always walk. His horizon did but widen when he rose, and enlarge as he moved. A great event indeed, in one sense, was his first step, but only as a beginning, not as the end. His true career was but then first entered on. The enfranchisement of humanity in the last century, from mental and physical absorption in working and scheming for the mere bodily necessities, may be regarded as a species of second birth of the race, without which its first birth to an existence that was but a burden would forever have remained unjustified, but whereby it is now abundantly vindicated. Since then, humanity has entered on a new phase of spiritual development, an evolution of higher faculties, the very existence of which in human nature our ancestors scarcely suspected. In place of the dreary hopelessness of the nineteenth century, its profound pessimism as to the future of humanity, the animating idea of the present age is an enthusiastic conception of the opportunities of our earthly existence, and the unbounded possibilities of human nature. The betterment of mankind from generation to generation, physically, mentally, morally, is recognized as the one great object supremely worthy of effort and of sacrifice. We believe the race for the first time to have entered on the realization of God's ideal of it, and each generation must now be a step upward.

"Do you ask what we look for when unnumbered generations shall have passed away? I answer, the way stretches far before us, but the end is lost in light. For twofold is the return of man to God 'who is our home,' the return of the individual by the way of death, and the return of the race by the fulfillment of the evolution, when the divine secret hidden in the germ shall be perfectly unfolded. With a tear for the dark past, turn we then to the dazzling future, and, veiling our eyes, press forward. The long and weary winter of the race is ended. Its summer has begun. Humanity has burst the chrysalis. The heavens are before it."

Herman Melville

✠

THE ISLAND
AND THE OCEAN

BRIT

Steering north-eastward from the Crozetts, we fell in with vast meadows of brit, the minute, yellow substance, upon which the Right Whale largely feeds. For leagues and leagues it undulated round us, so that we seemed to be sailing through boundless fields of ripe and golden wheat.

On the second day, numbers of Right Whales were seen, who, secure from the attack of a Sperm-Whaler like the

From *Moby Dick*, Chapters LVII and CXI, by Herman Melville. First published in 1851.

Pequod, with open jaws sluggishly swam through the brit, which, adhering to the fringing fibers of that wondrous Venetian blind in their mouths, was in that manner separated from the water that escaped at the lips.

As morning mowers, who side by side slowly and seethingly advance their scythes through the long wet grass of marshy meads; even so these monsters swam, making a strange, grassy, cutting sound; and leaving behind them endless swaths of blue upon the yellow sea.

But it was only the sound they made as they parted the brit which at all reminded one of mowers. Seen from the mast-heads, especially when they paused and were stationary for a while, their vast black forms looked more like lifeless masses of rock than anything else. And as in the great hunting countries of India, the stranger at a distance will sometimes pass on the plains recumbent elephants without knowing them to be such, taking them for bare, blackened elevations of the soil; even so, often, with him, who for the first time beholds this species of the leviathans of the sea. And even when recognized at last, their immense magnitude renders it very hard really to believe that such bulky masses of overgrowth can possibly be instinct, in all parts, with the same sort of life that lives in a dog or a horse.

Indeed, in other respects, you can hardly regard any creatures of the deep with the same feelings that you do those of the shore. For though some old naturalists have maintained that all creatures of the land are of their kind in the sea; and though taking a broad general view of the thing, this may very well be; yet coming to specialities, where, for example, does the ocean furnish any fish that in disposition answers to the sagacious kindness of the dog? The accursed shark alone can in any generic respect be said to bear comparative analogy to him.

But though, to landsmen in general, the native inhabitants of the seas have ever been regarded with emotions unspeakably unsocial and repelling; though we know the sea to be an everlasting terra incognita, so that Columbus sailed over numberless unknown worlds to discover his one superficial western one; though, by vast odds, the most

terrific of all mortal disasters have immemorially and indis-
criminately befallen tens and hundreds of thousands of those
who have gone upon the waters; though but a moment's
consideration will teach, that however baby man may brag
of his science and skill, and however much, in a flattering
future, that science and skill may augment; yet for ever
and for ever, to the crack of doom, the sea will insult and
murder him, and pulverize the stateliest, stiffest frigate he
can make; nevertheless, by the continual repetition of these
very impressions, man has lost that sense of the full awful-
ness of the sea which aboriginally belongs to it.

The first boat we read of, floated on an ocean, that with
Portuguese vengeance had whelmed a whole world without
leaving so much as a widow. That same ocean rolls now;
that same ocean destroyed the wrecked ships of last year.
Yea, foolish mortals, Noah's flood is not yet subsided; two
thirds of the fair world it yet covers.

Wherein differ the sea and the land, that a miracle upon
one is not a miracle upon the other? Preternatural terrors
rested upon the Hebrews, when under the feet of Korah and
his company the live ground opened and swallowed them
up for ever; yet not a modern sun ever sets, but in precisely
the same manner the live sea swallows up ships and crews.

But not only is the sea such a foe to man who is an
alien to it, but it is also a fiend to its own off-spring; worse
than the Persian host who murdered his own guests; sparing
not the creatures which itself hath spawned. Like a savage
tigress that tossing in the jungle overlays her own cubs, so
the sea dashes even the mightiest whales against the rocks,
and leaves them there side by side with the split wrecks of
ships. No mercy, no power but its own controls it. Panting
and snorting like a mad battle steed that has lost its rider,
the masterless ocean overruns the globe.

Consider the subtleness of the sea; how its most dreaded
creatures glide under water, unapparent for the most part,
and treacherously hidden beneath the loveliest tints of azure.
Consider also the devilish brilliance and beauty of many of
its most remorseless tribes, as the dainty embellished shape
of many species of sharks. Consider once more, the universal

cannibalism of the sea; all whose creatures prey upon each
other, carrying on eternal war since the world began.

Consider all this; and then turn to this green, gentle, and
most docile earth; consider them both, the sea and the land;
and do you not find a strange analogy to something in yourself? For as this appalling ocean surrounds the verdant
land, so in the soul of man there lies one insular Tahiti, full
of peace and joy, but encompassed by all the horrors of the
half known life. God keep thee! Push not off from that
isle, thou canst never return!

THE PACIFIC

When gliding by the Bashee isles we emerged at last
upon the great South Sea; were it not for other things I
could have greeted my dear Pacific with uncounted thanks,
for now the long supplication of my youth was answered;
that serene ocean rolled eastwards from me a thousand
leagues of blue.

There is, one knows not what sweet mystery about this
sea, whose gently awful stirrings seem to speak of some
hidden soul beneath; like those fabled undulations of the
Ephesian sod over the buried Evangelist St. John. And
meet it is, that over these sea-pastures, wide-rolling watery
prairies and Potters' Fields of all four continents, the waves
should rise and fall, and ebb and flow unceasingly; for here,
millions of mixed shades and shadows, drowned dreams,
somnambulisms, reveries; all that we call lives and souls,
lie dreaming, dreaming, still; tossing like slumberers in their
beds; the ever-rolling waves but made so by their restlessness.

To any meditative Magian rover, this serene Pacific, once
beheld, must ever after be the sea of his adoption. It rolls
the midmost waters of the world, the Indian ocean and
Atlantic being but its arms. The same waves wash the
moles of the new-built California towns, but yesterday
planted by the recentest race of men and lave the faded but
still gorgeous skirts of Asiatic lands, older than Abraham;
while all between float milky-ways of coral isles, and low-
lying, endless, unknown Archipelagoes, and impenetrable

Japans. Thus this mysterious, divine Pacific zones the
world's whole bulk about; makes all coasts one bay to it;
seems the tide-beating heart of earth. Lifted by those eternal
swells, you needs must own the seductive god, bowing your
head to Pan.

Henry David Thoreau

✠

LIFE IN THE WOODS

For a week I heard the circling, groping clangor of
some solitary goose in the foggy mornings, seeking its companion, and still peopling the woods with the sound of a
larger life than they could sustain. In April the pigeons were
seen again flying express in small flocks, and in due time I
heard the martins twittering over my clearing, though it had
not seemed that the township contained so many that it
could afford me any, and I fancied that they were peculiarly
of the ancient race that dwelt in hollow trees ere white men
came. In almost all climes the tortoise and the frog are
among the precursors and heralds of this season, and birds
fly with song and glancing plumage, and plants spring and
bloom, and winds blow, to correct this slight oscillation of
the poles and preserve the equilibrium of Nature.

As every season seems best to us in its turn, so the coming in of spring is like the creation of Cosmos out of Chaos
and the realization of the Golden Age.—

> Eurus ad Auroram, Nabathaeaque regna
>   recessit,
> Persidaque, et radiis juga subdita matutinis.

> The East-Wind withdrew to Aurora and the
>   Nabathaean kingdom,

From *Walden; or Life in the Woods*, by Henry David Thoreau.
First published in 1854.

And the Persian, and the ridges placed under
    the morning rays.

        .   .   .

Man was born. Whether that Artificer of
    things,
The origin of a better world, made him from
    the divine seed;
Or the earth being recent and lately sundered
    from the high
Ether, retained some seeds of cognate heaven.

A single gentle rain makes the grass many shades greener. So our prospects brighten on the influx of better thoughts. We should be blessed if we lived in the present always, and took advantage of every accident that befell us, like the grass which confesses the influence of the slightest dew that falls on it; and did not spend our time in atoning for the neglect of past opportunities, which we call doing our duty. We loiter in winter while it is already spring. In a pleasant spring morning all men's sins are forgiven. Such a day is a truce to vice. While such a sun holds out to burn, the vilest sinner may return. Through our own recovered innocence we discern the innocence of our neighbors. You may have known your neighbor yesterday for a thief, a drunkard, or a sensualist, and merely pitied or despised him, and despaired of the world; but the sun shines bright and warm this first spring morning, recreating the world, and you meet him at some serene work, and see how his exhausted and debauched veins expand with still joy and bless the new day, feel the spring influence with the innocence of infancy, and all his faults are forgotten. There is not only an atmosphere of good will about him, but even a savor of holiness groping for expression, blindly and ineffectually perhaps, like a new-born instinct, and for a short hour the south hill-side echoes to no vulgar jest. You see some innocent fair shoots preparing to burst from his gnarled rind and try another year's life, tender and fresh as the youngest plant. Even he has entered into the joy of his Lord. Why the jailer does not leave open his prison doors,—why the judge does not dismiss his case,

—why the preacher does not dismiss his congregation! It is because they do not obey the hint which God gives them, nor accept the pardon which he freely offers to all.

"A return to goodness produced each day in the tranquil and beneficent breath of the morning, causes that in respect to the love of virtue and the hatred of vice, one approaches a little the primitive nature of man, as the sprouts of the forest which has been felled. In like manner the evil which one does in the interval of a day prevents the germs of virtues which began to spring up again from developing themselves and destroys them.

"After the germs of virtue have thus been prevented many times from developing themselves, then the beneficent breath of evening does not suffice to preserve them. As soon as the breath of evening does not suffice longer to preserve them, then the nature of man does not differ much from that of the brute. Men seeing the nature of this man like that of the brute, think that he has never possessed the innate faculty of reason. Are those the true and natural sentiments of man?"

> The Golden Age was first created, which
>   without any avenger
> Spontaneously without law cherished fidelity
>   and rectitude.
> Punishment and fear were not; nor were
>   threatening words read
> On suspended brass; nor did the suppliant
>   crowd fear
> The words of their judge; but were safe with-
>   out an avenger.
> Not yet the pine felled on its mountains had
>   descended
> To the liquid waves that it might see a foreign
>   world,
> And mortals knew no shores but their own.
>
> There was eternal spring, and placid zephyrs
>   with warm
> Blasts soothed the flowers born without seed.

CONCLUSION

To the sick the doctors wisely recommend a change of air and scenery. Thank Heaven, here is not all the world. The buck-eye does not grow in New England, and the mocking-bird is rarely heard here. The wild-goose is more of a cosmopolite than we; he breaks his fast in Canada, takes a luncheon in the Ohio, and plumes himself for the night in a southern bayou. Even the bison, to some extent, keeps pace with the seasons, cropping the pastures of the Colorado only till a greener and sweeter grass awaits him by the Yellowstone. Yet we think that if rail-fences are pulled down, and stone-walls piled up on our farms, bounds are henceforth set to our lives and our fates decided. If you are chosen town-clerk, forsooth, you cannot go to Tierra del Fuego this summer: but you may go to the land of infernal fire nevertheless. The universe is wider than our views of it.

Yet we should oftener look over the tafferel of our craft, like curious passengers, and not make the voyage like stupid sailors picking oakum. The other side of the globe is but the home of our correspondent. Our voyaging is only great-circle sailing, and the doctors prescribe for diseases of the skin merely. One hastens to Southern Africa to chase the giraffe; but surely that is not the game he would be after. How long, pray, would a man hunt giraffes if he could? Snipes and woodcocks also may afford rare sport; but I trust it would be nobler game to shoot one's self.—

> Direct your eye right inward, and you'll find
> A thousand regions in your mind
> Yet undiscovered. Travel them, and be
> Expert in home-cosmography.

What does Africa,—what does the West stand for? Is not our own interior white on the chart? black though it may prove, like the coast, when discovered. Is it the source of the Nile, or the Niger, or the Mississippi, or a North-West Passage around this continent, that we would find? Are these the problems which most concern mankind? Is Franklin the only man who is lost, that his wife should be so earnest to find him? Does Mr. Grinnell know where he himself is? Be rather the Mungo Park, the Lewis and Clarke and Frobisher, of your own streams and oceans; explore your own higher latitudes,—with shiploads of preserved meats to support you, if they be necessary; and pile the empty cans sky-high for a sign. Were preserved meats invented to preserve meat merely? Nay, be a Columbus to whole new continents and worlds within you, opening new channels, not of trade, but of thought. Every man is the lord of a realm beside which the earthly empire of the Czar is but a petty state, a hummock left by the ice. Yet some can be patriotic who have no *self-respect*, and sacrifice the greater to the less. They love the soil which makes their graves, but have no sympathy with the spirit which may still animate their clay. Patriotism is a maggot in their heads. What was the meaning of that South-Sea Exploring Expedition, with all its parade and expense, but an indirect recognition of the fact, that there are continents and seas in the moral world, to which every man is an isthmus or an inlet, yet unexplored by him, but that it is easier to sail many thousand miles through cold and storm and cannibals, in a government ship, with five hundred men and boys to assist one, than it is to explore the private sea, the Atlantic and Pacific Ocean of one's being alone.—

> Erret, et extremos alter scrutetur Iberos.
> Plus habet hic vitae, plus habet ille viae.

> Let them wander and scrutinize the outlandish Australians.
> I have more of God, they more of the road.

It is not worth the while to go round the world to count the cats in Zanzibar. Yet do this even till you can do better, and you may perhaps find some "Symmes' Hole" by which to get at the inside at last. England and France, Spain and Portugal, Gold Coast and Slave Coast, all front on this private sea; but no bark from them has ventured out of sight of land, though it is without doubt the direct way to India. If you would learn to speak all tongues and conform to the customs of all nations, if you would travel farther than all travelers, be naturalized in all climes, and cause the Sphinx to dash her head against a stone, even obey the precept of the old philosopher, and Explore thyself. Herein are demanded the eye and the nerve. Only the defeated and deserters go to the wars, cowards that run away and enlist. Start now on that farthest western way, which does not pause at the Mississippi or the Pacific, nor conduct toward a worn-out China or Japan, but leads on direct a tangent to this sphere, summer and winter, day and night, sun down, moon down, and at last earth down too.

It is said that Mirabeau took to highway robbery "to ascertain what degree of resolution was necessary in order to place one's self in formal opposition to the most sacred laws of society." He declared that "a soldier who fights in the ranks does not require half so much courage as a foot-pad," —"that honor and religion have never stood in the way of a well-considered and a firm resolve." This was manly, as the world goes; and yet it was idle, if not desperate. A saner man would have found himself often enough "in formal opposition" to what are deemed "the most sacred laws of society," through obedience to yet more sacred laws, and so have tested his resolution without going out of his way. It is not for a man to put himself in such an attitude to society, but to maintain himself in whatever attitude he find himself through obedience to the laws of his being, which will never be one of opposition to a just government, if he should chance to meet with such.

I left the woods for as good a reason as I went there. Perhaps it seemed to me that I had several more lives to live, and could not spare any more time for that one. It is remarkable how easily and insensibly we fall into a particular route, and make a beaten track for ourselves. I had not lived there a week before my feet wore a path from my door to the pond-side; and though it is five or six years since I trod it, it is still quite distinct. It is true, I fear that others may have fallen into it, and so helped to keep it open. The surface of the earth is soft and impressible by the feet of men; and so with the paths which the mind travels. How worn and dusty, then, must be the highways of the world, how deep the ruts of tradition and conformity! I did not wish to take a cabin passage, but rather to go before the mast and on the deck of the world, for there I could best see the moonlight amid the mountains. I do not wish to go below now.

I learned this, at least, by my experiment; that if one advances confidently in the direction of his dreams, and endeavors to live the life which he has imagined, he will meet with a success unexpected in common hours. He will put some things behind, will pass an invisible boundary; new, universal, and more liberal laws will begin to establish themselves around and within him; or the old laws be expanded, and interpreted in his favor in a more liberal sense, and he will live with the license of a higher order of beings. In proportion as he simplifies his life, the laws of the universe will appear less complex, and solitude will not be solitude, nor poverty poverty, nor weakness weakness. If you have built castles in the air, your work need not be lost; that is where they should be. Now put the foundations under them. . . .

However mean your life is, meet it and live it; do not shun it and call it hard names. It is not so bad as you are. It looks poorest when you are richest. The fault-finder will find faults even in paradise. Love your life, poor as it is. You may perhaps have some pleasant, thrilling, glorious hours, even in a poor-house. The setting sun is reflected from the windows of the alms-house as brightly as from the rich man's abode; the snow melts before its door as early in the spring. I do not see but a quiet mind may live as contentedly there, and have as cheering thoughts, as in a palace. The town's poor seem to me often to live the most independent lives of any. May be they are simply great enough to receive without misgiving. Most think that they are above being supported by the town; but it oftener happens that they are not above supporting themselves by dishonest means, which should be more disreputable. Cultivate poverty like a garden herb, like sage. Do not trouble yourself much to get new things, whether clothes or friends. Turn the old; return to them. Things do not change; we change. Sell your clothes and keep your thoughts. God will see that you do not want society. If I were confined to a corner of a garret all my days, like a spider, the world would be just as large to me while I had my thoughts about me. The philosopher said: "From an army of three divisions one can take away its general, and put it in disorder; from the man the most abject and vulgar one cannot take away his thought." Do not seek so anxiously to be developed, to subject yourself to many influences to be played on; it is all dissipation. Humility like darkness reveals the heavenly lights. The shadows of poverty and meanness gather around us, "and lo! creation widens to our view." We are often reminded that if there were bestowed on us the wealth of Croesus, our aims must still be the same, and our means essentially the same. Moreover, if you are restricted in your range by poverty, if you cannot buy books and newspapers, for instance, you are but confined to the most significant and vital experiences; you are compelled to deal with the material which yields the most sugar and the most starch. It is life near the bone where it is sweetest. You are defended from being a trifler. No man loses ever on a lower level by magnanimity on a higher. Superfluous wealth can buy superfluities only. Money is not required to buy one necessary of the soul.

George Bernard Shaw

❈

31,920 A.D.

As Far as Thought Can Reach

Summer afternoon in the year 31,920 A.D. A sunlit glade at the southern foot of a thickly wooded hill. On the west side of it, the steps and columned porch of a dainty little classic temple. Between it and the hill, a rising path to the wooded heights begins with rough steps of stones in the moss.

On the opposite side, a grove. In the middle of the glade, an altar in the form of a low marble table as long as a man, set parallel to the temple steps and pointing to the hill. Curved marble benches radiate from it into the foreground; but they are not joined to it: there is plenty of space to pass between the altar and the benches.

A dance of youths and maidens is in progress. The music is provided by a few fluteplayers seated together on the steps of the temple. There are no children; and none of the dancers seems younger than eighteen. Some of the youths have beards. Their dress, like the architecture of the temple and the design of the altar and curved seats, resembles Grecian of the fourth century B.C., freely handled. They move with perfect balance and remarkable grace, racing through a figure like a farandole. They neither romp nor hug in our manner.

At the first full close they clap their hands to stop the musicians, who recommence with a saraband, during which a strange figure appears on the path beyond the temple. He is deep in thought, with his eyes closed and his feet feeling automatically for the rough irregular steps as he slowly descends them. Except for a sort of linen kilt consisting mainly of a girdle carrying a sporran and a few minor pockets, he is naked. In physical hardihood and uprightness he seems to be in the prime of life; and his eyes and mouth shew no signs of age; but his face, though fully and firmly fleshed, bears a network of lines, varying from furrows to hairbreadth reticulations, as if Time had worked over every inch of it incessantly through whole geologic periods. His head is finely domed and utterly bald. Except for his eyelashes he is quite hairless. He is unconscious of his surroundings, and walks right into one of the dancing couples, separating them. He wakes up and stares about him. The couple stop indignantly. The rest stop. The music stops. The youth whom he has jostled accosts him without malice, but without anything that we should call manners.

[In the following scene, the Youths and Maidens scoff at the He-Ancient for not enjoying their dances and love games; and he declares his indifference to such trivial activities, necessary to the early, brief stages of life. It is disclosed that human beings are hatched fully grown from eggs; they have passed embryonically through all the stages of evolution; and during their first four years, they move rapidly through all the stages of twentieth-century life-spans. At 3 or 4, they lose interest in clothes, sex, the "games" of art and science, at which point they become Ancients, contemplating abstract mathematics or philosophy. This contemplative existence lasts 700–800 years, until the Ancient is dispatched by a Fatal Accident, but not decay and death as they are known today–Ed.]

Pygmalion, with the smile of a simpleton, and the eager confidence of a fanatical scientist, climbs awkwardly on to the altar. They prepare for the worst.

PYGMALION. My friends: I will omit the algebra—

ACIS. Thank God!

PYGMALION (continuing)—because Martellus has made me promise to do so. To come to the point, I have succeeded in making artificial human beings. Real live ones, I mean.

INCREDULOUS VOICES. Oh, come! Tell us another. Really, Pyg! Get out. You havnt. What a lie!

PYGMALION. I tell you I have. I will shew them to you. It has been done before. One of the very oldest documents we possess mentions a tradition of a biologist who extracted certain unspecified minerals from the earth and, as it quaintly expresses it, 'breathed into their nostrils the breath of life.' This is the only tradition from the primitive ages which we can regard as really scientific. There are later documents which specify the minerals with great precision, even to their atomic weights; but they are utterly unscientific, because they overlook the element of life which makes all the difference between a mere mixture of salts and gases and a living organism. These mixtures were made over and over again in the crude laboratories of the Silly-Clever Ages; but nothing came of them until the ingredient which the old chronicler called the breath of life was added by this very remarkable early experimenter. In my view he was the founder of biological science.

ARJILLAX. Is that all we know about him? It doesn't amount to very much, does it?

PYGMALION. There are some fragments of pictures and documents which represent him as walking in a garden and advising people to cultivate their gardens. His name has come down to us in several forms. One of them is Jove. Another is Voltaire.

ECRASIA. You are boring us to distraction with your Voltaire. What about your human beings?

ARJILLAX. Aye: come to them.

PYGMALION. I assure you that these details are intensely interesting. (*Cries of* No! They are not! Come to the human beings! Conspuez Voltaire! Cut it short, Pyg! *interrupt him from all sides.*) You will see their bearing presently. I promise you I will not detain you long. We know, we children of science, that the universe is full of forces and powers and energies of one kind and another. The sap rising in a tree, the stone holding together in a definite crystalline structure, the thought of a philosopher holding his brain in form and operation with an inconceivably powerful grip, the urge of evolution: all these forces can be used by us. For instance, I use the force of gravitation when I put a stone on my tunic to prevent it being blown away when I am bathing. By substituting appropriate machines for the stone we have made not only gravitation our slave, but also electricity and magnetism, atomic attraction, repulsion, polarization, and so forth. But hitherto the vital force has eluded us; so it has had to create machinery for itself. It has created and developed bony structure of the requisite strength, and clothed them with cellular tissue of such amazing sensitiveness that the organs it forms will adapt their action to all the normal variations in the air they breathe, the food they digest, and the circumstances about which they have to think. Yet, as these live bodies, as we call them, are only machines after all, it must be possible to construct them mechanically.

ARJILLAX. Everything is possible. Have you done it? that is the question.

PYGMALION. Yes. But that is a mere fact. What is interesting is the explanation of the fact. Forgive my saying so;

but it is such a pity that you artists have no intellect.

ECRASIA (*sententiously*) I do not admit that. The artist divines by inspiration all the truths that the so-called scientist grubs up in his laboratory slowly and stupidly long afterwards.

ARJILLAX (*to Ecrasia, quarrelsomely*) What do you know about it? You are not an artist.

ACIS. Shut your heads, both of you. Let us have the artificial men. Trot them out, Pygmalion.

PYGMALION. It is a man and a woman. But I really must explain first.

ALL (*groaning*)!!!

PYGMALION. Yes: I—

ACIS. We want results, not explanations.

PYGMALION (*hurt*) I see I am boring you. Not one of you takes the least interest in science. Goodbye. (*He descends from the altar and makes for the temple.*)

SEVERAL YOUTHS AND MAIDENS (*rising and rushing to him*) No, no. Dont go. Dont be offended. We want to see the artificial pair. We will listen. We are tremendously interested. Tell us all about it.

PYGMALION (*relenting*) I shall not detain you two minutes.

ALL. Half an hour if you like. Please go on, Pygmalion. (*They rush him back to the altar, and hoist him on to it.*) Up you go.

They return to their former places.

PYGMALION. As I told you, lots of attempts were made to produce protoplasm in the laboratory. Why were these synthetic plasms, as they called them, no use?

ECRASIA. We are waiting for you to tell us.

THE NEWLY BORN (*molding herself on Ecrasia, and trying to outdo her intellectually*) Clearly because they were dead.

PYGMALION. Not bad for a baby, my pet. But dead and alive are very loose terms. You are not half as much alive as you will be in another month or so. What was wrong with the synthetic protoplasm was that it could not fix and conduct the Life Force. It was like a wooden magnet or a lightning conductor made of silk: it would not take the current.

ACIS. Nobody but a fool would make a wooden magnet, and expect it to attract anything.

PYGMALION. He might if he were so ignorant as not to be able to distinguish between wood and soft iron. In those days they were very ignorant of the differences between things, because their methods of analysis were crude. They mixed up messes that were so like protoplasm that they could not tell the difference. But the difference was there, though their analysis was too superficial and incomplete to detect it. You must remember that these poor devils were very little better than our idiots: we should never dream of letting one of them survive the day of its birth. Why, the Newly Born there already knows by instinct many things that their greatest physicists could hardly arrive at by forty years of strenuous study. Her simple direct sense of spacetime and quantity unconsciously solves problems which cost their most famous mathematicians years of prolonged and laborious calculations requiring such intense mental application that they frequently forgot to breathe when engaged in them, and almost suffocated themselves in consequence.

ECRASIA. Leave these obscure prehistoric abortions; and come back to your synthetic man and woman.

PYGMALION. When I undertook the task of making synthetic men, I did not waste my time on protoplasm. It was evident to me that if it were possible to make protoplasm in the laboratory, it must be equally possible to begin higher up and make fully evolved muscular and nervous tissues, bone, and so forth. Why make the seed when the making of the flower would be no greater miracle? I tried thousands of combinations before I succeeded in producing anything that would fix high-potential Life Force.

ARJILLAX. High what?

PYGMALION. High-po-tential. The Life Force is not so simple as you think. A high-potential current of it will turn a bit of dead tissue into a philosopher's brain. A low-potential current will reduce the same bit of tissue to a mass of corruption. Will you believe me when I tell you that, even in man himself, the Life Force used to slip suddenly down from its human level to that of a fungus, so that men found their flesh no longer growing as flesh, but proliferating horribly in a lower form which was called cancer, until the lower form of life killed the higher, and both perished together miserably?

MARTELLUS. Keep off the primitive tribes, Pygmalion. They interest you; but they bore these young things.

PYGMALION. I am only trying to make you understand. There was the Life Force raging all round me: there was I, trying to make organs that would capture it as a battery captures electricity, and tissues that would conduct it and operate it. It was easy enough to make eyes more perfect than our own, and ears with a larger range of sound; but they could neither see nor hear, because they were not susceptible to the Life Force. But it was far worse when I discovered how to make them susceptible; for the first thing that happened was that they ceased to be eyes and ears and turned into heaps of maggots.

ECRASIA. Disgusting! Please stop.

ACIS. If you dont want to hear, go away. You go ahead, Pyg.

PYGMALION. I went ahead. You see, the lower potentials of the Life Force could make maggots, but not human eyes nor ears. I improved the tissue until it was susceptible to a higher potential.

ARJILLAX (intensely interested) Yes; and then?

PYGMALION. Then the eyes and ears turned into cancers.

ECRASIA. Oh, hideous!

PYGMALION. Not at all. That was a great advance. It encouraged me so much that I put aside the eyes and ears, and made a brain. It wouldnt take the Life Force at all until I had altered its constitution a dozen times; but when it did, it took a much higher potential, and did not dissolve; and neither did the eyes and ears when I connected them up with the brain. I was able to make a sort of monster: a thing without arms or legs; and it really and truly lived for half-an-hour.

THE NEWLY BORN. Half-an-hour! What good was that? Why did it die?

PYGMALION. Its blood went wrong. But I got that right;

and then I went ahead with a complete human body: arms and legs and all. He was my first man.

ARJILLAX. Who modelled him?

PYGMALION. I did.

MARTELLUS. Do you mean to say you tried your own hand before you sent for me?

PYGMALION. Bless you, yes, several times. My first man was the ghastliest creature: a more dreadful mixture of horror and absurdity than you who have not seen him can conceive.

ARJILLAX. If you modelled him, he must indeed have been a spectacle.

PYGMALION. Oh, it was not his shape. You see I did not invent that. I took actual measurements and moulds from my own body. Sculptors do that sometimes, you know; though they pretend they dont.

MARTELLUS. Hm!

ARJILLAX. Hah!

PYGMALION. He was all right to look at, at first, or nearly so. But he behaved in the most appalling manner; and the subsequent developments were so disgusting that I really cannot describe them to you. He seized all sorts of things and swallowed them. He drank every fluid in the laboratory. I tried to explain to him that he must take nothing that he could not digest and assimilate completely; but of course he could not understand me. He assimilated a little of what he swallowed; but the process left horrible residues which he had no means of getting rid of. His blood turned to poison; and he perished in torments, howling. I then perceived that I had produced a prehistoric man; for there are certain traces in our own bodies of arrangements which enabled the earlier forms of mankind to renew their bodies by swallowing flesh and grains and vegetables and all sorts of unnatural and hideous foods, and getting rid of what they could not digest.

ECRASIA. But what a pity he died! What a glimpse of the past we have lost! He could have told us stories of the Golden Age.

PYGMALION. Not he. He was a most dangerous beast. He

was afraid of me, and actually tried to kill me by snatching up things and striking at me with them. I had to give him two or three pretty severe shocks before I· convinced him that he was at my mercy.

THE NEWLY BORN. Why did you not make a woman instead of a man? She would have known how to behave herself.

MARTELLUS. Why did you not make a man and a woman? Their children would have been interesting.

PYGMALION. I intended to make a woman; but after my experience with the man it was out of the question.

ECRASIA. Pray why?

PYGMALION. Well, it is difficult to explain if you have not studied prehistoric methods of reproduction. You see the only sort of men and women I could make were men and women just like us as far as their bodies were concerned. That was how I killed the poor beast of a man. I hadnt provided for his horrible prehistoric methods of feeding himself. Suppose the woman had reproduced in some prehistoric way instead of being oviparous as we are? She couldnt have done it with a modern female body. Besides, the experiment might have been painful.

ECRASIA. Then have you nothing to shew us at all?

PYGMALION. Oh yes I have. I am not so easily beaten as that. I set to work again for months to find out how to make a digestive system that would deal with waste products and a reproductive system capable of internal nourishment and incubation.

ECRASIA. Why did you not find out how to make them like us?

STREPHON (crying out in his grief for the first time) Why did you not make a woman whom you could love? That was the secret you needed.

THE NEWLY BORN. Oh yes. How true! How great of you, darling Strephon! (She kisses him impulsively.)

STREPHON (passionately) Leave me alone.

MARTELLUS. Control your reflexes, child.

THE NEWLY BORN. My what!

MARTELLUS. Your reflexes. The things you do without

thinking. Pygmalion is going to shew you a pair of human creatures who are all reflexes and nothing else. Take warning by them.

THE NEWLY BORN. But wont they be alive, like us?

PYGMALION. That is a very difficult question to answer, my dear. I confess I thought at first I had created living creatures; but Martellus declares they are only automata. But then Martellus is a mystic: *I* am a man of science. He draws a line between an automaton and a living organism. I cannot draw that line to my own satisfaction.

MARTELLUS. Your artificial men have no self-control. They only respond to stimuli from without.

PYGMALION. But they are conscious. I have taught them to talk and read; and now they tell lies. That is so very lifelike.

MARTELLUS. Not at all. If they were alive they would tell the truth. You can provoke them to tell any silly lie; and you can foresee exactly the sort of lie they will tell. Give them a clip below the knee, and they will jerk their foot forward. Give them a clip in their appetites or vanities or any of their lusts and greeds, and they will boast and lie, and affirm and deny, and hate and love without the slightest regard to the facts that are staring them in the face, or to their own obvious limitations. That proves that they are automata.

PYGMALION (*unconvinced*) I know, dear old chap; but there really is some evidence that we are descended from creatures quite as limited and absurd as these. After all, the baby there is three-quarters an automaton. Look at the way she has been going on!

THE NEWLY BORN (*indignantly*) What do you mean? How have I been going on?

ECRASIA. If they have no regard for truth, they can have no real vitality.

PYGMALION. Truth is sometimes so artificial: so relative, as we say in the scientific world, that it is very hard to feel quite sure that what is false and even ridiculous to us may not be true to them.

ECRASIA. I ask you again, why did you not make them like

us? Would any true artist be content with less than the best?

PYGMALION. I couldnt. I tried. I failed. I am convinced that what I am about to shew you is the very highest living organism that can be produced in the laboratory. The best tissues we can manufacture will not take as high potentials as the natural product: that is where Nature beats us. You dont seem to understand, any of you, what an enormous triumph it was to produce consciousness at all.

ACIS. Cut the cackle; and come to the synthetic couple.

SEVERAL YOUTHS AND MAIDENS. Yes, yes. No more talking. Let us have them. Dry up, Pyg; and fetch them along. Come on: out with them! The synthetic couple: the synthetic couple.

PYGMALION (*waving his hands to appease them*) Very well, very well. Will you please whistle for them? They respond to the stimulus of a whistle.

All who can, whistle like streetboys.

ECRASIA (*makes a wry face and puts her fingers in her ears*)!

PYGMALION. Sh-sh-sh! Thats enough: thats enough: thats enough. (*Silence.*) Now let us have some music. A dance tune. Not too fast.

The flutists play a quiet dance.

MARTELLUS. Prepare yourselves for something ghastly.

[*The human "dolls" created by Pygmalion and Martellus are ghastly: they are mere organisms, their human nature being nothing but reflexes to external stimuli. The man declares himself Ozymandias, King of Kings, and the woman is Semiramis-Cleopatra: both are vain, egotistical, selfish, violent, passionate, cowardly, and terrified of death. In a burst of madness, the woman bites Pygmalion and he dies. When the He-Ancient appears to judge them, they blame each other, like Adam and Eve before God. At last, the two creatures are disintegrated by Martellus; and in the ensuing discussion, the Ancients reveal the nature of man's unhappiness: his being the slave of the body. "The day will come when there will be no people, only thought. And that*

will be life eternal." After the Ancients depart and the
Youths and Maidens pair off once more, the spirits of Adam,
Eve, Cain, and the Serpent muse on the long distance man
has come through Evolution, and at last Lilith, the Earth-
Mother who preceded all, speaks the final words of the
drama—Ed.]

LILITH. They have accepted the burden of eternal life.
They have taken the agony from birth; and their life does
not fail them even in the hour of their destruction. Their
breasts are without milk: their bowels are gone: the very
shapes of them are only ornaments for their children to admire and caress without understanding. Is this enough; or
must I labor again? Shall I bring forth something that will
sweep them away and make an end of them as they have
swept away the beasts of the garden, and made an end of the
crawling things and the flying things and of all them that
refuse to live for ever? I had patience with them for many
ages: they tried me very sorely. They did terrible things:
they embraced death, and said that eternal life was a fable.
I stood amazed at the malice and destructiveness of the
things I had made: Mars blushed as he looked down on the
shame of his sister planet: cruelty and hypocrisy became so
hideous that the face of the earth was pitted with the graves
of little children among which living skeletons crawled in
search of horrible food. The pangs of another birth were already upon me when one man repented and lived three hundred years; and I waited to see what would come of that.
And so much came of it that the horrors of that time seem
now but an evil dream. They have redeemed themselves
from their vileness, and turned away from their sins. Best
of all, they are still not satisfied: the impulse I gave them
in that day when I sundered myself in twain and launched
Man and Woman on the earth still urges them: after passing
a million goals they press on to the goal of redemption from
the flesh, to the vortex freed from matter, to the whirlpool
in pure intelligence that, when the world began, was a
whirlpool in pure force. And though all that they have done
seems but the first hour of the infinite work of creation, yet

I will not supersede them until they have forded this last stream that lies between flesh and spirit, and disentangled their life from the matter that has always mocked it. I can wait: waiting and patience mean nothing to the eternal. I gave the woman the greatest of gifts: curiosity. By that her seed has been saved from my wrath; for I also am curious; and I have waited always to see what they will do tomorrow. Let them feed that appetite well for me. I say, let them dread, of all things, stagnation; for from the moment I, Lilith, lose hope and faith in them, they are doomed. In that hope and faith I have let them live for a moment; and in that moment I have spared them many times. But mightier creatures than they have killed hope and faith, and perished from the earth; and I may not spare them for ever. I am Lilith: I brought life into the whirlpool of force, and compelled my enemy, Matter, to obey a living soul. But in enslaving Life's enemy I made him Life's master; for that is the end of all slavery; and now I shall see the slave set free and the enemy reconciled, the whirlpool become all life and no matter. And because these infants that call themselves ancients are reaching out towards that, I will have patience with them still; though I know well that when they attain it they shall become one with me and supersede me, and Lilith will be only a legend and a lay that has lost its meaning. Of Life only is there no end; and though of its million starry mansions many are empty and many still unbuilt, and though its vast domain is as yet unbearably desert, my seed shall one day fill it and master its matter to its uttermost confines. And for what may be beyond, the eyesight of Lilith is too short. It is enough that there is a beyond. (*She vanishes.*)

Suggested Additional Readings

Hans Christian Andersen, *The Garden of Paradise*
Samuel Butler, *Erewhon*
Samuel Taylor Coleridge, "Kubla Khan"

Charles Darwin, *The Origin of Species* and *The Descent
    of Man*
Ralph Waldo Emerson, *Essays*
Karl Marx, *Das Kapital*
Herman Melville, *Omoo* and *Typee*
Book of Mormon
Mark Twain, *The Gilded Age*
Oscar Wilde, *The Selfish Giant*

Questions for Research and Writing

1. How is the Darwinian theory of evolution related to
utopian thinking? How does it appear in Shaw's *Back to
Methuselah* and Bellamy's *Looking Backward*?

2. Read all of *Back to Methuselah* and indicate the uses
Shaw has made of classical myths of Arcady, the Golden
Age, the Greek and Roman historians, the Heavenly City,
and the economic and biological theories of the nineteenth
century, as well as Genesis and *Paradise Lost*.

3. In what ways does Howells' satiric technique in *A Traveler from Altruria* compare with Swift's in *Gulliver's Travels*?
Are the anti-utopian satires based on the same fundamental
assumptions about human nature and human society? If
there are differences, what do these indicate about the
change in beliefs from the eighteenth to the nineteenth
centuries?

4. Does Bellamy's *Looking Backward* answer Howells' ob-
jections to nineteenth-century American practices in a credible way? Is Bellamy concerned with the same un-utopian
elements in nineteenth-century America as Howells or something else?

5. To what extent does Bellamy borrow the evolutionary
theories of Darwin and Marx to account for the change in
society between 1880 and 2000?

6. Do any of the utopias shown here depend on the utili-

tarian belief in the Greatest Good for the Greatest Number as the principle upon which happiness is to be based?

7. Which of the utopias are based on a strong emphasis on industrial and technological factors? Which, on natural and physical factors? Which on divine principles? Do any rest on several contradictory assumptions? Explain.

8. How does Melville use the traditional symbol of the island to illustrate his conception of human nature and human society? Is Melville's view of man like Swift's or Johnson's or Goldsmith's? Is it like Bellamy's or Thoreau's? Can it be described as "romantic" or "optimistic"?

9. Is *Walden* properly described as a "pastoral" utopian work or not? Does Thoreau emphasize reason or feeling as the right road to happiness (or self-fulfillment)?

10. Are the nineteenth-century utopias above primarily physical, emotional, economic, political, social, moral, or spiritual? Discuss.

11. Look up material about the following:
    a. The Pantisocracy
    b. Brook Farm
    c. The Shakers
    d. The Menonites
    e. The Dukhobors
    f. The Mormons
    g. Leo Tolstoy's Utopian Ideals
    h. The Dukhobor Communities in Canada
    i. Joseph Smith and the New Jerusalem
    j. Utopian Eschatology in the Nineteenth Century
    k. Marx and the Worker's Paradise
    l. J. S. Mill and Utopia
    m. Utopia and the Fairy Tale
    n. America: The Immigrant's Utopia

IX

The Twentieth Century

Introduction

Although all of the varieties of utopian thought—from the romantic depiction of the Pacific Island to the blessed race off on Asteroid X-3a—may be found in our own age, in general the twentieth century, like the eighteenth, has produced more anti-utopian sentiment than otherwise. Though James Michener may continue to exploit the primitivistic idea of the noble savage in such novels as *Return to Paradise* and James Hilton may capture the mass imagination with his dream of a Shangri-La hidden among the snowbound mountains of Tibet, more serious writers question sharply the belief that utopia is possible, especially under the conditions that characterize the present century.

The disillusionment with scientific utopianism may be found as early as H. G. Wells' novel *The Time Machine*, published in 1900. Still earlier, Jules Verne had shown that only the rare, highly cerebral man—the Nemo (or Nobody) —was capable of using the new technology wisely and well to promote his own happiness. H. G. Wells showed that the combination of technology and biological evolution must produce a divided race in which the brute controllers of the machine would eventually subjugate the golden, leisured class that benefited from industrial wealth. Wells saw the machine as the destroyer of all intelligence, virtue, initiative, and progress. Without challenge, men would revert to a brainless, sensual existence and become easy victims to the manipulators of the technology.

In a similar way, Aldous Huxley's *Brave New World* saw the dominant influences of twentieth-century life—industrialization, Freudian psychology, mass communications, capitalistic and Communistic economic theory, birth control—as conspiring to produce a race of controllers and controlled. The controlled, by far the large majority, were scientifically produced in bottles and conditioned to fill pre-established roles in a rigidly classed society. Kept docile by state-supervised programs of drug distribution, mindless entertainment, sexual orgies, and routine jobs on assembly-lines, Huxley's people are sensual robots, devoid of any of the hungers, needs, passions, and dreams that make men human. To be happy is simple, Huxley reminds his reader, if one merely ceases to be human.

Similarly, George Orwell, in *1984*, shows a strictly classed society of controllers and controlled, the former being politically totalitarian and the latter the manipulated masses. Like Huxley, Orwell shows that the supposed blessings of science—mass communications, psychological insights, medicine, technological power, controlled educational techniques—might all be subverted by cynical, ambitious politicians, who would keep the masses in ignorance, poverty, and fear in order to enjoy unlimited power. Orwell's citizens of Oceania re gray, joyless cogs in a political machine dedicated to the uthless exercise of authority and military power. Brainwashing is the tool of Big Brother, who tells his subjects that Error is Truth, Hate is Love, and War is Peace.

Both Huxley and Orwell deal extensively with the utopian concept in other works, invariably critically. British and American social critics have used the contrast between the theoretical utopia and the political actuality as the basis for satire, for example, Evelyn Waugh in *Scoop* and Kurt Vonnegut, Jr., in *God Bless You, Mr. Rosewater*. Other twentieth-century authors, notably the writers of science fiction in the tradition of Verne and Wells, have copied them in deploring the effects of science on man's potential for happiness. For example, Ray Bradbury's "There Will Come Soft Rains" not only points out the inhuman character of a technological utopia; it also shows a mechanical society first destroying man and his handiwork and finally all traces of human culture. Man's lust for happiness will destroy his petty devices for gaining it, leaving the physical world untouched by his vain utopian schemes.

At least two writers, however, have seriously presented blueprints for modern utopias. In *Islandia*, an "underground" novel written in the 1920's, Austin Tappan Wright depicts a society off the coast of South America which is an amalgam of world customs. Essentially agrarian, Wright's Islandians are isolated from the rest of the world by choice, largely to avoid the consequences of economic competition and outside influence. Their life is an updated version of More's Utopians, constructed on the author's view that happiness is pragmatically desirable and practically attainable. B. F. Skinner's *Walden Two*, on the other hand, is a serious presentation of the sort of scientifically controlled society that Huxley parodies in *Brave New World*. Thoreau would not like Skinner's view that human society can be conditioned through scientific techniques to be pleasurable, sensible, profitable, and utterly conformist. If Huxley's people are controlled by indulging their passions and Orwell's by playing on their passions, Skinner's ideal race is controllable because their passions are virtually eliminated —by means of psychological conditioning. The Waldenians may be contented but they strike many readers as living the pallid life to be found in Milton's Garden of Eden or Swift's Houyhnhnmland.

Two final works may be mentioned for their improvisations on the theme of utopia and the conditions that permit it. Franz Werfel's *Star of the Unborn* is a fictional glimpse into the future which obviously owes much to Bellamy's *Looking Backward* and to twentieth-century science fiction. Werfel's future beings are end products of evolution: hairless, frail, extremely intelligent and self-controlled. They can project themselves through space by thought power; war has been abolished; food is artificially synthesized; sex and marriage exist solely for the purpose of propagation. Most of the human race lives underground because the face of nature has altered and the earth's surface is largely sterile. So do the lives of Werfel's futurelings seem—until an accident occurs, evoking from beneath the passionless exteriors all of the subconscious drives and emotions that start another hideous, destructive war. Werfel feels that no amount of evolutionary development and natural alteration can change human nature in such a way as to make a lasting utopia possible.

Perhaps the most interesting of twentieth-century utopian thinkers is William Golding, whose novels appear largely anti-utopian. *Lord of the Flies* restates in terrible scenes Golding's belief in the innate savagery and barbarity of the human race, as his ultracivilized British choir boys lapse into bloodthirsty cannibalism and cruelty on an idyllic tropical island. Like the writer of Genesis, Golding firmly believes that man's depravity caused him to lose Eden and primitive innocence and that man can never regain that innocence, which is the basis of perfect happiness. In *The Inheritors,* Golding pursues this theme even further. His central figure is a Neanderthal caveman, Lok, whose mindless existence is centered in Now. A creature of instinct, Lok lives in a world without fear, except for certain nameless animal terrors that he expresses in totems, taboos, and the worship of Oa, the Earth-Mother. The amoral existence of "the people" (Lok's immediate family) ends suddenly with the appearance of a Cro-Magnon tribe, who represent the evolutionary gap between the higher anthropoids (Lok the ape-man) and *Homo sapiens*. It is easy for the Cro-Magnons to exterminate the brute Neanderthals, since the Cro-Magnons have lost the fear of water and travel by canoe and they have developed the spear as well as the bow and arrow. But the

Cro-Magnons are modern man in microcosm: they lust and fight for women and power. They worship demanding and contradictory gods. They depend upon an intricate social system that recalls its own past and prepares for the future. The Cro-Magnons have full-blown neuroses: fear of sterility, promiscuity, murderous desires, alcoholism. They are intellectually better equipped to survive than Neanderthal man; but they must take on the burden of dissatisfaction, fear, frustration, and guilt—Pandora's box of troubles, as it were—as the price of survival. The innocent life of the phylogenetic predecessors of *Homo sapiens*—the guiltless utopia—is forever lost. Thus in his anthropological allegory does Golding end the utopian tradition where it began: in the Garden of Eden.

B. F. Skinner

✠

WALDEN TWO

The quarters for children from one to three consisted of several small playrooms with Lilliputian furniture, a child's lavatory, and a dressing and locker room. Several small sleeping rooms were operated on the same principle as the baby-cubicles. The temperature and the humidity were controlled so that clothes or bedclothing were not needed. The cots were double-decker arrangements of the plastic mattresses we had seen in the cubicles. The children slept unclothed, except for diapers. There were more beds than necessary, so that the children could be grouped according to developmental age or exposure to contagious diseases or need for supervision, or for educational purposes.

Chapters 13–14. Reprinted with permission of The Macmillan Company from *Walden Two* by B. F. Skinner. Copyright 1948 by B. F. Skinner.

We followed Mrs. Nash to a large screened porch on the soutn side ot the building, where several children were playing in sandboxes and on swings and climbing apparatuses. A few wore "training pants"; the rest were naked. Beyond the porch was a grassy play yard enclosed by closely trimmed hedges, where other children, similarly undressed, were at play. Some kind of marching game was in progress.

As we returned, we met two women carrying food hampers. They spoke to Mrs. Nash and followed her to the porch. In a moment five or six children came running into the playrooms and were soon using the lavatory and dressing themselves. Mrs. Nash explained that they were being taken on a picnic.

"What about the children who don't go?" said Castle. "What do you do about the green-eyed monster?"

Mrs. Nash was puzzled.

"Jealousy. Envy," Castle elaborated. "Don't the children who stay home ever feel unhappy about it?"

"I don't understand," said Mrs. Nash.

"And I hope you won't try," said Frazier,[1] with a smile. "I'm afraid we must be moving along."

We said good-bye, and I made an effort to thank Mrs. Nash, but she seemed to be puzzled by that too, and Frazier frowned as if I had committed some breach of good taste.

"I think Mrs. Nash's puzzlement," said Frazier, as we left the building, "is proof enough that our children are seldom envious or jealous. Mrs. Nash was twelve years old when Walden Two was founded. It was a little late to undo her early training, but I think we were successful. She's a good example of the Walden Two product. She could probably recall the experience of jealousy, but it's not part of her present life."

"Surely that's going too far!" said Castle. "You can't be so god-like as all that! You must be assailed by emotions just as much as the rest of us!"

"We can discuss the question of godlikeness later, if you

[1] Frazier is the former Psychology professor who founded the Walden Two Community. Castle and Burris (the narrator) are visiting professors; Rodge is an ex-GI and Barbara is his girl friend.

wish," replied Frazier. "As to emotions—we aren't free of
them all, nor should we like to be. But the meaner and more
annoying—the emotions which breed unhappiness—are almost unknown here, like unhappiness itself. We don't need
them any longer in our struggle for existence, and it's easier
on our circulatory system, and certainly pleasanter, to dis-
pense with them."

"If you've discovered how to do that, you are indeed a
genius," said Castle. He seemed almost stunned as Frazier
nodded assent. "We all know that emotions are useless and
bad for our peace of mind and our blood pressure," he
went on. "But how arrange things otherwise?"

"We arrange them otherwise here," said Frazier. He was
showing a mildness of manner which I was coming to recognize as a sign of confidence.

"But emotions are—fun!" said Barbara. "Life wouldn't
be worth living without them."

"Some of them, yes," said Frazier. "The productive and
strengthening emotions—joy and love. But sorrow and hate
—and the high-voltage excitements of anger, fear, and rage
—are out of proportion with the needs of modern life, and
they're wasteful and dangerous. Mr. Castle has mentioned
jealousy—a minor form of anger, I think we may call it.
Naturally we avoid it. It has served its purpose in the evolution of man; we've no further use for it. If we allowed it
to persist, it would only sap the life out of us. In a cooper-
ative society there's no jealousy because there's no need
for jealousy."

"That implies that you all get everything you want," said
Castle. "But what about social possessions? Last night you
mentioned the young man who chose a particular girl or
profession. There's still a chance for jealousy there, isn't
there?"

"It doesn't imply that we get everything we want," said
Frazier. "Of course we don't. But jealousy wouldn't help.
In a competitive world there's some point to it. It energizes
one to attack a frustrating condition. The impulse and the
added energy are an advantage. Indeed, in a competitive
world emotions work all too well. Look at the singular lack

of success of the complacent man. He enjoys a more serene life, but it's less likely to be a fruitful one. The world isn't ready for simple pacifism or Christian humility, to cite two cases in point. Before you can safely train out the destructive and wasteful emotions, you must make sure they're no longer needed."

"How do you make sure that jealousy isn't needed in Walden Two?" I said.

"In Walden Two problems can't be solved by attacking others," said Frazier with marked finality.

"That's not the same as eliminating jealousy, though," I said.

"Of course it's not. But when a particular emotion is no longer a useful part of a behavioral repertoire, we proceed to eliminate it."

"Yes, but how?"

"It's simply a matter of behavioral engineering," said Frazier.

"Behavioral engineering?"

"You're baiting me, Burris. You know perfectly well what I mean. The techniques have been available for centuries. We use them in education and in the psychological management of the community. But you're forcing my hand," he added. "I was saving that for this evening. But let's strike while the iron is hot."

We had stopped at the door of the large children's building. Frazier shrugged his shoulders, walked to the shade of a large tree, and threw himself on the ground. We arranged ourselves about him and waited.

"Each of us," Frazier began, "is engaged in a pitched battle with the rest of mankind."

"A curious premise for a Utopia," said Castle. "Even a pessimist like myself takes a more hopeful view than that."

"You do, you do," said Frazier. "But let's be realistic. Each of us has interests which conflict with the interests of everybody else. That's our original sin, and it can't be helped. Now, 'everybody else' we call 'society.' It's a powerful opponent, and it always wins. Oh, here and there an individual prevails for a while and gets what he wants. Sometimes he storms the culture of a society and changes it slightly to his own advantage. But society wins in the long run, for it has the advantage of numbers and of age. Many prevail against one, and men against a baby. Society attacks early, when the individual is helpless. It enslaves him almost before he has tasted freedom. The 'ologies' will tell you how it's done. Theology calls it building a conscience or developing a spirit of selflessness. Psychology calls it the growth of the super-ego.

"Considering how long society has been at it, you'd expect a better job. But the campaigns have been badly planned and the victory has never been secure. The behavior of the individual has been shaped according to revelations of 'good conduct,' never as the result of experimental study. But why not experiment? The questions are simple enough. What's the best behavior for the individual so far as the group is concerned? And how can the individual be induced to behave in that way? Why not explore these questions in a scientific spirit?

"We could do just that in Walden Two. We had already worked out a code of conduct—subject, of course, to experimental modification. The code would keep things running smoothly if everybody lived up to it. Our job was to see that everybody did. Now, you can't get people to follow a useful code by making them into so many jacks-in-the-box. You can't foresee all future circumstances, and you can't specify adequate future conduct. You don't know what will be required. Instead you have to set up certain behavioral processes which will lead the individual to design his own 'good' conduct when the time comes. We call that sort of thing 'self-control.' But don't be misled, the control always rests in the last analysis in the hands of society.

"One of our Planners, a young man named Simmons, worked with me. It was the first time in history that the matter was approached in an experimental way. Do you question that statement, Mr. Castle?"

"I'm not sure I know what you are talking about," said Castle.

"Then let me go on. Simmons and I began by studying

the great works on morals and ethics—Plato, Aristotle, Confucius, the New Testament, the Puritan divines, Machiavelli, Chesterfield, Freud—there were scores of them. We were looking for any and every method of shaping human behavior by imparting techniques of self-control. Some techniques were obvious enough, for they had marked turning points in human history. 'Love your enemies' is an example—a psychological invention for easing the lot of an oppressed people. The severest trial of oppression is the constant rage which one suffers at the thought of the oppressor. What Jesus discovered was how to avoid these inner devastations. His technique was to *practice the opposite emotion*. If a man can succeed in 'loving his enemies' and 'taking no thought for the morrow,' he will no longer be assailed by hatred of the oppressor or rage at the loss of his freedom or possessions. He may not get his freedom or possessions back, but he's less miserable. It's a difficult lesson. It comes late in our program."

"I thought you were opposed to modifying emotions and instincts until the world was ready for it," said Castle. "According to you, the principle of 'love your enemies' should have been suicidal."

"It would have been suicidal, except for an entirely unforeseen consequence. Jesus must have been quite astonished at the effect of his discovery. We are only just beginning to understand the power of love because we are just beginning to understand the weakness of force and aggression. But the science of behavior is clear about all that now. Recent discoveries in the analysis of punishment—but I am falling into one digression after another. Let me save my explanation of why the Christian virtues—and I mean merely the Christian techniques of self-control—have not disappeared from the face of the earth, with due recognition of the fact that they suffered a narrow squeak within recent memory.

"When Simmons and I had collected our techniques of control, we had to discover how to teach them. That was more difficult. Current educational practices were of little value, and religious practices scarcely any better. Promising paradise or threatening hell-fire is, we assumed, generally admitted to be unproductive. It is based upon a fundamental fraud which, when discovered, turns the individual against society and nourishes the very thing it tries to stamp out. What Jesus offered in return for loving one's enemies was heaven *on earth*, better known as peace of mind.

"We found a few suggestions worth following in the practices of the clinical psychologist. We undertook to build a tolerance for annoying experiences. The sunshine of mid-day is extremely painful if you come from a dark room, but take it in easy stages and you can avoid pain altogether. The analogy can be misleading, but in much the same way it's possible to build a tolerance to painful or distasteful stimuli, or to frustration, or to situations which arouse fear, anger or rage. Society and nature throw these annoyances at the individual with no regard for the development of tolerances. Some achieve tolerances, most fail. Where would the science of immunization be if it followed a schedule of accidental dosages?

"Take the principle of 'Get thee behind me, Satan,' for example," Frazier continued. "It's a special case of self-control by altering the environment. Subclass A 3, I believe. We give each child a lollipop which has been dipped in powdered sugar so that a single touch of the tongue can be detected. We tell him he may eat the lollipop later in the day, provided it hasn't already been licked. Since the child is only three or four, it is a fairly diff——"

"Three or four!" Castle exclaimed.

"All our ethical training is completed by the age of six," said Frazier quietly. "A simple principle like putting temptation out of sight would be acquired before four. But at such an early age the problem of not licking the lollipop isn't easy. Now, what would you do, Mr. Castle, in a similar situation?"

"Put the lollipop out of sight as quickly as possible."

"Exactly. I can see you've been well trained. Or perhaps you discovered the principle for yourself. We're in favor of original inquiry wherever possible, but in this case we have a more important goal and we don't hesitate to give verbal help. First of all, the children are urged to examine their own behavior while looking at the lollipops. This helps them to recognize the need for self-control. Then the lollipops are concealed, and the children are asked to notice any gain in happiness or any reduction in tension. Then a strong distraction is arranged—say, an interesting game. Later the children are reminded of the candy and encouraged to examine their reaction. The value of the distraction is generally obvious. Well, need I go on? When the experiment is repeated a day or so later, the children all run with the lollpiops to their lockers and do exactly what Mr. Castle would do—a sufficient indication of the success of our training."

"I wish to report an objective observation of my reaction to your story," said Castle, controlling his voice with great precision. "I find myself revolted by this display of sadistic tyranny."

"I don't wish to deny you the exercise of an emotion which you seem to find enjoyable," said Frazier. "So let me go on. Concealing a tempting but forbidden object is a crude solution. For one thing, it's not always feasible. We want a sort of psychological concealment—covering up the candy by paying no attention. In a later experiment the children wear their lollipops like crucifixes for a few hours."

'Instead of the cross, the lollipop,
About my neck was hung,'

said Castle.

"I wish somebody had taught me that, though," said Rodge, with a glance at Barbara.

"Don't we all?" said Frazier. "Some of us learn control, more or less by accident. The rest of us go all our lives not even understanding how it is possible, and blaming our failure on being born the wrong way."

"How do you build up a tolerance to an annoying situation?" I said.

"Oh, for example, by having the children 'take' a more and more painful shock, or drink cocoa with less and less sugar in it until a bitter concoction can be savored without a bitter face."

"But jealousy or envy—you can't administer them in graded doses," I said.

"And why not? Remember, we control the social environment, too, at this age. That's why we get our ethical training in early. Take this case. A group of children arrive home after a long walk tired and hungry. They're expecting supper; they find, instead, that it's time for a lesson in self-control: they must stand for five minutes in front of steaming bowls of soup.

"The assignment is accepted like a problem in arithmetic. Any groaning or complaining is a wrong answer. Instead, the children begin at once to work upon themselves to avoid any unhappiness during the delay. One of them may make a joke of it. We encourage a sense of humor as a good way of not taking an annoyance seriously. The joke won't be much, according to adult standards—perhaps the child will simply pretend to empty the bowl of soup into his upturned mouth. Another may start a song with many verses. The rest join in at once, for they've learned that it's a good way to make the time pass."

Frazier glanced uneasily at Castle, who was not to be appeased.

"That also strikes you as a form of torture, Mr. Castle?" he asked.

"I'd rather be put on the rack," said Castle.

"Then you have by no means had the thorough training I supposed. You can't imagine how lightly the children take such an experience. It's a rather severe biological frustration, for the children are tired and hungry and they must stand and look at food; but it's passed off lightly as a five-minute delay at curtain time. We regard it as a fairly elementary test. Much more difficult problems follow."

"I suspected as much," muttered Castle.

"In a later stage we forbid all social devices. No songs, no jokes—merely silence. Each child is forced back upon his own resources—a very important step."

"I should think so," I said. "And how do you know it's successful? You might produce a lot of silently resentful children. It's certainly a dangerous stage."

"It is, and we follow each child carefully. If he hasn't picked up the necessary techniques, we start back a little. A still more advanced stage"—Frazier glanced again at Castle, who stirred uneasily—"brings me to my point. When it's time to sit down to the soup, the children count off—heads and tails. Then a coin is tossed and if it comes up heads, the 'heads' sit down and eat. The 'tails' remain standing for another five minutes."

Castle groaned.

"And you call that envy?" I said.

"Perhaps not exactly," said Frazier. "At least there's seldom any aggression against the lucky ones. The emotion, if any, is directed against Lady Luck herself, against the toss of the coin. That, in itself, is a lesson worth learning, for it's the only direction in which emotion has a surviving chance to be useful. And resentment toward things in general, while perhaps just as silly as personal aggression, is more easily controlled. Its expression is not socially objectionable."

Frazier looked nervously from one of us to the other. He seemed to be trying to discover whether we shared Castle's prejudice. I began to realize, also, that he had not really wanted to tell this story. He was vulnerable. He was treading on sanctified ground, and I was pretty sure he had not established the value of most of these practices in an experimental fashion. He could scarcely have done so in the short space of ten years. He was working on faith, and it bothered him.

I tried to bolster his confidence by reminding him that he had a professional colleague among his listeners. "May you not inadvertently teach your children some of the very emotions you're trying to eliminate?" I said. "What's the effect, for example, of finding the anticipation of a warm supper suddenly thwarted? Doesn't that eventually lead to feelings of uncertainty, or even anxiety?"

"It might. We had to discover how often our lessons could be safely administered. But all our schedules are worked out experimentally. We watch for undesired consequences just as any scientist watches for disrupting factors in his experiments.

"After all, it's a simple and sensible program," he went on

in a tone of appeasement. "We set up a system of gradually increasing annoyances and frustrations against a background of complete serenity. An easy environment is made more and more difficult as the children acquire the capacity to adjust."

"But *why?*" said Castle. "Why these deliberate unpleasantnesses—to put it mildly? I must say I think you and your friend Simmons are really very subtle sadists."

"You've reversed your position, Mr. Castle," said Frazier in a sudden flash of anger with which I rather sympathized. Castle was calling names, and he was also being unaccountably and perhaps intentionally obtuse. "A while ago you accused me of breeding a race of softies," Frazier continued. "Now you object to toughening them up. But what you don't understand is that these potentially unhappy situations are never very annoying. Our schedules make sure of that. You wouldn't understand, however, because you're not so far advanced as our children."

Castle grew black.

"But what do your children get out of it?" he insisted, apparently trying to press some vague advantage in Frazier's anger.

"What do they get out of it!" exclaimed Frazier, his eyes flashing with a sort of helpless contempt. His lips curled and he dropped his head to look at his fingers, which were crushing a few blades of grass.

"They must get happiness and freedom and strength," I said putting myself in a ridiculous position in attempting to make peace.

"They don't sound happy or free to me, standing in front of bowls of Forbidden Soup," said Castle, answering me parenthetically while continuing to stare at Frazier.

"If I must spell it out," Frazier began with a deep sigh, "what they get is escape from the petty emotions which eat the heart out of the unprepared. They get the satisfaction of pleasant and profitable social relations on a scale almost undreamed of in the world at large. They get immeasurably increased efficiency, because they can stick to a job without suffering the aches and pains which soon beset most of us. They get new horizons, for they are spared the emotions characteristic of frustration and failure. They get—" His eyes searched the branches of the trees. "Is that enough?" he said at last.

"And the community must gain their loyalty," I said, when they discover the fears and jealousies and diffidences in the world at large."

"I'm glad you put it that way," said Frazier. "You might have said that they must feel superior to the miserable products of our public schools. But we're at pains to keep any feeling of superiority or contempt under control, too. Having suffered most acutely from it myself, I put the subject first on our agenda. We carefully avoid any joy in a personal triumph which means the personal failure of somebody else. We take no pleasure in the sophistical, the disputative, the dialectial." He threw a vicious glance at Castle. "We don't use the motive of domination, because we are always thinking of the whole group. We could motivate a few geniuses that way—it was certainly my own motivation—but we'd sacrifice some of the happiness of everyone else. Triumph over nature and over oneself, yes. But over others, never."

"You've taken the mainspring out of the watch," said Castle flatly.

"That's an experimental question, Mr. Castle, and you have the wrong answer."

Frazier was making no effort to conceal his feeling. If he had been riding Castle, he was now using his spurs. Perhaps he sensed that the rest of us had come round and that he could change his tactics with a single holdout. But it was more than strategy, it was genuine feeling. Castle's undeviating skepticism was a growing frustration.

"Are your techniques really so very new?" I said hurriedly. "What about the primitive practice of submitting a boy to various tortures before granting him a place among adults? What about the disciplinary techniques of Puritanism? Or of the modern school, for that matter?"

"In one sense you're right," said Frazier. "And I think you've nicely answered Mr. Castle's tender concern for our little ones. The unhappinesses we deliberately impose are far milder than the normal unhappinesses from which we offer protection. Even at the height of our ethical training, the un-happiness is ridiculously trivial—to the well-trained child.

"But there's a world of difference in the way we use these annoyances," he continued. "For one thing, we don't punish. We never administer an unpleasantness in the hope of re-pressing or eliminating undesirable behavior. But there's an-other difference. In most cultures the child meets up with annoyances and reverses of uncontrolled magnitude. Some are imposed in the name of discipline by persons in authority. Some, like hazings, are condoned though not authorized. Others are merely accidental. No one cares to, or is able to, prevent them.

"We all know what happens. A few hardy children emerge, particularly those who have got their unhappiness in doses that could be swallowed. They become brave men. Others become sadists or masochists of varying degrees of pathology. Not having conquered a painful environment, they become preoccupied with pain and make a devious art of it. Others submit—and hope to inherit the earth. The rest—the crav-ens, the cowards—live in fear for the rest of their lives. And that's only a single field—the reaction to pain. I could cite a dozen parallel cases. The optimist and the pessimist, the con-tented and the disgruntled, the loved and the unloved, the ambitious and the discouraged—these are only the extreme products of a miserable system.

"Traditional practices are admittedly better than nothing," Frazier went on. "Spartan or Puritan—no one can question the occasional happy result. But the whole system rests upon the wasteful principle of selection. The English public school of the nineteenth century produced brave men—by setting up almost insurmountable barriers and making the most of the few who came over. But selection isn't education. Its crops of brave men will always be small, and the waste enormous. Like all primitive principles, selection serves in place of edu-cation only through a profligate use of material. Multiply extravagantly and select with rigor. It's the philosophy of the 'big litter' as an alternative to good child hygiene.

"In Walden Two we have a different objective. We make every man a brave man. They all come over the barriers.

Some require more preparation than others, but they all come over. The traditional use of adversity is to select the strong. We control adversity to build strength. And we do it deliberately, no matter how sadistic Mr. Castle may think us, in order to prepare for adversities which are beyond control. Our children eventually experience the 'heartache and the thousand natural shocks that flesh is heir to.' It would be the cruelest possible practice to protect them as long as possible, especially when we could protect them so well."

Frazier held out his hands in an exaggerated gesture of appeal.

"What alternative *had* we?" he said, as if he were in pain. "What else could we do? For four or five years we could provide a life in which no important need would go unsatisfied, a life practically free of anxiety or frustration or annoyance. What would you do? Would you let the child enjoy this paradise with no thought for the future—like an idolatrous and pampering mother? Or would you relax control of the environment and let the child meet accidental frustrations? *But what is the virtue of accident?* No, there was only one course open to us. We had to *design* a series of adversities, so that the child would develop the greatest possible self-control. Call it deliberate, if you like, and accuse us of sadism; there was no other course." Frazier turned to Castle, but he was scarcely challenging him. He seemed to be waiting, anxiously, for his capitulation. But Castle merely shifted his ground.

"I find it difficult to classify these practices," he said. Frazier emitted a disgruntled "Ha!" and sat back. "Your system seems to have usurped the place as well as the techniques of religion."

"Of religion and family culture," said Frazier wearily. "But I don't call it usurpation. Ethical training belongs to the community. As for techniques, we took every suggestion we could find without prejudice as to the source. But not on faith. We disregarded all claims of revealed truth and put every principle to an experimental test. And by the way, I've very much misrepresented the whole system if you suppose that any of the practices I've described are fixed. We try

out many different techniques. Gradually we work toward
the best possible set. And we don't pay much attention to
the apparent success of a principle in the course of history.
History is honored in Walden Two only as entertainment. It
isn't taken seriously as food for thought. Which reminds me,
very rudely, of our original plan for the morning. Have you
had enough of emotion? Shall we turn to intellect?"

Frazier addressed these questions to Castle in a very
friendly way and I was glad to see that Castle responded in
kind. It was perfectly clear, however, that neither of them
had ever worn a lollipop about the neck or faced a bowl of
Forbidden Soup.

Aldous Huxley

✖

BRAVE NEW WORLD

The room into which the three were ushered was the Controller's study.

"His fordship will be down in a moment." The Gamma
butler left them to themselves.

Helmholtz laughed aloud.

"It's more like a caffeine-solution party than a trial," he
said, and let himself fall into the most luxurious of the pneumatic arm-chairs. "Cheer up, Bernard," he added, catching
sight of his friend's green unhappy face. But Bernard would
not be cheered; without answering, without even looking at
Helmholtz, he went and sat down on the most uncomfort-
able chair in the room, carefully chosen in the obscure hope
of somehow deprecating the wrath of the higher powers.

The Savage meanwhile wandered restlessly round the room,

Chapter 16 from *Brave New World*, by Aldous Huxley. Copy-
right 1932 by Aldous Huxley. Renewed 1960 by Aldous Huxley.
Reprinted by permission of Harper & Row, Publishers, Mrs. Laura
Huxley, and Chatto and Windus Ltd.

peering with a vague superficial inquisitiveness at the books in the shelves, at the sound-track rolls and the reading machine bobbins in their numbered pigeon-holes. On the table under the window lay a massive volume bound in limp black leather-surrogate, and stamped with large golden T's. He picked it up and opened it. MY LIFE AND WORK, BY OUR FORD. The book had been published at Detroit by the Society for the Propagation of Fordian Knowledge. Idly he turned the pages, read a sentence here, a paragraph there, and had just come to the conclusion that the book didn't interest him, when the door opened, and the Resident World Controller for Western Europe walked briskly into the room.

Mustapha Mond shook hands with all three of them; but it was to the Savage that he addressed himself. "So you don't much like civilization, Mr. Savage," he said.

The Savage looked at him. He had been prepared to lie, to bluster, to remain sullenly unresponsive; but, reassured by the good-humored intelligence of the Controller's face, he decided to tell the truth, straightforwardly. "No." He shook his head.

Bernard started and looked horrified. What would the Controller think? To be labeled as the friend of a man who said that he didn't like civilization—said it openly and, of all people, to the Controller—it was terrible. "But, John," he began. A look from Mustapha Mond reduced him to an abject silence.

"Of course," the Savage went on to admit, "there are some very nice things. All that music in the air, for instance . . ."

"Sometimes a thousand twangling instruments will hum about my ears and sometimes voices."

The Savage's face lit up with a sudden pleasure. "Have you read it too?" he asked. "I thought nobody knew about that book here, in England."

"Almost nobody. I'm one of the very few. It's prohibited, you see. But as I make the laws here, I can also break them. With impunity, Mr. Marx," he added, turning to Bernard. "Which I'm afraid you *can't* do."

Bernard sank into a yet more hopeless misery.

"But why is it prohibited?" asked the Savage. In the excitement of meeting a man who had read Shakespeare he had momentarily forgotten everything else.

The Controller shrugged his shoulders. "Because it's old; that's the chief reason. We haven't any use for old things here."

"Even when they're beautiful?"

"Particularly when they're beautiful. Beauty's attractive, and we don't want people to be attracted by old things. We want them to like the new ones."

"But the new ones are so stupid and horrible. Those plays, where there's nothing but helicopters flying about and you *feel* the people kissing." He made a grimace. "Goats and monkeys!" Only in Othello's words could he find an adequate vehicle for his contempt and hatred.

"Nice tame animals, anyhow," the Controller murmured parenthetically.

"Why don't you let them see *Othello* instead?"

"I've told you; it's old. Besides, they couldn't understand it."

Yes, that was true. He remembered how Helmholtz had laughed at *Romeo and Juliet*. "Well then," he said, after a pause, "something new that's like *Othello*, and that they could understand."

"That's what we've all been wanting to write," said Helmholtz, breaking a long silence.

"And it's what you never will write," said the Controller. "Because, if it were really like *Othello* nobody could understand it, however new it might be. And if it were new, it couldn't possibly be like *Othello*."

"Why not?"

"Yes, why not?" Helmholtz repeated. He too was forgetting the unpleasant realities of the situation. Green with anxiety and apprehension, only Bernard remembered them; the others ignored him. "Why not?"

"Because our world is not the same as Othello's world. You can't make flivvers without steel—and you can't make tragedies without social instability. The world's stable now. People are happy; they get what they want, and they never want what they can't get. They're well off; they're safe;

they're never ill; they're not afraid of death; they're bliss-
fully ignorant of passion and old age; they're plagued with
no mothers or fathers; they've got no wives, or children, or
lovers to feel strongly about; they're so conditioned that they
practically can't help behaving as they ought to behave. And
if anything should go wrong, there's *soma*. Which you go
and chuck out of the window in the name of liberty, Mr.
Savage. *Liberty!*" He laughed. "Expecting Deltas to know
what liberty is! And now expecting them to understand
Othello! My good boy!"

The Savage was silent for a little. "All the same," he insisted obstinately, *"Othello's* good, *Othello's* better than
those feelies."

"Of course it is," the Controller agreed. "But that's the
price we have to pay for stability. You've got to choose between happiness and what people used to call high art.
We've sacrificed the high art. We have the feelies and the
scent organ instead."

"But they don't mean anything."

"They mean themselves; they mean a lot of agreeable
sensations to the audience."

"But they're . . . they're told by an idiot."

The Controller laughed. "You're not being very polite
to your friend, Mr. Watson. One of our most distinguished
Emotional Engineers . . ."

"But he's right," said Helmholtz gloomily. "Because it
is idiotic. Writing when there's nothing to say . . ."

"Precisely. But that requires the most enormous in-
genuity. You're making flivvers out of the absolute minimum
of steel—works of art out of practically nothing but pure
sensation."

The Savage shook his head. "It all seems to me quite
horrible."

"Of course it does. Actual happiness always looks pretty
squalid in comparison with the over-compensations for
misery. And, of course, stability isn't nearly so spectacular
as instability. And being contented has none of the glamor
of a good fight against misfortune, none of the picturesque-

ness of a struggle with temptation, or a fatal overthrow by passion or doubt. Happiness is never grand."

"I suppose not," said the Savage after a silence. "But need it be quite so bad as those twins?" He passed his hand over his eyes as though he were trying to wipe away the re-membered image of those long rows of identical midgets at the assembling tables, those queued-up twin-herds at the entrance to the Brentford monorail station, those human maggots swarming round Linda's bed of death, the end-lessly repeated face of his assailants. He looked at his ban-daged left hand and shuddered. "Horrible!"

"But how useful! I see you don't like our Bokanovsky Groups; but, I assure you, they're the foundation on which everything else is built. They're the gyroscope that stabilizes the rocket plane of state on its unswerving course." The deep voice thrillingly vibrated; the gesticulating hand im-plied all space and the onrush of the irresistible machine. Mustapha Mond's oratory was almost up to synthetic stand-ards.

"I was wondering," said the Savage, "why you had them at all—seeing that you can get whatever you want out of those bottles. Why don't you make everybody an Alpha Double Plus while you're about it?"

Mustapha Mond laughed. "Because we have no wish to have our throats cut," he answered. "We believe in happi-ness and stability. A society of Alphas couldn't fail to be unstable and miserable. Imagine a factory staffed by Alphas —that is to say by separate and unrelated individuals of good heredity and conditioned so as to be capable (within limits) of making a free choice and assuming responsibili-ties. Imagine it!" he repeated.

The Savage tried to imagine it, not very successfully.

"It's an absurdity. An Alpha-decanted, Alpha-conditioned man would go mad if he had to do Epsilon Semi-Moron work—go mad, or start smashing things up. Alphas can be completely socialized—but only on condition that you make them do Alpha work. Only an Epsilon can be expected to make Epsilon sacrifices, for the good reason that for him they aren't sacrifices; they're the line of least resistance. His conditioning has laid down rails along which he's got to run. He can't help himself; he's foredoomed. Even after decanting, he's still inside a bottle—an invisible bottle of infantile and embryonic fixations. Each one of us, of course," the Controller meditatively continued, "goes through life inside a bottle. But if we happen to be Alphas, our bottles are, relatively speaking, enormous. We should suffer acutely if we were confined in a narrower space. You cannot pour upper-caste champagne-surrogate into lower-caste bottles. It's obvious theoretically. But it has also been proved in actual practice. The result of the Cyprus experiment was convincing."

"What was that?" asked the Savage.

Mustapha Mond smiled. "Well, you can call it an experiment in rebottling if you like. It began in A.F. 473. The Controllers had the island of Cyprus cleared of all its existing inhabitants and re-colonized with a specially prepared batch of twenty-two thousand Alphas. All agricultural and industrial equipment was handed over to them and they were left to manage their own affairs. The result exactly fulfilled all the theoretical predictions. The land wasn't properly worked; there were strikes in all the factories; the laws were set at naught, orders disobeyed; all the people detailed for a spell of low-grade work were perpetually intriguing for high-grade jobs, and all the people with high-grade jobs were counter-intriguing at all costs to stay where they were. Within six years they were having a first-class civil war. When nineteen out of the twenty-two thousand had been killed, the survivors unanimously petitioned the World Controllers to resume the government of the island. Which they did. And that was the end of the only society of Alphas that the world has ever seen."

The Savage sighed, profoundly.

"The optimum population," said Mustapha Mond, "is modeled on the iceberg—eight-ninths below the water line, one-ninth above."

"And they're happy below the water line?"

"Happier than above it. Happier than your friend here, for example." He pointed.

"In spite of that awful work?"

"Awful? *They* don't find it so. On the contrary, they like it. It's light, it's childishly simple. No strain on the mind or the muscles. Seven and a half hours of mild, unexhausting labor, and then the *soma* ration and games and unrestricted copulation and the feelies. What more can they ask for? True," he added, "they might ask for shorter hours. And of course we could give them shorter hours. Technically, it would be perfectly simple to reduce all lower-caste working hours to three or four a day. But would they be any the happier for that? No, they wouldn't. The experiment was tried, more than a century and a half ago. The whole of Ireland was put on to the four-hour day. What was the result? Unrest and a large increase in the consumption of *soma*; that was all. Those three and a half hours of extra leisure were so far from being a source of happiness, that people felt constrained to take a holiday from them. The Inventions Office is stuffed with plans for labor-saving processes. Thousands of them." Mustapha Mond made a lavish gesture. "And why don't we put them into execution? For the sake of the laborers; it would be sheer cruelty to afflict them with excessive leisure. It's the same with agriculture. We could synthesize every morsel of food, if we wanted to. But we don't. We prefer to keep a third of the population on the land. For their own sakes—because it takes *longer* to get food out of the land than out of a factory. Besides, we have our stability to think of. We don't want to change. Every change is a menace to stability. That's another reason why we're so chary of applying new inventions. Every discovery in pure science is potentially subversive; even science must sometimes be treated as a possible enemy. Yes, even science."

Science? The Savage frowned. He knew the word. But what it exactly signified he could not say. Shakespeare and the old men of the pueblo had never mentioned science, and from Linda he had only gathered the vaguest hints:

science was something you made helicopters with, something that caused you to laugh at the Corn Dances, something that prevented you from being wrinkled and losing your teeth. He made a desperate effort to take the Controller's meaning.

"Yes," Mustapha Mond was saying, "that's another item in the cost of stability. It isn't only art that's incompatible with happiness; it's also science. Science is dangerous; we have to keep it most carefully chained and muzzled."

"What?" said Helmholtz, in astonishment. "But we're always saying that science is everything. It's a hypnopaedic platitude."

"Three times a week between thirteen and seventeen," put in Bernard.

"And all the science propaganda we do at the College . . ."

"Yes; but what sort of science?" asked Mustapha Mond sarcastically. "You've had no scientific training, so you can't judge. I was a pretty good physicist in my time. Too good —good enough to realize that all our science is just a cookery book, with an orthodox theory of cooking that nobody's allowed to question, and a list of recipes that mustn't be added to except by special permission from the head cook. I'm the head cook now. But I was an inquisitive young scullion once. I started doing a bit of cooking on my own. Unorthodox cooking, illicit cooking. A bit of real science, in fact." He was silent.

"What happened?" asked Helmholtz Watson.

The Controller sighed. "Very nearly what's going to happen to you young men. I was on the point of being sent to an island."

The words galvanized Bernard into a violent and unseemly activity. "Send me to an island?" He jumped up, ran across the room, and stood gesticulating in front of the Controller. "You can't send me. I haven't done anything. It was the others. I swear it was the others." He pointed accusingly to Helmholtz and the Savage. "Oh, please don't send me to Iceland. I promise I'll do what I ought to do. Give me another chance. Please give me another chance." The tears began to flow. "I tell you, it's their fault," he sobbed. "And not to Iceland. Oh please, your fordship, please . . ." And in a paroxysm of abjection he threw himself on his knees before the Controller. Mustapha Mond tried to make him get up; but Bernard persisted in his groveling; the stream of words poured out inexhaustibly. In the end the Controller had to ring for his fourth secretary.

"Bring three men," he ordered, "and take Mr. Marx into a bedroom. Give him a good *soma* vaporization and then put him to bed and leave him."

The fourth secretary went out and returned with three green-uniformed twin footmen. Still shouting and sobbing, Bernard was carried out.

"One would think he was going to have his throat cut," said the Controller, as the door closed. "Whereas, if he had the smallest sense, he'd understand that his punishment is really a reward. He's being sent to an island. That's to say, he's being sent to a place where he'll meet the most interesting set of men and women to be found anywhere in the world. All the people who, for one reason or another, have got too self-consciously individual to fit into community-life. All the people who aren't satisfied with orthodoxy, who've got independent ideas of their own. Every one, in a word, who's any one. I almost envy you, Mr. Watson."

Helmholtz laughed. "Then why aren't you on an island yourself?"

"Because, finally, I preferred this," the Controller answered. "I was given the choice: to be sent to an island, where I could have got on with my pure science, or to be taken on to the Controllers' Council with the prospect of succeeding in due course to an actual Controllership. I chose this and let the science go." After a little silence, "Sometimes," he added, "I rather regret the science. Happiness is a hard master—particularly other people's happiness. A much harder master, if one isn't conditioned to accept it unquestioningly, than truth." He sighed, fell silent again, then continued in a brisker tone, "Well, duty's duty. One can't consult one's own preferences. I'm interested in truth, I like science. But truth's a menace, science is a public danger. As dangerous as it's been beneficent. It has given us the stablest equilibrium in history. China's was hopelessly insecure by comparison; even the primitive matriarchies weren't steadier than we are. Thanks, I repeat, to science. But we can't allow science to undo its own good work. That's why we so carefully limit the scope of its researches—that's why I almost got sent to an island. We don't allow it to deal with any but the most immediate problems of the moment. All other enquiries are most sedulously discouraged. It's curious," he went on after a little pause, "to read what people in the time of Our Ford used to write about scientific progress. They seemed to have imagined that it could be allowed to go on indefinitely, regardless of everything else. Knowledge was the highest good, truth the supreme value; all the rest was secondary and subordinate. True, ideas were beginning to change even then. Our Ford himself did a great deal to shift the emphasis from truth and beauty to comfort and happiness. Mass production demanded the shift. Universal happiness keeps the wheels steadily turning; truth and beauty can't. And, of course, whenever the masses seized political power, then it was happiness rather than truth and beauty that mattered. Still, in spite of everything, unrestricted scientific research was still permitted. People still went on talking about truth and beauty as though they were the sovereign goods. Right up to the time of the Nine Years' War. *That* made them change their tune all right. What's the point of truth or beauty or knowledge when the anthrax bombs are popping all around you? That was when science first began to be controlled—after the Nine Years' War. People were ready to have even their appetites controlled then. Anything for a quiet life. We've gone on controlling ever since. It hasn't been very good for truth, of course. But it's been very good for happiness. One can't have something for nothing. Happiness has got to be paid for. You're paying for it, Mr. Watson—paying because you happen to be too much interested in beauty. I was too much interested in truth; I paid too."

"But *you* didn't go to an island," said the Savage, breaking a long silence.

The Controller smiled. "That's how I paid. By choosing to serve happiness. Other people's—not mine. It's lucky," he added, after a pause, "that there are such a lot of islands in the world. I don't know what we should do without them. Put you all in the lethal chamber, I suppose. By the way, Mr. Watson, would you like a tropical climate? The Marquesas, for example; or Samoa? Or something rather more bracing?"

Helmholtz rose from his pneumatic chair. "I should like a thoroughly bad climate," he answered. "I believe one would write better if the climate were bad. If there were a lot of wind and storms, for example . . ."

The Controller nodded his approbation. "I like your spirit, Mr. Watson. I like it very much indeed. As much as I officially disapprove of it." He smiled. "What about the Falkland Islands?"

"Yes, I think that will do," Helmholtz answered. "And now, if you don't mind, I'll go and see how poor Bernard's getting on."

Robert Frost

✖

DEPARTMENTAL

An ant on the table cloth
Ran into a dormant moth
Of many times his size.
He showed not the least surprise.
His business wasn't with such.
He gave it scarcely a touch,

And was off on his duty run.
Yet if he encountered one
Of the hive's enquiry squad
Whose work is to find out God
And the nature of time and space,
He would put him onto the case.
Ants are a curious race;
One crossing with hurried tread
The body of one of their dead
Isn't given a moment's arrest—
Seems not even impressed.
But he no doubt reports to any
With whom he crosses antennae,
And they no doubt report
To the higher up at court.
Then word goes forth in Formic:
"Death's come to Jerry McCormic,
Our selfless forager Jerry.
Will the special Janizary
Whose office it is to bury
The dead of the commissary
Go bring him home to his people.
Lay him in state on a sepal.
Wrap him for shroud in a petal.
Embalm him with ichor of nettle.
This is the word of your Queen."
And presently on the scene
Appears a solemn mortician;
And taking formal position
With feelers calmly atwiddle,
Seizes the dead by the middle,
And heaving him high in air,
Carries him out of there.
No one stands round to stare.
It is nobody else's affair.

It couldn't be called ungentle.
But how thoroughly departmental.

Ray Bradbury

THERE WILL COME
SOFT RAINS

In the living room the voice-clock sang, *Tick-tock, seven o'clock, time to get up, time to get up, seven o'clock!* as if it were afraid that nobody would. The morning house lay empty. The clock ticked on, repeating and repeating its sounds into the emptiness. *Seven-nine, breakfast time, seven-nine!*

In the kitchen the breakfast stove gave a hissing sigh and ejected from its warm interior eight pieces of perfectly browned toast, eight eggs sunnyside up, sixteen slices of bacon, two coffees, and two cool glasses of milk.

"Today is August 4, 2026," said a second voice from the kitchen ceiling, "in the city of Allendale, California." It repeated the date three times for memory's sake. "Today is Mr. Featherstone's birthday. Today is the anniversary of Tilita's marriage. Insurance is payable, as are the water, gas, and light bills."

Somewhere in the walls, relays clicked, memory tapes glided under electric eyes.

Eight-one, tick-tock, eight-one o'clock, off to school, off to work, run, run, eight-one! But no doors slammed, no carpets took the soft tread of rubber heels. It was raining outside. The weather box on the front door sang quietly: "Rain, rain, go away; rubbers, raincoats for today . . ." And the rain tapped on the empty house, echoing.

Outside, the garage chimed and lifted its door to reveal

the waiting car. After a long wait the door swung down
again.

At eight-thirty the eggs were shriveled and the toast was
like stone. An aluminum wedge scraped them into the sink,
where hot water whirled them down a metal throat which
digested and flushed them away to the distant sea. The
dirty dishes were dropped into a hot washer and emerged
twinkling dry.

Nine-fifteen, sang the clock, *time to clean.*

Out of warrens in the wall, tiny robot mice darted. The
rooms were acrawl with the small cleaning animals, all rubber and metal. They thudded against chairs, whirling their
mustached runners, kneading the rug nap, sucking gently
at hidden dust.

Then, like mysterious invaders, they popped into their
burrows. Their pink electric eyes faded. The house was clean.

Ten o'clock. The sun came out from behind the rain.
The house stood alone in a city of rubble and ashes. This
was the one house left standing. At night the ruined city
gave off a radioactive glow which could be seen for miles.

Ten-fifteen. The garden sprinklers whirled up in golden
founts, filling the soft morning air with scatterings of bright-
ness. The water pelted windowpanes, running down the
charred west side where the house had been burned evenly
free of its white paint. The entire west face of the house
was black, save for five places. Here the silhouette in paint
of a man mowing a lawn. Here, as in a photograph, a woman
bent to pick flowers. Still farther over, their images burned
on wood in one titanic instant, a small boy, hands flung into
the air; higher up, the image of a thrown ball, and opposite
him a girl, hands raised to catch a ball which never came
down.

The five spots of paint—the man, the woman, the children, the ball—remained. The rest was a thin charcoaled
layer.

The gentle sprinkler rain filled the garden with falling
light.

Until this day, how well the house had kept its peace.
How carefully it had inquired, "Who goes there? What's

the password?" and, getting no answer from lonely foxes and whining cats, it had shut up its windows and drawn shades in an old-maidenly preoccupation with self-protection which bordered on a mechanical paranoia.

It quivered at each sound, the house did. If a sparrow brushed a window, the shade snapped up. The bird, startled, flew off! No, not even a bird must touch the house!

The house was an altar with ten thousand attendants, big, small, servicing, attending, in choirs. But the gods had gone away, and the ritual of the religion continued senselessly, uselessly.

Twelve noon.

A dog whined, shivering, on the front porch.

The front door recognized the dog voice and opened. The dog, once huge and fleshy, but now gone to bone and covered with sores, moved in and through the house, tracking mud. Behind it whirred angry mice, angry at having to pick up mud, angry at inconvenience.

For not a leaf fragment blew under the door but what the wall panels flipped open and the copper scrap rats flashed swiftly out. The offending dust, hair, or paper seized in miniature steel jaws, was raced back to the burrows. There, down tubes which fed into the cellar, it was dropped into the sighing vent of an incinerator which sat like evil Baal in a dark corner.

The dog ran upstairs, hysterically yelping to each door, at last realizing, as the house realized, that only silence was here.

It sniffed the air and scratched the kitchen door. Behind the door, the stove was making pancakes which filled the house with a rich baked odor and the scent of maple syrup.

The dog frothed at the mouth, lying at the door, sniffing, its eyes turned to fire. It ran wildly in circles, biting at its tail, spun in a frenzy, and died. It lay in the parlor for an hour.

Two o'clock, sang a voice.

Delicately sensing decay at last, the regiments of mice hummed out as softly as blown gray leaves in an electrical wind.

Two-fifteen.

The dog was gone.

In the cellar, the incinerator glowed suddenly and a whirl of sparks leaped up the chimney.

Two thirty-five.

Bridge tables sprouted from patio walls. Playing cards fluttered onto pads in a shower of pips. Martinis manifested on an oaken bench with egg-salad sandwiches. Music played.

But the tables were silent and the cards untouched.

At four o'clock the tables folded like great butterflies back through the paneled walls.

Four-thirty.

The nursery walls glowed.

Animals took shape: yellow giraffes, blue lions, pink antelopes, lilac panthers cavorting in crystal substance. The walls were glass. They looked out upon color and fantasy. Hidden films clocked through well-oiled sprockets, and the walls lived. The nursery floor was woven to resemble a crisp cereal meadow. Over this ran aluminum roaches and iron crickets, and in the hot still air butterflies of delicate red tissue wavered among the sharp aroma of animal spoors! There was the sound like a great matted yellow hive of bees within a dark bellows, the lazy bumble of a purring lion. And there was the patter of okapi feet and the murmur of a fresh jungle rain, like other hoofs, falling upon the summer-starched grass. Now the walls dissolved into distances of parched weed, mile on mile, and warm endless sky. The animals drew away into thorn brakes and water holes.

It was the children's hour.

Five o'clock. The bath filled with clear hot water.

Six, seven, eight o'clock. The dinner dishes manipulated like magic tricks, and in the study a *click*. In the metal stand opposite the hearth where a fire now blazed up warmly, a cigar popped out, half an inch of soft gray ash on it, smoking, waiting.

Nine o'clock. The beds warmed their hidden circuits, for nights were cool here.

Nine-five. A voice spoke from the study ceiling:

"Mrs. McClellan, which poem would you like this evening?"

The house was silent.

The voice said at last, "Since you express no preference, I shall select a poem at random." Quiet music rose to back the voice. "Sara Teasdale. As I recall, your favorite. . . .

There will come soft rains and the smell of the ground,
And swallows circling with their shimmering sound;

And frogs in the pools singing at night,
And wild plum trees in tremulous white;

Robins will wear their feathery fire,
Whistling their whims on a low fence-wire;

And not one will know of the war, not one
Will care at last when it is done.

Not one would mind, neither bird nor tree,
If mankind perished utterly;

And Spring herself, when she woke at dawn
Would scarcely know that we were gone.

The fire burned on the stone hearth and the cigar fell away into a mound of quiet ash on its tray. The empty chairs faced each other between the silent walls, and the music played.

At ten o'clock the house began to die.

The wind blew. A falling tree bough crashed through the kitchen window. Cleaning solvent, bottled, shattered over the stove. The room was ablaze in an instant!

"Fire!" screamed a voice. The house lights flashed, water pumps shot water from the ceilings. But the solvent spread on the linoleum, licking, eating, under the kitchen door, while the voices took it up in chorus: "Fire, fire, fire!"

The house tried to save itself. Doors sprang tightly shut,

but the windows were broken by the heat and the wind blew and sucked upon the fire.

The house gave ground as the fire in ten billion angry sparks moved with flaming ease from room to room and then up the stairs. While scurrying water rats squeaked from the walls, pistoled their water, and ran for more. And the wall sprays let down showers of mechanical rain.

But too late. Somewhere, sighing, a pump shrugged to a stop. The quenching rain ceased. The reserve water supply which had filled baths and washed dishes for many quiet days was gone.

The fire crackled up the stairs. It fed upon Picassos and Matisses in the upper halls, like delicacies, baking off the oily flesh, tenderly crisping the canvases into black shavings.

Now the fire lay in beds, stood in windows, changed the colors of drapes!

And then, reinforcements.

From attic trapdoors, blind robot faces peered down with faucet mouths gushing green chemical.

The fire backed off, as even an elephant must at the sight of a dread snake. Now there were twenty snakes whipping over the floor, killing the fire with a clear cold venom of green froth.

But the fire was clever. It had sent flame outside the house, up through the attic to the pumps there. An explosion! The attic brain which directed the pumps was shattered into bronze shrapnel on the beams.

The fire rushed back into every closet and felt of the clothes hung there.

The house shuddered, oak bone on bone, its bared skeleton cringing from the heat, its wire, its nerves revealed as if a surgeon had torn the skin off to let the red veins and capillaries quiver in the scalded air. Help, help! Fire! Run, run! Heat snapped mirrors like the first brittle winter ice. And the voices wailed Fire, fire, run, run, like a tragic nursery rhyme, a dozen voices, high, low, like children dying in a forest, alone, alone. And the voices fading as the wires popped their sheathings like hot chestnuts. One, two, three, four, five voices died.

In the nursery the jungle burned. Blue lions roared, purple giraffes bounded off. The panthers ran in circles, changing color, and ten million animals, running before the fire, vanished off toward a distant steaming river. . . .

Ten more voices died. In the last instant under the fire avalanche, other choruses, oblivious, could be heard announcing the time, playing music, cutting the lawn by remote-control mower, or setting an umbrella frantically out and in the slamming and opening front door, a thousand things happening, like a clock shop when each clock strikes the hour insanely before or after the other, a scene of maniac confusion, yet unity; singing, screaming, a few last cleaning mice darting bravely out to carry the horrid ashes away! And one voice, with sublime disregard for the situation, read poetry aloud in the fiery study, until all the film spools burned, until all the wires withered and the circuits cracked.

The fire burst the house and let it slam flat down, puffing out skirts of spark and smoke.

In the kitchen, an instant before the rain of fire and timber, the stove could be seen making breakfasts at a psychopathic rate, ten dozen eggs, six loaves of toast, twenty dozen bacon strips, which, eaten by fire, started the stove working again, hysterically hissing!

The crash. The attic smashing into kitchen and parlor. The parlor into cellar, cellar into sub-cellar. Deep freeze, armchair, film tapes, circuits, beds, and all like skeletons thrown in a cluttered mound deep under.

Smoke and silence. A great quantity of smoke.

Dawn showed faintly in the east. Among the ruins, one wall stood alone. Within the wall, a last voice said, over and over again and again, even as the sun rose to shine upon the heaped rubble and steam:

"Today is August 5, 2026, today is August 5, 2026, today is . . ."

William Golding

THE PEOPLE

Now that the day was almost done the sun lay in the gap and dazzled from the water. Across the water the current slid by sheer mountain that was black and hidden from the sun; but this side of the gap was less uncompromising. There was a slanting shelf, a terrace that gradually became a cliff. Lok ignored the unvisited island and the mountain beyond it on the other side of the gap. He began to hurry after the people as he remembered how safe the terrace was. Nothing could come at them out of the water because the current would snatch it over the fall; and the cliff above the terrace was for foxes, goats, the people, hyenas and birds. Even the way down from the terrace to the forest was defended by an entry so narrow that one man with a thorn bush could hold it. As for this trail on the sheer cliff above the spray pillars and the confusion of waters, it was worn by nothing but the feet of the people.

When Lok edged round the corner at the end of the trail the forest was already dark behind him, and shadows were racing through the gap towards the terrace. The people relaxed noisily on the terrace but then Ha swung his thorn bush so that the prickly head lay on the ground before him. He bent his knees and sniffed the air. At once the people were silent, spreading in a semicircle before the overhang. Mal and Ha stole forward, thorn bushes at the ready, moved up a little slope of earth until they could look down into the overhang.

But the hyenas had gone. Though the scent clung to the scattered stones that had dropped from the roof and the scanty grass that grew in the soil of generations, it was a day old. The people saw Ha lift his thorn bush until it was no longer a weapon and relaxed their muscles. They moved a few paces up the slope and stood before the overhang while the sunlight threw their shadows sideways. Mal quelled the cough that rose from his chest, turned to the old woman and waited. She knelt in the overhang and laid the ball of clay in the center of it. She opened the clay, smoothing and patting it over the old patch that lay there already. She put her face to the clay and breathed on it. In the very depth of the overhang there were recesses on either side of a pillar of rock and these were filled with sticks and twigs and thicker branches. She went quickly to the piles and came again with twigs and leaves and a log that was fallen almost to powder. She arranged this over the opened clay and breathed till a trickle of smoke appeared and a single spark shot into the air. The branch cracked and a flame of amethyst and red coiled up and straightened so that the side of her face away from the sun was glowing and her eyes gleamed. She came again from the recesses and put on more wood so that the fire gave them a brilliant display of flame and sparks. She began to work the wet clay with her fingers, tidying the edges so that now the fire sat in the middle of a shallow dish. Then she stood up and spoke to them.

"The fire is awake again."

At that the people talked again excitedly. They hurried into the hollow. Mal crouched down between the fire and the recess and spread out his hands, while Fa and Nil brought more wood and placed it ready. Liku brought a branch and gave it to the old woman. Ha squatted against the rock and shuffled his back till it fitted. His right hand found a stone and picked it up. He showed it to the people.

"I have a picture of this stone. Mal used it to cut a branch. See! Here is the part that cuts."

Mal took the stone from Ha, felt the weight, frowned a moment, then smiled at them.

"This is the stone I used," he said. "See! Here I put my thumb and here my hand fits round the thickness."

He held up the stone, miming Mal cutting a branch.

"The stone is a good stone," said Lok. "It has not gone away. It has stayed by the fire until Mal came back to it."

He stood up and peered over the earth and stones down the slope. The river had not gone away either or the mountains. The overhang had waited for them. Quite suddenly he was swept up by a tide of happiness and exultation. Everything had waited for them: Oa had waited for them. Even now she was pushing up the spikes of the bulbs, fattening the grubs, reeking the smells out of the earth, bulging the fat buds out of every crevice and bough. He danced on to the terrace by the river, his arms spread wide.

"Oa!"

Mal moved a little way from the fire and examined the back of the overhang. He peered at the surface and swept a few dried leaves and droppings from the earth at the base of the pillar. He squatted and shrugged his shoulders into place.

"And this is where Mal sits."

He touched the rock gently as Lok or Ha might touch Fa.

"We are home!"

Lok came in from the terrace. He looked at the old woman. Freed from the burden of the fire she seemed a little less remote, a little more like one of them. He could look her in the eye now and speak to her, perhaps even be answered. Besides, he felt the need to speak, to hide from the others the unease that the flames always called forth in him.

"Now the fire sits on the hearth. Do you feel warm, Liku?"

Liku took the little Oa from her mouth.

"I am hungry."

"To-morrow we shall find food for all the people."

Liku held up the little Oa.

"She is hungry too."

"She shall go with you and eat."

He laughed round at the others.

"I have a picture—"

Then the people laughed too because this was Lok's picture, almost the only one he had, and they knew it as well as he did.

"—a picture of finding the little Oa."

Fantastically the old root was twisted and bulged and smoothed away by age into the likeness of a great-bellied woman.

"—I am standing among the trees. I feel. With this foot I feel—" He mimed for them. His weight was on his left foot and his right was searching in the ground. "—I feel. What do I feel? A bulb? A stick? A bone?" His right foot seized something and passed it to up his left hand. He looked. "It is the little Oa!" Triumphantly he sunned himself before them. "And now where Liku is there is the little Oa."

The people applauded him, grinning, half at Lok, half at the story. Secure in their applause, Lok settled himself by the fire and the people were silent, gazing into the flames.

The sun dropped into the river and light left the overhang. Now the fire was more than ever central, white ash, a spot of red and one flame wavering upwards. The old woman moved softly, pushing in more wood so that the red spot ate and the flame grew strong. The people watched, their faces seeming to quiver in the unsteady light. Their freckled skins were ruddy and the deep caverns beneath their brows were each inhabited by replicas of the fire and all their fires danced together. As they persuaded themselves of the warmth they relaxed limbs and drew the reek into their nostrils gratefully. They flexed their toes and stretched their arms, even leaning away from the fire. One of the deep silences fell on them, that seemed so much more natural than speech, a timeless silence in which there were at first many minds in the overhang; and then perhaps no mind at all. So fully discounted was the roar of the water that the soft touch of the wind on the rocks became audible. Their ears as if endowed with separate life sorted the tangle of tiny sounds and accepted them, the sound of breathing, the sound of wet clay flaking and ashes falling in.

Then Mal spoke with unusual diffidence.

"It is cold?"

Called back into their individual skulls they turned to him. He was no longer wet and his hair curled. He moved forward decisively and knelt so that his knees were on the clay, his arms as supports on either side and the full heat beating on his chest. Then the spring wind flicked at the fire and sent the thin column of smoke straight into his open mouth. He choked and coughed. He went on and on, the coughs seeming to come out of his chest without warning or consultation. They threw his body about and all the time he gaped for his breath. He fell over sideways and his body began to shake. They could see his tongue and the fright in his eyes.

The old woman spoke.

"This is the cold of the water where the log was."

She came and knelt by him and rubbed his chest with her hands and kneaded the muscles of his neck. She took his head on her knees and shielded him from the wind till his coughing was done and he lay still, shivering slightly. The new one woke up and scrambled down from Fa's back. He crawled among the stretched legs with his red thatch glistening in the light. He saw the fire, slipped under Lok's raised knee, took hold of Mal's ankle and pulled himself upright. Two little fires lit in his eyes and he stayed, leaning forward, holding on to the shaking leg. The people divided their attention between him and Mal. Then a branch burst so that Lok jumped and sparks shot out into the darkness. The new one was on all fours before the sparks landed. He scuttled among the legs, climbed Nil's arm and hid himself in the hair of her neck. Then one of the little fires appeared by her left ear, an unwinking fire that watched warily. Nil moved her face sideways and rubbed her cheek gently up and down on the baby's head. The new one was enclosed again. His own thatch and his mother's curls made a cave for him. Her mop hung down and sheltered him. Presently the tiny point of fire by her ear went out.

Mal pulled himself up so that he sat leaning against the

old woman. He looked at each of them in turn. Liku opened her mouth to speak but Fa hushed her quickly.

Now Mal spoke.

"There was the great Oa. She brought forth the earth from her belly. She gave suck. The earth brought forth woman and the woman brought forth the first man out of her belly."

They listened to him in silence. They waited for more, for all that Mal knew. There was the picture of the time when there had been many people, the story that they all liked so much of the time when it was summer all year round and the flowers and fruit hung on the same branch. There was also a long list of names that began at Mal and went back choosing always the oldest man of the people at that time: but now he said nothing more.

Lok sat between him and the wind.

"You are hungry, Mal. A man who is hungry is a cold man."

Ha lifted up his mouth.

"When the sun comes back we will get food. Stay by the fire, Mal, and we will bring you food and you will be strong and warm."

Then Fa came and leaned her body against Mal so that three of them shut him in against the fire. He spoke to them between coughs.

"I have a picture of what is to be done."

He bowed his head and looked into the ashes. The people waited. They could see how his life had stripped him. The long hairs on the brow were scanty and the curls that should have swept down over the slope of his skull had receded till there was a finger's-breadth of naked and wrinkled skin above his brows. Under them the great eye-hollows were deep and dark and the eyes in them dull and full of pain. Now he held up a hand and inspected the fingers closely.

"People must find food. People must find wood."

He held his left fingers with the other hand; he gripped them tightly as though the pressure would keep the ideas inside and under control.

"A finger for wood. A finger for food."

He jerked his head and started again.

"A finger for Ha. For Fa. For Nil. For Liku—"

He came to the end of his fingers and looked at the other hand, coughing softly. Ha stirred where he sat but said nothing. Then Mal relaxed his brow and gave up. He bowed down his head and clasped his hands in the grey hair at the back of his neck. They heard in his voice how tired he was.

"Ha shall get wood from the forest. Nil will go with him, and the new one." Ha stirred again and Fa moved her arm from the old man's shoulders, but Mal went on speaking.

"Lok will get food with Fa and Liku."

Ha spoke:

"Liku is too little to go on the mountain and out on the plain!"

Liku cried out:

"I will go with Lok!"

Mal muttered under his knees:

"I have spoken."

Now the thing was settled the people became restless. They knew in their bodies that something was wrong, yet the word had been said. When the word had been said it was as though the action was already alive in performance and they worried. Ha clicked a stone aimlessly against the rock of the overhang and Nil was moaning softly again. Only Lok, who had fewest pictures, remembered the blinding pictures of Oa and her bounty that had set him dancing on the terrace. He jumped up and faced the people and the night air shook his curls.

"I shall bring back food in my arms"—he gestured hugely—"so much food that I stagger—so!"

Fa grinned at him.

"There is not as much food as that in the world."

He squatted.

"Now I have a picture in my head. Lok is coming back to the fall. He runs along the side of the mountain. He carries a deer. A cat has killed the deer and sucked its blood, so there is no blame. So. Under this left arm. And under this right one"—he held it out—"the quarters of a cow."

He staggered up and down in front of the overhang under

the load of meat. The people laughed with him, then at him. Only Ha sat silent, smiling a little until the people noticed him and looked from him to Lok.

Lok blustered:

"That is a true picture!"

Ha said nothing with his mouth but continued to smile. Then as they watched him, he moved both ears round, slowly and solemnly aiming them at Lok so that they said as clearly as if he had spoken: I hear you! Lok opened his mouth and his hair rose. He began to gibber wordlessly at the cynical ears and the half-smile.

Fa interrupted them.

"Let be. Ha has many pictures and few words. Lok has a mouthful of words and no pictures."

At that Ha shouted with laughter and wagged his feet at Lok and Liku laughed without knowing why. Lok yearned suddenly for the mindless peace of their accord. He put his fit of temper on one side and crept back to the fire, pretending to be very miserable so that they pretended to comfort him. Then there was silence again and one mind or no mind in the overhang.

Quite without warning, all the people shared a picture inside their heads. This was a picture of Mal, seeming a little removed from them, illuminated, sharply defined in all his gaunt misery. They saw not only Mal's body but the slow pictures that were waxing and waning in his head. One above all was displacing the others, dawning through the cloudy arguments and doubts and conjectures until they knew what it was he was thinking with such dull conviction.

"To-morrow or the day after, I shall die."

Suggested Additional Readings

William Golding, *Lord of the Flies*
Aldous Huxley, *Ape and Essence*
               Brave New World Revisited
Nicolai Lenin, *Philosophical Writings*

George Orwell, *Animal Farm*
                1984
Boris Pasternak, *Dr. Zhivago*
Kurt Vonnegut, Jr., *God Bless You, Mr. Rosewater, or, Pearls Before Swine*
H. G. Wells, *The Shape of Things to Come*
                The Time Machine
Franz Werfel, *Star of the Unborn*
Andrew Wright, *Islandia*

Questions for Discussion and Writing

1. B. F. Skinner's description of the children's nurseries and conditioning begins with a reference to Lilliput. Is the conditioning process shown in *Walden Two* like that in *Gulliver's Travels*? See pp. 194–201 above. What important difference is there between Skinner's process and Swift's?

2. Is Frazier's evaluation of Jesus' teachings an accurate one? Is Jesus' system of ethics based only in the Pleasure-Pain Principle? Is the happiness promised by Jesus really "peace of mind," as Frazier says?

3. To what extent is the conditioning of the little Waldenians like that of the young Spartan? Why has punishment been dispensed with in Walden Two?

4. Frazier speaks of Plato's theories of ethical good. Is "good" the same in Walden Two as "good" in the Republic?

5. To what extent do you think Castle's criticism of Frazier's methods is fair and accurate? Do Castle's emotional reactions indicate that Frazier's system represents an improvement over the sort of education Castle (and Frazier himself) had?

6. Compare life in Walden Two with life in Aldous Huxley's Brave New World. Does Huxley's criticism of the New World apply to Walden Two and its values or not?

7. Discuss Aldous Huxley's satiric treatment of the philosopher-king in the passage given above.

8. What resemblances does Huxley's brave new society bear to Plato's Republic? Is Huxley's novel really an attack on Plato or something else? Elaborate.

9. Compare Huxley's utopian satire with Goldsmith's *Asem*. Does Huxley agree with Goldsmith in any vital ways or not?

10. Discuss Frost's use of the animal fable in "Departmental." Is it like or unlike that of the Neo-Classical anti-utopians? Why?

11. Is the society of Frost's ants basically like that shown in *Brave New World*? Comment in detail.

12. What is the implied manner of life in Bradbury's short story? What did the destroyed race obviously hold as its ideal of happiness?

13. How does Bradbury suggest that an ideal leads to its own destruction? How does the mechanized house symbolize this?

14. In what important ways is the amorality of Golding's "people" different from that of Huxley's humanoids? How does this difference affect the nature of the writers' utopian views?

15. Read Orwell's *Animal Farm* and evaluate it as: 1. an animal fable (like Swift's or Frost's) 2. a condemnation of utopian thought 3. an attack on the Communists' perversions of utopian thought.

16. What virtues or attractive qualities are possessed by Golding's people? Are they shown as living utopian lives or not?

17. How does the attitude toward the natural world affect these anti-utopian works of our century? Has man's view of the physical world changed from the last century to this one? Explain.

18. Contemporary critics use a new term to describe certain kinds of utopian thinking: the *dystopia*. The same set of utopian conditions may be viewed as good or bad, depending on the point of view taken, thus reflecting a different set of assumptions used in judging the utopia.

   a. Read some of the recent works listed in the Selective Bibliography and summarize the dystopic theories.

   b. Read and make a comparison of Huxley's utopian views in *Brave New World* and *The Island*.

   c. Select one of the utopias described above and show how it can be treated as a dystopia.

19. Write a paper on one of these subjects:

   a. Marx, Lenin, and the Utopian Goal of Communism

   b. Pasternak's Anti-Communism (or Anti-Utopianism)

   c. Wright's *Islandia* and More's *Utopia*

   d. Freudian Theory and Utopia

   e. B. F. Skinner and Behavioral Psychology in Utopia

   f. Utopianism in American Advertising

   g. Science Fiction and Utopia

   h. Capitalism and Utopia

   i. Science and Utopianism in the Twentieth Century

   j. Utopia and Hollywood

   k. The Psychedelic Drugs and Utopia

   l. Henry Miller and the Sexual Utopia

   m. Utopia in Contemporary Popular Music

   n. Contemporary Revivalism and the New Jerusalem

General Questions

1. Apart from a chronological order, what principle of categorization might be used to group together the utopias alike in one way or another? Begin by identifying the underlying, basic assumptions of the utopia (physical, geographical, political, etc.) and then putting them in categories that help to identify their essential nature.

2. Outline the role played by women in utopian thought from Eve to Lenina (in *Brave New World*) and the old woman (in *The Inheritors*). Does utopian thinking seem to be more a masculine pastime than a feminine one? Would this affect the character of utopian literature or not?

3. Utopian writing incorporates detailed investigations of heterosexual relationships. Summarize the chief varieties of attitudes on the subject. Has there been any direct, linear development of attitudes from early to more recent utopian literature?

4. Discuss the place that death has in utopian writing. Are the utopianists unanimously agreed that death is an evil and a deterrent to utopia?

5. Population control (and thus birth control) has occupied the attention of utopian writers from the beginning, and not only those interested in political utopia. What are the basic attitudes toward birth control in utopian literature? What seems to determine them?

6. Trace the alterations in the views of a utopia in the sky from the Greek legends of the gods on Mount Olympus to the science fiction of today.

7. What is the place of these items in four or five of the utopias you have studied: clothing, books, music, athletics, diet, war?

8. Trace the changes in pastoral utopianism from the Garden of Eden to Walden Pond.

9. Trace the evolution of the idea of the Noble Savage from the Scythian to Huxley's Savage and Golding's Lok.

10. Which of the utopias depend upon a basic alteration of human nature as we traditionally know it? How does each suppose this alteration is to take place?

11. Compare and contrast the Christian utopia as it is shown by John the Divine, Dante, Milton, and Bellamy. How does each reflect the dominant views of the author's age?

12. Each of these countries has been depicted as a utopia: ancient Egypt, the Roman Republic, Incan Peru, eighteenth-century America, nineteenth-century Polynesia. In what ways did the utopian representation repress or overlook or distort actual facts in order to show these cultures as perfect? (Ancient Sparta, Ethiopia, or Scythia might also be used.)

13. Many utopian thinkers have been mystics and visionaries. Outline the forms of mystical or visionary utopianism from the early prophets to the modern psychedelic "vision."

14. Trace the use of the island in utopian literature from its first forms to those in the twentieth century. Why is the island such a useful symbol to utopian thinkers?

15. Utopian writing is often used as a way of criticizing contemporary social or political conditions. How do these writers level charges against their societies in their utopian compositions; what are they protesting against; and how do they frame their protests: Strabo, Diodorus Siculus, Plato, Jesus, St. Augustine, Montaigne, More, Swift, Howells, Bellamy, Shaw, Huxley, Frost?

16. In what important ways are Student Protest Movements in contemporary America related to utopianism? Is the Civil Rights movement utopian in any way? The Psychedelic cults? The Anti-Vietnam rallies?

17. The Russian Revolution of 1917–1918 is an obvious instance of theoretical utopianism (formulated by Marx,

Engels, and Lenin) producing significant social changes. What other important historical changes can be seen as the effects of utopian thinking? Is utopian thought empirically "practical" or not?

18. What is *your* definition of utopia? Does it correspond to the version of any of the writers in this book? In what ways does your utopia depart from theirs? Can you actually give a definition of the term itself? If not, why?

Postscript

After the reader has worked his way through the foregoing selection of utopian writing—or perhaps even through the full body of utopian literature—he may feel that he still lacks a clear notion of what utopia is. He will know what Herodotus, Dante and Johnson thought it was (or was not); but he will probably find trouble in reconciling the opinions expounded by the utopianists or even in choosing from them a few basic ones that provide a workable definition of utopia.

What, then, has the reader learned? The first is the difficulty of defining accurately, or even coherently, terms we take for granted. "Utopia" is nearly always a synonym for total happiness; the writers in this collection implicitly equate *eutopia* ("the good place") with *euphoria* ("the good feeling"). And each writer propounds the system he thinks most likely to eliminate the causes of human unhappiness, of dissatisfaction with life, and to replace misery with the state of euphoria.

What is happiness? This collection shows that there are as many ideas of "happiness" as there are writers. The author of Genesis clearly believes it is the enjoyment of God's favor. Herodotus thinks of it as freedom from want and worry, as "security." Plato is confident that happiness is moral goodness. St. Augustine explicitly says that only freedom from the fear of death permits happiness: it is eternal life. Swift insists happiness is the control of the passions by reason. Aldous Huxley scorns the twentieth-century belief that happiness is sensual gratification and lack of responsibility, that is, being uninhibited. And William Golding says happiness is a deficiency of intelligence or a lack of the sense of right and wrong. They all seem to agree that whatever it is, happiness is in short supply among mankind and that every man desires more of it than he has—as much, in fact, as he can get.

As the condition under which man finds total, lasting happiness, utopia will vary according to the idea of happiness the utopianist chooses. If physical sensation is the criterion and happiness is sensual gratification, one sort of utopian system will result. But can man's senses be a satisfactory basis for constructing a utopian system? Man sensually experiences pain and death, yet these do not provide pleasure or physical gratification in the usual meaning of the word. Faced with this problem, the framer of a utopia of the senses may decide that pain and death would have to be done away with in order for men to be perfectly happy. To do so, however, is to change human nature as we know it or else to give up the possibility of perfect happiness.

Should the utopianist decide that it is possible to change man's physical nature—as G. B. Shaw and others suggest —then man's psychological nature must alter as well. To be mortal is to be human, as all of us know the state of humanity. What if we suddenly became immortal, through evolution or medicine or God's grace? Would we not then be happy? Many philosophers do not think so. Milton showed Adam and Eve in a state of complete happiness and grace, which they deliberately rejected. Milton insisted that death is in truth a blessing to man as the means of his ceasing to be "human" and "mortal" (thus in a state of sin). And Swift argued that eternal life would be a horrible curse if man had to continue to live forever in the pain and misery that constitute human existence. The sum of all these antisensual arguments is that pain is essential to the senses and to eradicate it entirely from human experience would alter man's very being, his essential humanity. *Brave New World* takes this as its central thesis.

Suppose, then, that the utopian writer argues that happiness is not to be reached through the physical senses or even through the rational thought processes which depend on the senses. Both Jesus and St. Augustine insisted that to be human is to be sinful (thus in misery), that perfect happiness is not to be found on this earth, and that bliss comes only to those who rely upon the supernatural or metaphysical, "beyond physical nature," and faith. This position has the advantage of accepting the conditions of human life as all men experience them; but it also asserts that utopian perfection exists under conditions untestable by our physical senses or our reasonable (empirical) faculties. The prospect of a distant—perhaps nonexistent—utopia after death has not served for many thinkers, who assert that such an optimistic reliance on future, undemonstrable possibilities is escapism: they scorn the idea of "pie in the sky by and by." They point out that spiritual utopianism depends on Platonic dualism and that a utopia for the spirit does little to alleviate suffering on earth.

Similarly, if the theorist tries to construct a utopia on empiric grounds, asserting that somewhere in the past, earthly conditions were such as to grant men a state of euphoria now impossible because things have changed, critics will assault this position. If twentieth-century man cannot be happy because the H-Bomb has been invented, then why were men just as unhappy before the Bomb? Or perhaps ancient Rome was a utopia because gunpowder was not yet known. History indicates that Rome was far from utopian. Perhaps men were more virtuous and happier in primitive Egypt, as Diodorus said? Evidence shows not. Then was Neanderthal man or his ape-forebears happier than we, lacking a highly developed brain and sense of time and ethics? He was hardly happy by twentieth-century standards of happiness; and even if he had an animal contentment, that is not the same as a utopia in human terms.

One must conclude that if utopia does not exist for us today, right now, it is not likely to exist somewhere else now for the Polynesian or Eskimo, at least in the mind of the Polynesian or Eskimo. Will men alter in such a way as to make utopia a future possibility? Maybe, but we are selfish beings and want utopia for ourselves now. Did it exist in the past? Perhaps, but once again it helps us very little to think the Spartans or Scythians were entirely happy when we are not. Can utopia be found after death? Not everyone thinks so, and those who do think so base their belief in unarguable and unprovable faith.

Must we conclude that utopia is a worthless, time-consuming daydream, then? Far from it. Though the utopian writers in this collection may not have formulated precise answers to the vital questions of human existence, they have at least confronted those questions. To read utopian literature is to see defined the basic questions that all of us must face, alone and together, if we wish to be educated. The first step toward knowledge is the acknowledgment of specific questions; and the men who write about utopia are more fully, passionately aware of these questions than most men. They confront us with the very problems we must deal with in our own lives.

What *is* human life and what meaning has it, if any? Do we seek for meaning through our bodies (sensual experience), through our minds (the capacity for observation and synthesis), or through our spirits (our emotions and intuitive knowledge)? If we rely on the senses, what value do we place on such physically animal drives as sex, hunger, and thirst in constructing a system of desirables? What is the significance of pain and death? And how do we accept the limitations of the senses (deafness, blindness, and so forth) in searching for life's meaning? If we believe that the intellect is the best indicator of the values in life, how are we to relate it to its dependence on the body? Can the intellect be "happy" if the body suffers? Does the mind die when the body dies? And if the intellect is the guide to life, why do men differ in the ways their minds construct contradictory views of life? Is the meaning (truth) of life to be found by the individual or the group? Through withdrawal or cooperation? And if by cooperation, what sort: social, political, economic, physical, mystic? How are the operative principles of cooperation to be arrived at? And if life's truth is to be found and happiness to be reached through the spirit rather than the body or mind, how is it done? Can a group of people arrive at a mystic communion or does the saint reach spiritual happiness alone? Can the spiritual process be taught? Does it depend on some supernatural grace? And if men live by the spirit entirely, what happens to the worldly society of which we all are part?

These eternal questions relate to the issues most pressing

today. Sexual liberty, birth control, war and bloodshed, military service, the value of education, psychedelic drugs, the relations between the generations, authority, pain, choice of life, suffering and death—these "twentieth-century" issues absorbed the utopian writers as well. We find in Plato and Plutarch, Jesus and Augustine, More and Milton some provocative answers to the matters that trouble us. Though we live in the world shown by Huxley, Skinner, Orwell, and Bradbury, that world was developed in the centuries covered by the selections from Genesis to Shaw. By becoming acquainted with its treatment of one core theme (together with a cluster of related topics), we can gain a fuller awareness of the contemporary world. And we may begin the difficult process of altering our own subjective utopian dreams to accommodate life's most basic realities.

INDEX

MODERN LIBRARY COLLEGE EDITIONS